£3.00

General Revelation

BOOKS BY G. C. BERKOUWER

MODERN UNCERTAINTY AND CHRISTIAN FAITH

THE TRIUMPH OF GRACE IN THE THEOLOGY OF KARL BARTH

STUDIES IN DOGMATICS SERIES —

THE PROVIDENCE OF GOD

FAITH AND SANCTIFICATION

FAITH AND JUSTIFICATION

FAITH AND PERSEVERANCE

THE PERSON OF CHRIST

GENERAL REVELATION

DIVINE ELECTION

MAN: THE IMAGE OF GOD

Studies in Dogmatics

GENERAL REVELATION

BY

G. C. BERKOUWER

PROFESSOR OF SYSTEMATIC THEOLOGY
FREE UNIVERSITY OF AMSTERDAM

WM. B. EERDMANS PUBLISHING COMPANY
GRAND RAPIDS, MICHIGAN

© Copyright Wm. B. Eerdmans Publishing Co. 1955

Library of Congress Catalog Card No., 53-8142

First printing, May 1955
Second printing, October 1964
Third printing, February 1968
Fourth printing, April 1971

This American edition is published
by special arrangement with the Dutch publisher
J. H. KOK — KAMPEN
and is translated from the Dutch edition
Algemene Openbaring

Printed in the United States of America

Contents

Background

CHAPTER I

Background

WHEN one reflects upon what theology calls God's general revelation, he immediately faces a number of significant questions which have aroused agitated and even violent discussions in our day. These discussions chiefly concern the question of the legitimacy of acknowledging general revelation. It appears that the time when reformed theology could take the distinction between general and special revelation for granted is gone forever. It is no exaggeration to say that we have come to the crossroads. Stiff opposition to the distinction between "general" and "special" has arisen, and it is therefore desirable to give careful consideration to the questions that are asked in this connection.

We must study the material in detail because some charge that the distinction between general and special revelation does not do justice to the *unique* and "once-for-all" character of the redemptive revelation in Jesus Christ. It is said that the distinction is the bitter fruit of abstract reason which has, consciously or unconsciously, been stimulated by a feeling of insufficiency in the redemptive revelation of Christ. Along this road, they say, many have proceeded from special revelation to something more *general* and *universal,* and have thereby done injustice to the sufficiency and absoluteness of revelation in Christ.

This criticism, which was often voiced as a warning in the midst of the theological discussions, places us before the decisive question, as to whether a certain estrangement from redemption in Christ is actually the result of accepting general

9

revelation. Does this confession really owe its existence to a flight, perhaps unconscious, from the sufficiency and absoluteness of the revelation in Christ? Is it desirable to break with the traditional distinction at this point and reject it as an impure and unacceptable element in our creeds and theology?

If it were true that the confession of general revelation would necessarily cast a shadow upon the revelation in Jesus Christ, then it would certainly conflict with the testimony of Holy Scripture which always posits the unique, overpowering and decisive character of the revelation in Christ Jesus. The Scriptures everywhere emphasize the mystery of the ages and sound the hymn of praise concerning *this* act of God: "And without controversy great is the mystery of godliness; he who was manifested in the flesh, [is] justified in the spirit . . ." (I Tim. 3:16).

According to the word of Scripture, revelation in Christ concerns the revelation of the mystery, "which hath been kept in silence through times eternal, but now is manifested" (Rom. 16:25-26). The word became flesh, and dwelt among us (John 1:14). All lines which point to Him meet in the focal point of Scripture, for in Jesus Christ dwelleth all the *fulness* of the Godhead bodily (Col. 2:9), and He is the revelation of God in the *fulness* of time (Gal. 4:4). With ecstasy the testimony of this unique mystery is sent into the world: "We beheld his glory" (John 1:14). It was Christ who revealed the name of the Father (John 17:6). "No man hath seen God at any time; the only begotten Son, who is in the bosom of the Father, he hath declared *him*" (John 1:18).

Is not the knowledge of God in his revelation *always* and *everywhere* dependent upon the knowledge of Christ, and is there anyone who comes to the Father except *through Him*? (John 14:6). "If ye had known me, ye would have known my Father also: from hence forth ye know him, and have seen him" (John 14:7). And when Philip then asks for revelation: "Lord, show us the Father, and it sufficeth us," Christ replies, "Have I been so long time with you, and dost thou not know me, Philip? He that hath seen me hath seen the Father; how sayest thou, Show us the Father?" (John 14:8-9). Does not this answer, from the highest authority Himself, once and for all solve the question of revelation? And is not the exclusively *Christian* character of the knowledge of God, and therefore of revelation, permanently expressed in Christ's own words: "And no one knoweth the Son, save the Father; neither doth any know the Father, save the Son, and he to whomsoever the Son willeth to reveal him" (Matt. 11:27 cf. Luke 10:22)? Who would want to do injustice to those expressions concerning the exclusiveness of the redeeming grace of God in Christ Jesus who has appeared unto all men? (Titus 3:4 f). How can one then, it is asked, come to a revelation different from this decisive act of God? Does not one do injustice to the *unity,* seriousness and finality of God's revelatory activity, if he speaks of *general* in addition to *special* revelation? Is not the reality of special revelation endangered when one thinks that there is also another revelation to be found in nature, history, and in man himself, in short, in the whole of created reality?

These questions are significant just because men have often referred to "general" revelation in such a way that the unique significance of revelation in Christ was relativized and endangered. That was especially true when the view of the unique-historical character of the Christ-revelation was considered untenable and an offensive delimitation of revelation. It was held that one must not lose sight of the more "general" manifestations of God in the world on the basis of which the diverse religious expressions could be more easily explained. Thus, from the special, historically-concrete and limited, they deliberately took the road to the general and universal.

Especially in the Hegelian influenced theology of the 19th century, this emphasis upon general revelation is clearly seen. Here it concerned the "correlation between the absolute and the finite Spirit" as the *essence* of religion.[1] This theology spoke of the immediate revelation of the absolute Spirit in the human ego, reason and freedom.[2] This conception of revelation strongly opposed the view then current which started out from the "revelation of God in Jesus as the only source from which Christians and theologians too had to draw all their knowledge of God."[3] The Hegelian wanted to view God's revelation as richer and broader than simply that revelation in Christ. Christ was indeed of special significance for God's revelation, but then only as a special *illustration* of the *general* revelation of God in the world.

The increased knowledge of the various religions also led to further generalization of revelation. For many the denial of the absoluteness of Christianity became the background of the dilemma: general or special revelation? They thought they could see one broad, universal revelation of God in the background of the various religions, and they hesitated to accept the uniqueness and exclusiveness of the revelation in Christ on the basis of an *a priori* of faith. They rejected this position as "the old method of the supranaturalistic theology."[4]

This method became an offense to many,[5] and therefore they advocated *general* revelation in the place of, or in addition to, special revelation. The more emphasis that was laid upon "general," the less "special" could receive. The significance of the revelation in Christ was gradually relativized by a *general* divine manifestation in the world. This conception of

1. A. E. Biedermann, *Christliche Dogmatik* I, 1884, p. 264.
2. *Ibid.* p. 270f.
3. *Ibid.* p. 265f. Compare the corresponding criticism of orthodox Christology: Biedermann, *op. cit.* II, p. 403f. The religious principle has its realization in Jesus Christ and has "as the fact of the religious personality of Jesus entered into human history." p. 403. Orthodox Christology is, according to Biedermann, a mythological form of the religious principle (cf. II, 425). These and similar ideas are found in all Hegelian influenced theology.
4. E. Troeltsch, *Gesammelte* Aufs. II, p. 341.
5. "Since the new beginning of the history of religious investigation in the nineteenth century, the appeal to truth as made by the prophets and apostles has become a rock of offense." Karl Heim, *Glaube und Leben*, 1928, p. 445.

"general revelation" is widely held in the modern theological world. It is the fruit of a rapidly growing relativism. When Brunner speaks of "the antithesis: general and special revelation,"[6] he demonstrates this tendency of modern theology, namely, the failure to appreciate the uniqueness of the Christ-revelation and the attempt to defend a "general-religion," which becomes concrete and particularized in the various religions. It can be said that in many respects modernism defends a "general revelation," although it does not at all mean what reformed theology does. It is obvious that the road from special to a more general, universal revelation is being followed, and in this we can see that men take offense at the fact that God has revealed himself *in Christ* and that no one comes to the Father except *through Him*.

Particularly in view of this flight into a "general" revelation, it is necessary to consider whether *every* confession of general (in addition to special) revelation is based upon this offense, and whether special revelation is *always* absorbed by general revelation.[7]

We hear this criticism repeatedly from those who oppose general revelation. They see in it a fatal generalization of revelation. In reaction against all "general-religion" and "general-revelation," they wish to point the way back to the uniqueness (*Einmaligkeit*) of the revelation of Christ. They desire a return from breadth to depth, from hesitation to decision, from the abstract to the concrete-historical revelation in Christ.

It it thus by way of reaction to the abstract and relativizing thought of modern theology that recently some oppose the confession of general revelation. They emphasize that God is

---

6. E. Brunner, *Der Mittler*, 1927, p. 3f.
7. One must always guard against this danger. Frequently a "widening" of revelation has led to its actual rejection. Think of how revelation and reason, Scripture and tradition, revelation and feeling were at first placed side by side but in the end reason and tradition and feeling had taken control. A typical example is the Mormon religion in which the Bible is placed along side of the book of Mormon. Appeal is frequently made to *continuing* revelation.

not simply revealed in nature and history, and they appeal to those words in Scripture which speak of Christ who has revealed God. This reaction makes it doubly necessary to give careful consideration to the conflict concerning general revelation. Against this background of modern theological thought and its general, universal revelation, everyone who believes in general revelation must prove that he does absolutely no *injustice* to the revelation in Christ. There may be no *competition* between God's general and special revelation, and every conception of general revelation which is the result of doubt as to the absoluteness of the revelation in Christ is to be condemned.

It is true that belief in general revelation was often the symptom and result of a rejection of special revelation, but this is certainly not *always* the case. The distinction between general and special revelation is found also where there is no rejection of special revelation and where no offense is taken at the "here and now" of the historical Christ-revelation. This distinction was reached as a result of careful listening to the Holy Scriptures which spoke of a revelation of God in the works of his hands, as *distinguished* from the revelation in Christ.

No wonder, then, that the appeal to Scripture has played such an important role in the discussions. Those who oppose general revelation oversimplify matters when they attack those only who have consciously moved from special to general revelation. For there is another view of general revelation which cannot be characterized in that way. It is the view which appeals to Scripture as the final authority in every controversy. All theological problems, also our views of revelation, must be decided there.

But the discussion of general revelation has still another aspect. The question has been asked whether the doctrine of a general revelation does not irresistibly lead to what is called a *natural theology*. Is it true that in admitting general revelation one has opened the door to natural theology and guaranteed it a legitimate place in the theological system? An affirmative reply is frequently given. General revelation and natural theology are thought to be on the *same plane* structurally, They admit, for the fact can hardly be denied, that the confession of general revelation has frequently gone parallel to a *refutation* of natural theology, but this is considered an inconsistency. Consistently — it is said — the idea of general revelation *must* lead to natural theology. Therefore, we must discuss the background of natural theology and ask whether general revelation and natural theology are indissoluably united. This investigation is doubly necessary because the history of theology shows one form of theology, Roman Catholicism, in which this relation is openly accepted. Naturally the question also arises as to whether this may be true in reformed theology too.

As a result of the dialectical movement, the conflict about general revelation and natural theology has flared again in our day. Karl Barth especially has launched a heavy offensive against natural theology and has also attacked the distinction between general and special revelation. In the midst of this offensive, the intensity of which continuously increased, a new conflict developed within the dialectical movement itself on *this* very point. It is the split between Karl Barth and Emil Brunner. Thus we see how tense the discussions concerning this doctrine have become.

First of all there is the struggle between Rome and the Reformation. Next we see the offensive of Barth and then the divergence between Barth and Brunner concerning the foundations of theology, *both of whom* declared war against the so called "General Religion" and the flight from the absolute revelation in Christ. The underlying question in all of these discussions concerns the *knowledge of God*. The question which momentarily dominates the whole conflict is this one: is there a "natural" knowledge of God and his will possible outside of the revelation in Jesus Christ? It is remarkable that new reactions have already been voiced over against Barth, not only by Brunner, but also from Althaus, Dillschneider and Rudolph Hermann and others. Many believed that Barth's protest against "general religion" and "general revelation" did contain some worthwhile elements, but that he was side-tracked because of a onesided reaction. This could be demonstrated by means of a constructive exegesis of the various scriptural passages. Thus yeas and nays sound over against each other with all the dangers of new one-sidedness.

These reactions make a careful analysis difficult. One must not think that an all out affirmative or negative has made the situation perfectly clear. Whoever wishes to maintain general revelation by accepting the view of Brunner or Althaus over against Barth would fall into a new danger which a careful analysis must make clear. Only one who truly bows to the Word of God will be able to find his way through the underbrush in these discussions, and to speak responsibly concerning the revelation of God.

A final aspect in the various discussions must be mentioned. It is the approach to these questions by means of the phenomenology of religion. In studying the various religious phenomena one repeatedly faces the question of revelation. Van der Leeuw speaks of the *two* ways of theology, viz., the way from revelation to the world (the truly theological way), and the way from the world to revelation (the way of the science of religion).[8] In this connection he raises the question of natural theology and general revelation. He feels that this question has received new actuality and calls the relation between general and special revelation an *urgent* question.

On the one hand he warns against the science of religion which all too often recognizes only general revelation and believes that a natural theology is the only one possible. On the other hand he also rejects the standpoint — obviously the

---

8. G. v.d. Leeuw, "De Twee Wegen der Theologie," *Vox Theologica,* 13e Jrg. (1941), 20.

Barthian, which completely discards natural theology as well as its methods.

Thus we see that the phenomenology of religion has given new impetus to the questions of natural theology and general revelation. One is amazed how often old theological and confessional questions are suddenly elevated to new actuality. A careful examination will uncover the main lines of thought. In the phenomenology of religion this will be evident also because here the question of the relation to God's revelation is acute.

And from all this — the background of our subject — it is clear that we are not dealing with a purely theoretical question. The subject that demands our full attention is of great importance. There is no more significant question in the whole of theology and in the whole of human life than that of the nature and reality of revelation.

Karl Barth's Offensive Against Natural Theology

CHAPTER II

Karl Barth's Offensive Against Natural Theology

I T IS certainly no exaggeration to speak of Barth's offensive. Barth has centered his attack more and more upon natural theology as *the* great enemy of faith, and general revelation was always involved in his attack as well. When Barth was invited to deliver the Gifford lectures, he faced a unique predicament. In his will in 1887, Gifford had stipulated that the lectures were to be given on the subject of natural theology and should serve the "promoting, advancing, teaching and diffusing" of the study of natural theology.

Could Barth accept that invitation? He was convinced that natural theology always owes its existence to "a radical error" and "how then should (he) be in a position to further and to spread it?"[1] He did not see how he could fulfill Gifford's requirement without being unfaithful to Reformed theology. However, when the invitation was upheld, Barth accepted, explaining that perhaps he could serve the interest of natural theology indirectly. For natural theology lives by its opposition to another theology. Thus if Barth would strongly defend this other, viz. *reformed,* theology, then by way of reaction there would probably be others who would give more emphasis to natural theology!

* * *

This historical sketch clearly emphasizes the severity of Barth's offensive. He wants his rejection of natural theology

---

1. Barth *Gotteserkentnis und Gottesdienst nach reformatorischer Lehre,* 1938, p. 43.

to be *radical*. In his attempted renovation of dogmatics, he opposes natural theology in its every form. It appears that this offensive is closely related to the subject of general revelation because the *central* question in the conflict directly concerns the reality and nature of God's revelation. Barth maintains that both Rome and modern Protestantism have an erroneous view of revelation. And although the Reformers' conception is much better and has done greater justice to revelation *in Christ*, yet not even they have sufficiently recognized the demonic character of natural theology. In a certain sense both Luther and Calvin have made use of it. Their unique significance, however, lies in the fact that they recognized that the church and our salvation are based exclusively upon the revelation of God in Jesus Christ. In that they *actually* stood opposed to all natural theology "which declares that man himself possesses the capacity and the power to inform himself about God, the world and man."[2] From this it is clear that Barth considers natural theology to be one of the most dangerous enemies of church and theology, an enemy in which everything is at stake. It is necessary to analyze the background of Barth's fierce attack.

* * *

All will certainly agree that Barth's rejection of natural theology is motivated by his conception of God's revelation in Christ as the *unique* and *exclusive* revelation in the world. He does not believe that one first knows something about revelation and then learns to know the revelation in Christ as a *special* form of that revelation. On the contrary, one must know about *Jesus Christ* in order to know *anything* about revelation.[3] Revelation concerns something *new*, which was not

---

2. *Ibid.*, p. 46.
3. *Revelation*, ed. John Baille & Hugh Martin, (New York: Macmillan, 1937) p. 42, 48.

previously known *in any manner whatsoever.*[4] The revelation
of God in Jesus Christ is "once for all" (*einmalig*) in an absolute sense; *apart from* that revelation there may be *signs*
and *witnesses,* but there cannot be a repetition of the unique
reality of that revelation. This revelation is not the appearance
of a "being" who is already known, namely God, nor the realization of some general possibility of revelation. Only Jesus
Christ can be called revelation in the *true* and *strict* and *original*
sense of the word:[5] the *Word* became flesh. Apart from the
incarnation we cannot speak of revelation. In the incarnation
revelation comes to us as revelation of God's grace and reconciliation.[6] Through this reconciliation which conquers and
destroys the radical enmity, man learns to know God. Apart
from this revelation, apart from this self-revealing activity of
God, man only walks in darkness and cannot know God. True,
there are "signs" which reflect the first sign of revelation and
agree with it and *in so far repeat it.* The one revelation expresses itself in nature and in the history of the world in fixed
forms, "but these forms are not revelation,"[7] nor multipli-
cations of the incarnation, but only useful as *signs* of the revelation which call for faith in the one revelation of God: Jesus
Christ. According to Barth the words and deeds of Christ, the
virgin birth and the empty grave, the prophetic and apostolic
testimony and the Holy Scriptures belong to these signs of the
revelation. Even the Bible is not itself revelation,[8] but only a
sign of revelation. Furthermore, *preaching* and *sacraments* also belong to the signs of revelation as does also the *church*
which is a secondary sign of revelation. All of these signs are
important as pointers (*Hinweis*) to the revelation, but they

---

4. *Ibid.,* p. 45.   5. *Ibid.,* p. 49.

6. *Ibid.,* p. 49-50. Cf. H. Kraemer, *The Christian Message in the Non-
Christian World,* 1938. p. 119 for a summary of Barth's view of revelation.
Also pp. 118, 125ff. See also H. Kraemer, "Continuity or Discontinuity"
in *The Authority of the Faith,* 1938. p. 3ff and note his dissatisfaction with
Barth's solution on p. 22.

7. *Revelation,* pp. 63-64.   8. *Ibid.,* p. 67.

are not themselves revelation. Jesus Christ is revelation, alone and exclusively.[9]

In all of this Barth wants to emphasize the absolute uniqueness and unrepeatableness of God's revelation in Jesus Christ, the incarnation of the Word: "an absolute once-and-for-all reality."[10] The divine revelation is "this absolutely fixed event never having occurred previously nor successively."[11] It is as once-and-for-all as God is once-and-for-all (*einmalig*) even as there is only one Name given unto salvation and only one Mediator. An "antiquity"[12] precedes this revelation in Christ, viz. that of the Old Testament. "The revelation in the Old Testament is really the expectation of the revelation or the expected revelation."[13] The Old Testament is not itself revelation, but is pointed toward the revelation. In the Old Testament Jesus Christ is revealed *as* the expected one. The Old Testament is concerned with pointing (*Hinweis*) to *the* revelation: Christ. In this *pointing,* the nature of the Old Testament's witness is expressed.

In addition to the time of expectation, there is also the time of recollection.[14] The New Testament is a witness to this recollection. Just as the period of expectation goes out to meet the revelation, so the period of recollection starts out from it, viz. from "the finished revelation."

Both the witness of the Old as well as that of the New Testament point to an "eternal presence in time," [15] point to birth

---

9. *Ibid.,* p. 81.
10. Barth, *Kirchliche Dogmatik,* I/2, p. 13.
11. *Ibid.* 12. *Ibid.,* p. 77.
13. *Ibid.,* p. 78. In this quotation a unique problem arises in relation to the word *oder* (or). A jump is made from the "expectation of the revelation" to "the expected revelation." Barth says that "Christ was also revealed in the Old Testament as the expected one." p. 81. The same thing is said of the covenant in the OT.: "This declared covenant in the OT is God's revelation because it is the expectation of the revelation of Jesus Christ." p. 89. This "because" (*weil*) is like the "or" (*oder*) of our quotation. See further the relation of the "expected" (*erwartete*) and the "occurred" (*geschehene*) revelation, p. 111.
14. Barth, *Kirchliche Dogmatik* I/2, p. 111f.
15. *Ibid.,* pp. 126-127.

and resurrection, to the definitive "free self-activity of God to man."[16] And that is unrepeatable: *this* here and now is "the unique, in no way problematical, Now."[17]

Here and here *only* has God's revelation *taken place*: "the pure presence of God."[18] This divine revelation is the reconciling revelation of Jesus Christ in whom God himself as sovereign Person, is *redemptively* with us in judgment and grace. In this connection Barth had to ask the question why there is real revelation only *here*, "in the existence of Jesus Christ."[19] Here Barth mentions Troeltsch, who opposed an exclusive supernaturalism, and Barth adds that in all these powerful impressions and 'revelations' about us, one thing is lacking, viz. "a final, simply binding *authority*."[20] Here we see the heart of Barth's conception of revelation, which is frequently called "Christomonism." In his dogmatics[21] Barth refers to this charge of "Christomonism" and adds that his only motive has been to hold fast at all cost to the Christological thread throughout, and he asks whether a *Christian* theologian may with good conscience do anything else but think of "Christ only." None the less it does appear that this "Christ only" of Barth is given so special a form that it can rightly be called a "Christomonism." Barth's negations are sharp here. He says that when we think of the many revelations about us, we then consider the greatness, power, goodness and beauty of "the earth created by God"[22] or of the heavenly revelation which is "that invisible and inconceivable reality of creation with which we are girded about."[23] But all of this lacks "ultimate authority"[24] because it concerns "creaturely revelation." It is at most the herald of the King, but not the King himself.[25] But the revelation of God himself is completely different. *Here* we do

---

16. *Ibid.,* p. 114 17. *Ibid.,* p. 115. 18. *Ibid.,* p. 127
19. Barth, *Dogmatik im Grundriss*, 1947. p. 97.
20. *Ibid.,* p. 97.
21. *Kirchliche Dogmatik* III/3, p. v.
22. *Dogmatik im Grundriss,* p. 97.
23. *Ibid.*   24. *Ibid.,* p. 98.   25. *Ibid.*

not speak of "such earthly or heavenly revelations, but of the Power which is above all powers; not of the revelation of a divine Above or Below, but the *revelation of God himself.*"[26]

We do not face a reality *differentiated* from God, but we face *God himself.* He himself is revealed and *this* revelation "confronts the whole world of creatures, excellent beyond compare."[27]

This revelation in Jesus Christ is the revelation of *reconciliation.* God through his Son comes to us in grace and reconciliation. Therefore it is a radical error to think that God can also be known by us through another way, a way *outside of this revelation.* This error rests upon the idea that God is knowable apart from his *grace.* And against that point Barth's entire offensive is directed. "We think of God's grace when we say: God is knowable. For it is through God's grace that he is knowable to us."[28] In Christ the *gracious* decision has been made for us as a divine "approach" (*Ubergriff*). "In his good pleasure God is God in our midst and for us; the approach is completely and entirely on his initiative and in it he gives himself unto us in his good pleasure and is revealed unto us with the openness with which he is revealed unto himself."[29] This is the only way to know God because here we, in our need, are known by God. "There is no way which can bypass the grace and mercy of God's good pleasure by which we can assure ourselves of the knowability of God and of the certainty of our knowledge."[30] At this point Barth's opposition to natural theology is also evident. Natural theology stands for the possibility of knowing God in such a way that the knowledge of his grace and mercy is *not* yet included. Natural theology assumes the possibility of a certain "foreknowledge" (*Vorherwissen*) which is *not* yet the knowledge of the merciful Father of Jesus Christ.

---

26. *Ibid.*   27. *Ibid.*, p. 99.   28. *K. D.* II/1, pp. 74, 76.
29. *Ibid.*, p. 80.   30. *Ibid.*, p. 81.

This *being able to know in advance,* apart from revelation in Christ, is considered possible by means of *analogy.* By means of analogy it is thought possible to arrive at the knowledge of the *existence,* the *being* of God, while not yet knowing *anything* of the grace and mercy of God. Barth holds that this position of natural theology injures the *unity* of God because it abstracts the *being* aspect in God from the fullness of God's activity and thus comes to an independent theology of the *first* article: *God as Creator.* Barth speaks of an "assault (*Attentat*) upon the Christian idea of God."[31] One attempts to reach a certain and true knowledge of God's *being* "which has nothing to do with grace and faith." Barth maintains that this aspect-knowledge (*being* apart from *grace*) is absolutely impossible. The unity of God would then be destroyed, and Barth claims the Vatican Council did just that when it spoke of the knowledge of God *as* Creator.

The Christian idea of God is then split up by this conception of *"being"* in itself. In this Barth sees the essence and heart of natural theology. There must be some special reason why it has repeatedly appeared with such stubborn vitality throughout the history of theology. Barth maintains that the reason cannot lie in any supposed Scriptural witness, which he says does not exist. There must be some other motif which accounts for the remarkable sympathy for natural theology. This deepest motif Barth finds in the fact that there is no receptivity in man for *grace.* Because man is *by nature* shut up to the grace of God, therefore he seeks some way to knowledge *apart from grace,* in short, another way to know God. The man who is shut up to God's *grace* still desires to have at his disposal a certain openness to God. In the nature of the case, natural theology is nothing else but the self-justification of the *natural* man. Only in this way can we understand the vitality of this natural theology, namely as man's opposition to grace.[32] Here man

---

31. *Ibid.,* p. 93.   32. *Ibid.,* p. 158.

sees his *own* possibilities. In nature and history, God is *already* revealed and man is *already* receptive for this God. Here God is not seen in his gracious activity but in his "being." Natural theology is concerned with this "being" of God. God can be known from the analogy between divine and human being. Because this analogy exists, there is a certain *true* knowledge of God possible outside of the revelation in Christ, by way of the analogy of being there is a way which leads from human thought to God, to God *as* being.

This "being" of God can be known simply by the natural light of reason. But the result, according to Barth, is that one does not thus come into contact with the true God of revelation but at best with an Aristotelian concept of abstract being. For this reason natural theology is so dangerous and fatal. Barth considers this analogy of being, the cardinal doctrine of the Roman Catholic church, to be the "invention of the Antichrist."[33]

Later we shall have to deal separately with the natural theology of Rome. Our purpose here is to show that Barth's view of natural theology is inseparably related to his Christological conception of revelation. For him the relationship rests upon a correct insight into the *knowability of God*. We have seen that Barth does not believe that there is any Scriptural support for natural theology. In order to understand Barth fully, we must note his interpretation of those Scriptural passages which are generally understood as expressions of a general revelation of God in his works.

To begin, Barth does agree that there is a line running through the whole Bible in relation to which one *must* ask the question: Is not natural theology posited here in principle both as to its possibility and reality? Are there not various passages which speak of a knowability of God apart from Jesus Christ?[34] Barth answers by referring to "a deciding line, the chief line

---

33. *K. D.* I/1, p. viii.; I/2, pp. 48ff; II/1, p. 88ff, 275, 658.
34. *K. D.* II/1, p. 109.

of the biblical message"[35] which speaks to us of the knowability of God in the revelation of his Word. The question remains however whether there is not in addition another way
by which God is knowable, a way directly related to man *in the
cosmos*. Is there a voice which man can recognize in and
through the cosmos as God's revelation in addition to and independent of God's revelation in his Word?

In response to these questions of the main line and the subsidiary line, Barth discusses the main passages of Scripture
which have usually been thought to prove a general revelation
as well as a natural theology. The main question here is
whether this subsidiary line has independent status.

Barth feels that in view of the testimony of the apostles and
prophets, this is in itself highly improbable. The revelation to
which they testify always concerns grace and judgment, God's
turning to us in love and reconciliation: "and looked at from
the main line, how would it be possible that there be also a
subsidiary line from which man in the world would be able to
approach God in another way which is not grounded in his
election nor directed by his grace in judgment?"[36] *If* this is a
subsidiary line parallel to the main line, then it can never under
any circumstances replace (blurr) the main line. Therefore
when the Bible speaks of this subsidiary line in relation to
man in the world, then it cannot mean to indicate "another,
second source for knowing God."[37] The only possibility, which
does *not* blurr the main line, is that the one revelation of God
produces an *echo*, or casts a *light*: "the place where revelation
occurs, becomes, now that it is the place of revelation, objectively a different place."[38] It is to this that the subsidiary line
in Scripture points. Therefore it is not an independent revelation next to Christ; it is not a prior revelation of God in the
cosmos, but it concerns a light *which comes out of the revelation in Christ* and shines upon the world. *In itself* the cosmos is not a revelation of God. It is true that Psalm 19 says

35. *Ibid.*, p. 112. 36. *Ibid.*, p. 114. 37. *Ibid.*, p. 121. 38. *Ibid.*

that the heavens declare the glory of God, but whatever the
Bible says concerning the glory of God in his works, is "itself
read into the text of the cosmos."[39] "In itself and as such the
text of the cosmos is dumb, as is clearly stated in Psalm 19:3:
'There is no speech nor language; their voice is not heard.' "[40]
It might be thought that by this "reading-into" Barth means
about the same that Calvin meant by the use of the figure of the
spectacles of special revelation which are needed in order to
read the revelation in creation.[41] But careful analysis shows
that something different is involved. Calvin means an objective
revelation of God in his works which man however can no
longer read correctly because of the darkening of his understanding. Through the Word, the special revelation, according to "the rule of eternal truth,"[42] he again learns to understand revelation correctly.

For Barth the situation is entirely different. There is no
original revelation of God through the work of his hands: the
text of the cosmos is itself dumb, but the light of revelation
in Christ *shines into the cosmos* and only then does the Scripture speak of a subsidiary line. By means of the revelation in
Christ we receive, as it were, a specific interpretation and qualification of the cosmos. An objective knowability of God
through the created reality which, according to Calvin, already bears the traces of its Creator, is rejected by Barth.
But for Calvin this knowability exists. Calvin recognizes the
rupture on the part of man's reaction to the revelation, but he
refuses to determine the revelation out of this subjective reaction. His problem is completely different from that of Barth.
We can say that Calvin always distinguishes sharply between

---

39. *Ibid.*, p. 123. 40. *Ibid.*
41. Cf. Calvin's *Institutes*, I, vi, 1, 3. 4. In I, vi, 4 Calvin also speaks of
the *deafness* of unbelievers "to all the voices of God which resound in the
air." The Bible is the *guide* which is needed because otherwise we could
not find our way. Cf. also T. H. L. Parker, "Calvin's Concept of Revelation," in the *Scottish Journal of Theology*, 1949, No. 1 and 2.
42. *Institutes*, I, vi, 3.

the *noetic* and the *ontic,* between *knowing* and *being.* Therefore the *deafness* and *blindness* of which Calvin speaks in no way
denies the reality of revelation. The not-knowing is unmasked
in its guilty character precisely because there is and remains
revelation. Calvin based this mainly upon what Romans 1
says about God's revelation and man's response to that revelation. Barth's exegesis of Romans 1 is radically different; of
man in the cosmos it is said, "God is knowable to him; God
himself reveals himself to him." And then he adds, "Without
a doubt knowledge of God and the knowability of God are ascribed to man in the cosmos."[43]

But at once Barth adds that this passage must be read in
the *light of the whole.* It follows then that Paul is not here
speaking of the heathen as such and in general, but in the light
of the revelation in Christ, in the light of the cross and the resurrection,[44] in the light of the confrontation of the heathen by
the revelation in the Gospel. The Epistle to the Romans was
not written by a Stoic but by an apostle of Jesus Christ. It is
in the light of Golgotha that the heathen are no longer without
excuse. What is referred to is not some specific knowledge
which the heathen have from a revelation in creation apart
from the cross, but rather the revelation preached by Paul, and
what is said of the heathen concerns "the truth ascribed to,
reckoned to and imputed to the heathen over and above himself."[45] Again Barth speaks of a "reading-into." Paul does not
speak of a "natural relation to God and knowledge of God as
such," but God's revelation is *read-into* man in the cosmos by
the sovereignty of the prophetic-apostolic authority."[46] It is
an *interpretation,* an objective qualification of man in relation
to the cross which is the content of Paul's preaching. Therefore Barth does not here deal with the question of an original
revelation in creation. He warns against taking what Paul

43. Barth, *K.D.,* II/1. p. 131.
44. *Ibid.,* p. 132. Cf. also O. Cullmann, *Christus und die Zeit. Die
Urchristliche Zeit- und Geschichtsauffassung,* 1946, p. 160f.
45. Barth, *K.D.* II/1, p. 133. 46. *Ibid.,* p. 134.

says in Romans 1:19-20 as "an abstract matter concerning the heathen as such, concerning the revelation possessed by the heathen as such."[47] Apart from the incarnation of the Word, the only aspect from which one can approach the knowability of God is the Christological, and that exclusively.[48] By combining the noetic and the ontic aspects, the question concerning the reality of a revelation of God in his works disappears for Barth. He sees the entire question of revelation Christologically, and he does not take into account the rupture which became visible in history from paradise to the fall, upon which Calvin's conception of the inexcusableness of man wholly rests. For Barth the problem is not that of the heathen and an original revelation in creation but through the cross of Christ the state of the heathen has become different from what it was previously. It is in this new light that the heathen now "know God" (Rom. 1:21) even though they have not subjectively realized it.[49] This "inexcusableness" is not related to an original revelation in creation but to the *cross of Christ* alone.

Barth's entire interpretation of Romans 1 is conditioned by his fear that in addition to the revelation in Christ there be accepted another independent source of knowledge of God, one preceding the cross. Such a second source of knowledge would, he thinks, be in sharp conflict with the redemptive character of God's revelation. Since Barth identifies revelation and reconciliation, he considers the search for a revelation which does not imply reconciliation to be a search for revelation apart from grace. Then there would be knowledge of God by means of which one would not actually need the revelation of God's *grace*. Thus in this whole search man displays his opposition to God!

Barth cannot conceive of a general revelation which would already in itself be in conflict with man who opposes *this* revelation. Therefore his offensive against natural theology is at

---

47. *K.D.* I/2, p. 334.   48. *K. D.* II/1, p. 166.   49. *Ibid.*, p. 335.

the same time a denial of "general" revelation. Although it is true that in the reconciliation of the cross, the whole cosmos and the whole of life are seen in the light of the Creator and the Redeemer, yet he cannot conceive of an *actual, objective* revelation in God's works. Therefore Barth writes, and here all misunderstanding is certainly impossible, "the conception of an indirect revelation in nature, in history and in our self-consciousness, is destroyed by the recognition of grace. . ."[50] His fierce opposition to the second article of the Belgic Confession is just as clear; thus his offensive is creedal as well as theological.[51] For Barth *general* revelation and *natural* theology are inseparably united. The root idea of Barth's violent attack lies in the fact that he considers them to be on the same plane.

---

50. *Revelation,* p. 51.   51. Cf. Chapter XI.

Reaction to Barth's Offensive

CHAPTER III

Reaction to Barth's Offensive

A SIGNIFICANT aspect of the discussions concerning dialectical theology is undoubtedly the reaction which Barth's offensive has aroused. It is desirable to study this reaction in order to see clearly the important questions involved. We must limit ourselves chiefly to two contemporary theologians, Emil Brunner and Paul Althaus, who have differed sharply with Barth at this point. Although there are important differences between the two, yet in their reaction to Barth there is remarkable similarity. It is therefore our task to carefully analyze this difference concerning general revelation, and we may not *a priori* express our full agreement with these theologians on important criticism directed toward details.

A. *Emil Brunner*

After 1930, when the tension between Barth and Brunner on the question of the point-of-contact had already become evident, the conflict came to a head regarding the relation of "nature" and "grace." Brunner began a counter offensive against his former friend, Barth, even though he still considered Barth his confederate in the attempt to build a theology of the Word.[1] He still recognized their mutual starting-point and felt that Barth's basic error lay in his inconsistent conclusions.[2] From their mutual starting-point, Barth drew false conclusions and called those who hesitated to accept those conclusions traitors.[3] What they have in common, according to Brunner, is the message of the Bible, the Word of God, the

---

1. Brunner, *Natur und Gnade,* 1934, p. 1.
2. *Ibid.,* p. 7.   3. *Ibid.,* p. 4.

revelation in Jesus Christ. It is the radical and exclusive message of *"sola gratia — sola fide,"* the message of free grace
and sovereign redemption over against free will and synergism,
the message of God's revelation over against historism and psychologism and every kind of experience-theology. Brunner explains this common starting-point as the conviction that the
church's message is not based upon two sources, viz. revelation
and reason, revelation and nature, revelation and history. The
fight against this "and" is the same struggle Elijah had upon
Mt. Carmel against those who were halting between two opinions. "In all of this there is no difference of opinion between
Barth and myself, except for the fact that Barth does suppose
that a difference exists."[4]

However, Brunner does object to the conclusions which
Barth draws from the central Biblical-Reformed message. He
summarizes Barth's two chief conclusions as follows:

1. The sinner has completely lost the image of God so
    that no element of it remains.

2. Since Holy Scripture is the only norm for our
    knowledge of God, every attempt "to assert a general revelation of God in nature, consciousness and
    history" must be resisted.

We are mainly concerned with the second conclusion. Brunner considers it almost superfluous to point out that at this
point Barth is in direct conflict with Scripture. For it is clear
that according to the Old and New Testaments the creation
of the world is *at once* revelation, "self-communication of God."
"This is not a heathen tenet, but a fundamental Christian
proposition."[5]

Indeed, he is convinced that "Barth denies Paul's conclusions"[6] in relation to Romans 1 and 2, and adds that Paul
presupposes the Old Testament with "its hundred-fold testi-

4. *Ibid.,* p. 6.   5. *Ibid.,* p. 12.   6. *Ibid.*

mony to the Creator's divine majesty in his works." Whether
there be two revelations is really no problem for Brunner:
"This question should be answered positively once and for all
according to the Bible."[7] The only question is that of the
relation between the two, between revelation in creation and
revelation in Jesus Christ. The universal Christian answer to
this question is that, for us sinful people, the revelation in creation is not sufficient to bring us to a saving knowledge of
God.[8]

In itself this revelation was certainly sufficient to bring everyone to a knowledge of the majesty and wisdom of the Creator. But sin has changed all this so that the sinner is now
darkened in his heart and turns God's revelation into a caricature.[9] Only in the light of the revelation of Jesus Christ can
we again understand God's revelation in creation and thus discover "that God has already revealed himself previously."

Acceptance of this two-fold revelation does not imply that
Brunner means to tone down the antithesis between Rome and
the Reformation. Although Barth accuses Brunner of wandering
off in this direction and even characterizes Brunner's position
as "Thomistic," Brunner means to keep the Reformed antithesis against Rome wholly intact. He wants to follow Calvin
who emphasized revelation in creation. What Brunner means
by "natural theology" is certainly quite different from the
natural theology of Rome which can be called an *unbroken*
natural theology. Rome believes in natural theology as a system, "a rational system which is sufficient unto itself."[10] It is
of a purely rational nature. But the impossibility of *such* a
natural theology does *not* mean that we must set aside *all* natural theology as Barth does. Barth does that only because he
has a onesided conception of revelation as complete actuality.[11]
As a result Barth denies that God speaks, upon the ground that
he *has* spoken.

---

7. *Ibid.*, p. 13.   8. *Ibid.*, p. 13.   9. *Ibid.*, p. 31.   10. *Ibid.*, p. 32.
11. *Ibid.*, p. 35.

Over against Barth, Brunner contends that we must emphasize that God has revealed himself in his works, so that the
whole world is a "manifestation of God."[12]   Only a *false* natural theology is dangerous for church and theology.[13]   The
church may never allow itself to be driven to a onesided reaction. "The church may no more tolerate the continuous rejection of natural theology than an erroneous use of it." [14]
According to Brunner, it is therefore the task of our generation
"to find the way back to a *true* natural theology."[15]

* * *

From this, one might think that Brunner only wants to
stress the objective possibility of knowing God from the revelation in creation, although this would not yet mean, the *subjective* possibility of this knowledge, because sin has wrecked
man's receptivity for revelation.   God's revelation still *exists*
in the created reality, but man cannot perceive this revelation
because his whole nature has been darkened.   Revelation now
stands over against the sinful ignorance of man, and therefore
man is inexcusable.

Brunner has repeatedly referred to Calvin and Scripture for
these aspects of guilt and revelation, objective knowability and
subjective ignorance.   But it sounds strange when he adds that
the task of the present generation must be to pave the way
toward a "natural theology" again.   Careful scrutiny soon
shows that Brunner is really after something more than simply
"objective knowability" without the knowledge that flows from
it.   His doctrine of general revelation is closely linked to his
view of the divine image in man.   He is therefore not simply
concerned with the knowability of God through the work of
creation, but with the problem of *knowledge*.

Brunner always distinguishes between the *formal* and the
material aspects of the image of God.[16]   The formal image is the

---

12. *Ibid.*, p. 36.   13. *Ibid.*, p. 44.   14. *Ibid.*, p. 44.   15. *Ibid.*
16. *Ibid.*, p. 10.

humanity (*humanum*) of man, that is, that which distinguishes man, be he sinner or not, from the rest of creation; it indicates man as a responsible subject. He is someone "with whom man can speak, and with whom God can speak."[17] That is man's capacity for the Word (*Wortfähigkeit*) and his responsibility (*Verantwortlichkeit*).[18]

Sin has not in the least impaired this formal image of God, and it now constitutes the point of contact for redeeming grace. Sin has affected the material image of God since every part of man has been affected by sin.[19] But just the same the point of contact is "the formal image of God, present also in the sinner, the humanness (*Menschsein*) of man, his humanity . . . . subject to the Word (*Wortmächtigkeit*) and responsibility (*Verantwortlichkeit*)."[20] There is a purely *formal* addressability. This does not include the receptivity or disposition to accept grace and the Word of God. "*Wortmächtigkeit*" is formally only the "presupposition for the possibility of hearing the Word of God."[21] Only the *creative* word has power to bring man to a positive decision. It is completely due to the grace of God so that the confession of *sola gratia — sola fide* is not in the least endangered by the doctrine of the point of contact.

The formal image of God, according to Brunner, refers to man with his natural knowledge of God and everything else connected with it.[22]

It is clear that we are dealing here with something different from the objective knowability of God through his works. Brunner here passes over to the subjective side and, via the addressability and the *humanum*, he arrives at conscience and God-consciousness, both of which belong to the formal image of God.

Therefore, by way of the objective knowability, he arrives at the subjective qualities of knowledge and consciousness of

17. *Idid.*   18. *Ibid.*, p. 11.   19. *Ibid.*   20. *Ibid.*, p. 18.
21. *Ibid.*, p. 19.   22. *Ibid.*

the natural man, viz. those "of God, of law and of his own responsibility to God," [23] as the "point of contact" for divine grace.

In response to Barth's reply, Brunner made certain corrections in the second edition of 1935.[24] Now he formulates it more emphatically: "One now arrives at true knowledge from the first revelation only by way of the second. That does not mean, however, that it may not be known as the *first* nor that it does not retain its own validity."[25] Here Brunner emphasizes Calvin's statement, to which his attention was called by many, concerning the knowledge of God that man would have had, *"if* Adam had *not* fallen." What God revealed in creation "would have been (objectively) known to everyone if sin had not entered the world."[26] For Brunner a Christian natural theology asserts "the objective knowability of God through the creation which is now possible only within a Christian theology, i. e., only on the basis of the revelation of Christ and the Holy Scriptures through the illumination of the Holy Spirit."[27]

Brunner continues, however, to emphasize the two-fold character of revelation. In a later book he again opposes a so-called theological monism.[28] He will not allow that the diverse ways of God's speaking may simply be called *signs,* and without denying its unity, he calls attention to the manifold revelation of God.[29]

There is a general or creational revelation. In it God is *objectively* knowable, but that does not mean that the natural man is himself able to receive this revelation and develop a natural theology. On the basis of this revelation in creation, Luther and Calvin did not derive a doctrine of a true natural

23. *Ibid.,* p. 20.
24. Brunner, *Natur und Gnade,* 1935.
25. *Ibid.,* p. 46.   26. *Ibid.,* p. 47.   27. *Ibid.,* p. 50.
28. Brunner, *Offenbarung und Vernunft,* 1941, p. 60.
29. *Ibid.,* p. 59.

knowledge but a doctrine of paganism.[30] Rejection of general revelation was often the result of fear of natural theology *rationally* derived independently of the special revelation. As a result some have put general revelation, even though clearly expressed in Scripture, under the same suspicion as natural theology.[31] Although Brunner had previously emphasized the great significance of natural theology for this generation, in this book he declares: "in short, Biblical and natural theology can never be harmonized."[32] "They stand in an exclusive relationship to each other." The problem of general revelation and the problem of natural theology "concern two completely different things."[33]

General revelation does not compete with special historical revelation, but is rather its *presupposition*. Only by means of Christian faith is one able to understand this revelation correctly. The fact that this way to knowledge has been disturbed does not in the least impair the *reality* of the original revelation, nor does it discontinue the "inexcusableness" but rather establishes it.[34] Although this revelation does not lead to the "actual reception of the knowledge of God,"[35] yet the *suppression* of this revelation is the presupposition of its *existence*. The "source of his false ideas of God" lies in the suppression of this revelation. Brunner maintains that it is at this point that the Reformation differs fundamentally from Rome: there is *general revelation but no natural theology*. It is the corruption of nature which accounts for this and prevents true knowledge of God. Man's *knowledge* is no better than his works.

But the acknowledgment of this may not lead to the denial of general revelation. To do so would destroy the basis of man's responsibility.[36] This revelation is the "inescapable presupposition of the gospel message." If only it is remembered that Christ alone "reopens the obstructed entrance to this orig-

---

30. *Ibid.*, p. 61.　31. *Ibid.*　32. *Ibid.*, p. 62.　33. *Ibid.*, p. 63.
34. *Ibid.*, p. 65.　35. *Ibid.*, p. 66.　36. *Ibid.*, p. 67.

inal source of the knowledge of God,"[37] then the doctrine of general revelation will in no way diminish the glory of Christ. At this point Brunner again refers to his conflict with Barth. In this "sideline" (*Nebenlinie*) he detects the old error appearing again.[38] Barth does not distinguish between the ontic and noetic principles and therefore thinks that the doctrine of general revelation must necessarily lead to natural theology.[39] Brunner detects the same error in Barth's criticism of the analogy of being. It is certainly true that the analogy of being does not enable one to build a natural theology. The analogies in the creation are no legitimate theological way for sinful man to follow, but they do exist, even though they are only recognized in faith.[40] Thus by way of an ever more careful formulation, Brunner attempts to withstand the offensive of Barth. We can say that the *central* problem with which he deals is that of *objective knowability* and *subjective knowledge*. Here he touches a problem which Reformed theology has long discussed in relation to Romans 1.

This must be kept clearly in mind even though one should conclude that in his opposition to Barth, Brunner has also reached unacceptable conclusions. This is regrettable because these false conclusions have made it difficult again for Barth to give careful attention to the *clear motives* of Brunner's opposition. The main cause lay in Brunner's development of the doctrine of the point of contact. To the elements which are the givens of man's existence, Brunner mentions human reason,[41] the experience of the limitation of our life by the world and the necessity of dying, the natural knowledge of God and conscience. Thus he speaks of "the knowledge of God which belongs to human nature as such."[42] He sets these negative, immanent possibilities or givens of human nature over against the Word of God, but it is not altogether clear why he speaks

---

37. *Ibid.*, p.78.　38 *Ibid.*, p. 80 ff.　39. *Ibid.*, p. 80.　40. *Ibid.*, p. 81.
41. Brunner, *Zwischen den Zeiten*, 1932, p. 514.　42. *Ibid.*, p. 516.

only of "negative" possibilities. It is difficult to believe that by the formal image of God, Brunner only means something simply formal especially when one takes note of the illustration he uses of the *spearhead* (*spits*) of the image of God "meeting" the spearhead of the Word of God, and then goes on to speak of the "*actualization of the negative possibility of the point of contact.*" Consider merely the way Brunner speaks of these things in his anthropology. Every person, says Brunner, "knows about responsibility."[43] Indeed, "the consciousness of a divine obligation is ineradicable; it outlasts the whole destructive development of human thought."[44]

From his conception of the formal image of God, Brunner came to consider conscience as pointing to the "natural" self-consciousness of man and to consider it a part of the existence of the natural man as such.[45] Although a miracle of grace is needed to bring man to faith, yet Brunner says that "latent despair breaks forth in order to bring the guilt-consciousness to maturity."[46] And when Brunner *in this context* mentions penance as "the presupposition of faith" and deals with "the sickness unto death" as the "natural man's state of being,"[47] we can understand why Barth cannot agree with *such* conceptions. He cannot be convinced by *this* plea for a point of contact. Here we see that which occurs so frequently in theology — a counter-offensive *fails to achieve the desired result* because not all of the weapons employed are sound. Then a new reaction begins again so that the possibility that the telling blows will actually be felt is small. This has happened in the discussions between Barth and Brunner. One who follows the discussion carefully cannot deny that Brunner has at least

43. Brunner. *Der Mensch im Widerspruch,* p. 39.
44. *Ibid.,* p. 39.
45. Brunner, *"Die Frage nach dem Anknüpfungspunkt als Problem der Theologie."* *Zwischen den Zeiten,* 1932, p. 516.
46. *Ibid.* p. 518.   47. *Ibid.*

pointed out this *one* important point: i.e., *that general revelation and a rational natural theology are not to be identified.*

Barth has unjustly referred to the problem which Brunner has indicated as only an apparent problem. This is not true because the problem is real even for those who differ from Brunner at many points. Precisely this distinction, yes, the *separation* of general revelation and natural theology, is the most important question in the whole debate. It is impossible and unjustified to conclude that because man lacks the true knowledge of God, therefore *God's revelation* is also absent. Barth's criticism of Brunner in no way gives him the right to consider this question closed. When Rome claims to possess the formula "by which theology completely remains theology, and yet the pre-theological is fully justified,"[48] then Barth, as a Protestant theologian, will reject that formula. Neither does he want to make theology dependent upon an anthropological analysis. He is concerned only with the miracle of grace which itself "creates" the point of contact, and only then is man able to receive the Word of God.[49]

We can understand the dangers which Barth fears. They are acutely present, life-size, in the natural theology of Rome. But Barth's polemic may not attack the confession of general revelation. No one makes this more clear than Calvin in his penetrating comments upon general revelation. True, Barth says it is "astounding" that Brunner should appeal to Calvin.[50] But even if one cannot at all agree with Brunner's position, he cannot deny that an appeal to Calvin for a confession of general revelation is certainly in order. That is certainly clear even

---

48. L. Fendt, "Natürliche Theologie im Katholizismus." *Zeitschrift für Theologie und Kirche,* 1934. p. 331.

49. Barth, *Kirchliche Dogmatik,* II/1, p. 251.

50. Barth's own position here is too simplistic a reproduction of the penetrating views of Calvin. He thinks that Calvin held only that *in principle* there was the possibility of knowledge from creation but *not in fact.*

from Peter Barth's book written against Brunner.[51]   When
Brunner rejects the identity of general revelation and natural
theology, he can rightly appeal to Calvin.   For Calvin the solution does not lie in *identification* but in *separation* between general revelation and the knowledge of this revelation, so that the
acceptance of general revelation does not *automatically* open the
door to natural theology.   Therefore, upon the basis of Scripture, Calvin can always point to God's works in nature, but at
the same time emphasize the word of John, "Whosoever de-
nieth the Son, the same hath not the Father . . ." (I John 2 :23),
And whatever claims to be "knowledge" of God, must be judged
by the only norm which is given for the true knowledge of God
in Christ.[52]

B. *Paul Althaus*

The polemic of Althaus against Barth bears a striking similarity in many respects to that of Brunner. Althaus, like Brunner, begins by saying that the revelation in Jesus Christ is *not*
"the first and only self-communication of God to mankind and
individual men," but that it rests upon an earlier revelation.[53]

He says that this is so obvious that it had become a matter
of course for theology to deal "with a twofold revelation,"[54]
until recently when the idea of general revelation was given up
and revelation was limited to Jesus Christ. Here Althaus directs himself primarily against Barth and refers to what he
considers the irrefutable testimony of Romans 1 and 2.   He

51. Peter Barth. "Das Problem der natürlichen Theologie bei Calvin,"
Theologisch Existenz Heute, 1935, No. 18.   Cf. also Peter Brunner,
"Allgemeine und besondere Offenbarung in Calvins Institutio," *Evang.
Theol.* I, p. 189ff. and Günter Gloede. *Theologia naturalis bei Calvin*, 1935.
Cf. also T.H.L. Parker, "Calvin's Concept of Revelation." *Scottish
Journal of Theology*, 1949, p. 36: "that Calvin undoubtedly teaches a self-
manifestation of the Creator in the universe, in history and in experience."
"The revelation, however, does not cease to be revelation, because man
does not recognize it as such." p. 37.
52. Calvin: *Institutes of the Christian Religion*, II, vi, 4.
53. P. Althaus, *Die Christliche Wahrheit*, I, 1947, p. 45.
54. *Ibid.*, p. 45.

calls Barth's exegesis an "act of pure despair."[55] If one really wants to listen to Scripture, he *must* speak of a two-fold revelation — the redemptive revelation in Christ and the "original self communication, or primary, foundational revelation."[56] It is necessary to speak of the latter as well because *guilt* is anchored to it.

There is a general revelation, a *logos,* which lighteth every man.[57] This confession in no way signifies defection from the Reformed view. Of course there is always the danger that general revelation will *supplant* special revelation, but this is not necessarily so. In the nineteenth century, largely under influence of Kantian criticism, revelation was Christologically narrowed. W. Herrmann, once a teacher of Karl Barth, did that. The natural sciences and positivism have had the same influence. "Nature and history are emptied of God, so that knowledge of them has absolutely no significance any more as the basis for certainty of God."[58]

Reaction to this narrowing of revelation now arose from the side of the history-of-religions school. It wanted nothing to do with a Christomonistic view of revelation, but stressed the close relation between Christianity and the other religions, thereby denying that Christianity was *the* absolute religion and holding that it was only a special form of the general "revelation which lay behind all religions."[59]

Then in the twentieth century the tidal wave of Christomonistic revelation came along, especially through K. Heim and K. Barth.[60] Althaus' critique is directed mainly at Barth. He, like Brunner, accuses Barth of confusing original revelation and rational natural theology.[61] General revelation, says Althaus, must be freed from this confusing identification. God communicates himself, reveals himself in the reality of our lives, "in the immediate consciousness, in active experience of

---

55. *Ibid.,* p. 48.   56. *Ibid.,* p. 50.   57. *Ibid.,* p. 53.   58. *Ibid.,* p. 65.
59. *Ibid.,* p. 65.   60. *Ibid.,* p. 67.   61. *Ibid.,* p. 69.

the reality of our lives."[62] Man, because he is a man, becomes
conscious of God.[63] That is not to say that we arrive at God
by way of causality.[64] On the contrary, it is an *immediate experience.*

Here already we can see that Althaus wants more than an
objective knowability of God through his works. He is
actually concerned with a true natural knowledge of God.
Who this God is, as in Rome's natural theology, is not under
consideration at the outset. This is clear when Althaus writes
that we become conscious of being "in the hands of the power
of providence,"[65] or even more characteristically, "we are in
the hands of *a* Lord who is over us."[66] This expression,
"*a* Lord," displays the *heart* of Althaus' natural theology.
For *this* "Lord" is still undetermined and bears striking resemblance to the first cause of the unmoved mover of Roman
Catholic theology, even though Althaus here (as does the
Vaticanum, too, however), calls him *Lord.* We notice a turn
(*sprong*) in Althaus' argument: "Thus the experience of our
absolute creation (*Gewirktheit*) is the first moment of our existence, in which that power *which we call God* testifies of himself, and the omnipotent, omniscient living power of providence
is the first thing we mean by the word 'God.' Through this
experience we are *called to humble obedience.*"[67] Althaus
agrees with Schleiermacher who identifies the feeling of absolute dependence with the consciousness of God, and it is not
at all surprising then that Althaus should defend the thesis:
"Theology must start out, therefore, from anthropology."[68]
He is concerned with man's immediate experience. Here God
is near to us. In this nearness of God we become aware of an
"unconditional demand" upon us. God reveals himself in our
being (*sein*) and in our obligation (*sollen*), in our loneliness
and suffering. He is the mystery of our humanity.[69] "We were

---

62. *Ibid.,* p. 75.   63. *Ibid.,* p. 76.   ʒʒ. Ibid., p. 76.   64. *Ibid.*
65. *Ibid.,* p. 78.   66. *Ibid.,* Italics ours.   67. *Ibid.,* p. 78. Italics ours.
68. *Ibid.,* p. 78.   69. *Ibid.,* p. 84.

made by him and therefore we are conscious of him." Furthermore, one also gains certainty concerning God from the passing
of history. This experience of God is not bound up with the
gospel. and faith in Christ.[70] It is "essential, foundational,
'pre-Christian,' i.e., it is both possible and real prior to the confrontation of God in Jesus Christ."[71] We experience God in
history when we experience God's call to carry out a special
task through regulations and conditions in which a man is
placed at a significant period of history.[72] This call can only
be understood in faith, but that does not yet mean *Christian*
faith. There is also a *general, non-Christian* faith, and theology
must "esteem every faith equally as truly possessing the Lord
of history."[73] It is irrefutable : God comes to us *through* history
with the seriousness of his laws and in the exceptional events,
"in the miracle of turning to a hopeless situation."[74] "That
turning comes to pass mainly as the act of man.[75] It is then
a gift "of the Lord of history."

Besides history, God is revealed also in theoretical thought
and in nature. It is true that we do not know the God of the
gospel from nature,[76] but that is not decisive. There is
order, harmony and teleology in nature; and although much
disorder can be observed, this does not destroy the self-witness
of God.[77]

For Althaus, then, natural knowledge of God is not simply
a possibility, but an all important reality, [78] which theology can
not afford to neglect.

* * *

In Althaus we see again, even more clearly than in Brunner,
that we must not rejoice too quickly when general revelation
is stressed over against those who have rejected it. For here
we see a defense of the doctrine of general revelation bound

70. *Ibid.*, p. 86.   71. *Ibid.*   72 *Ibid.* (Germany?)   73. *Ibid.*, p. 87.
74. *Ibid.*, p. 90.
75. *Ibid.*, p. 90. Unconsciously one asks at what time this part of Althaus'
dogmatics was written.
76. *Ibid.*, p. 99.   77. *Ibid.*, pp. 105, 107.   78. *Ibid.*, p. 108.

up with natural theology in a remarkable but illegitimate way.
It is a natural theology built upon nature, history, great men,
and self-consciousness; a natural theology of pre-Christian
character which receives *independent* status. It is not necessary
to describe the theology of Althaus further. But it is valuable
to understand the nature of this reaction or counter-offensive, so that we in our reactions may avoid Charybdis as well
as Scylla.

Althaus has opposed the so-called Christomonistic view of
revelation for a long time. In it he sees at work a modern relativism which no longer recognizes God in nature and history;
and he felt that this modern relativism had now become a fel-
low-laborer with theology as tutor to Christ."[79]

Althaus protests against this relativistic conception of nature
and history and its unwarranted conclusion that revelation is
exclusively in Christ. In those days already (1935) he thought
he understood the times. He says, "the surprising birth of a
vigorous national ethos has superseded and relativized every
relativism."[80] Christomonistic theology and ethics[81] have had
their day: "these thoughts are of yesterday and the day before,
no longer of today."[82]

The irony of history in dogmatics! When the idea of general revelation is worked out in *this* way, then the dangers facing us are very great. Althaus' dogmatics of 1948 are on the
whole more sober, but his views on Christomonism in 1935
were more clear, for there his view of God's revelation reached
a vague unrecognizableness by way of the German national
ethos and *this* Lord of history. Yet we may no more get rid of
Althaus than of Brunner by simply saying that their counter-
offensive shows how strong Barth's offensive had been. No

79. Althaus, *Uroffenbarung, Luthertum,* 1935, p. 4.
80. *Ibid.,* p. 5.   81. *Ibid.*
82. *Ibid.* Cf. also P. Althaus, "Die Inflation des Begriffs der Offenbarung in der gegenwärtigen Theologie" *Zeitschr. für systematische
Theologie,* 18e Jrg. and P. Althaus, "Natürliche Theologie und Christus-
glaube," *Z.F. syst. Theol.* 1939, p. 417ff.

matter how unacceptable Althaus' "natural theology" may be, yet in this conception which led him to such dangerous consequences in 1935, there are forces at work which show how complex a theological conception is. We have seen above that Althaus, as well as Brunner, appeals to Romans 1. Although Romans 1 does not support Althaus' natural theology — on the contrary!— yet we may not lose sight of the significant questions involved here. Althaus has referred to the relation between general revelation and guilt[83] and to what Scripture says of the revelation of God in his works. One can only regret that Althaus weaves these Scriptural ideas into such a pattern that Barth will probably feel no more force in these criticisms than he does in those of Brunner.

* * *

In Brunner's and Althaus' reaction to Barth, we now see that in spite of the dangerous way in which they sometimes reproduce Scriptural ideas, they have nevertheless emphasized some questions which theology may not and cannot neglect. It must be admitted that their reaction is gaining influence.[84] The conviction is growing that the identification of the *noetic* and the *ontic*[85] is wrong, and that in spite of its suggestiveness, the christological (Christ only!) limitation of revelation does not do justice to the full teaching of Scripture.

The power of this suggestion made progress for some time because it reminded men of the absoluteness of the Christian religion and the exclusiveness of salvation through Christ who is the only way to the Father. But upon further reflection, the conviction grew, that, although the idea of "Christ only" was derived from the Reformation, as were the preaching of the

---

83. *Luthertum,* 1935, p. 8ff. Cf. also P. Althaus. *Der Brief an der Römer* (Das N.T. deutsch) 1949, p. 15.

84. E.g. F.W. A. Korff, *Het Christelijk geloof en de niet-Christelijke godsdiensten,* 1946, p. 72.

85. Noetic refers to knowledge, ontic to being.

only name and the exclusiveness of salvation, Scripture also speaks of a revelation of God in his works, a revelation which in no way conflicts with this "Christ only."

In the reactions to Barth, we see how the search for the extent and the place of revelation continues, together with all the dangers of a universalism in revelation which accompanies it. A dangerous situation thus arose out of this reaction, so that even those who denied the uniqueness of Christ could readily agree with the reaction. Because this has often been true, one might get the impression that the whole reaction can be traced back to a *relativizing* universalism in revelation which so often appears in the history of church and theology. To understand these reactions to Barth, we shall have to make careful distinctions and always investigate its background. Not all that glitters here is gold. Our purpose is not to give a complete description of the reaction. Besides Brunner and Althaus, we shall indicate a few others who have likewise discussed this problem.

* * *

A remarkable representative of this reaction is Dillschneider, who also objects to the limitation of revelation to Jesus of Nazareth. In his dogmatics he sets forth the doctrine of the "cosmic Christ."[86] All creation owes its origin (*ontstaan*) and continued existence (*bestaan*) to Christ.[87] "In creation we deal with the cosmic Christ."[88] We meet Christ in creation, perhaps not *personally,* but *really.*[89] Revelation in creation is the form of the really active Christ,[90] as distinguished from other forms of the Son's operation, even as Calvin distinguished them. In this connection, Dillschneider refers to Romans 1, where Paul speaks of mankind which is unexcusable, mankind

---

86. O. A. Dillschneider, *Gegenwart Christi.* I, 1948, p. 214. Cf. also his *Evangelische Offenbarung,* 1939.
87. Cf. Col. 1:14-17.
88. Dillschneider, *Gegenwart Christi,* p. 219.
89. *Ibid.,* p. 218.   90. *Ibid.,* p. 219.

which "lives on the other side of the *'Deus dixit,'* which does not have God's Word."[91] God's eternal power and divinity become visible in the "Christus-cosmos." Dillschneider distinguishes also between revelation "in Jesus Christ" and in the "Christus-cosmos,"[92] but at the same time he rejects the side line (*Nebenlinie*) of Barth, as well as his criticism of Article II of the Belgic Confession.[93] Dillschneider maintains that it is the duty of theology to find a cure for her long endured "blindness of nature."[94]

Evidently, Dillschneider's view could also in a sense be called Christological — perhaps even Christomonistic — but the nature of this Christomonism is completely different from that of Barth. The distinction between the Logos-Christ who is already active in creation and Jesus Christ is radically different from that of Barth. Barth's relation between creation and Christ is entirely different from that of Dillschneider. Therefore Dillschneider also belongs to the reaction against Barth, and in spite of his many speculative tendencies, he too points us to an *important* problem.

* * *

Wilhelm Lütgert has also dealt at length with the relation between creation and revelation.[95] He feels that since the beginning of the nineteenth century the doctrine of creation has been gradually pushed into the background in favor of the doctrine of redemption. The necessary result of this has been a Christomonistic theology. "If this doctrine means to say that Christ must be central in Christian doctrine, then it is, of course, true. However, in principle, it means a limitation of revelation to the person and work (history) of Christ."[96] Over

91. *Ibid.,* pp. 229 and 233.   92. *Ibid.,* p. 230.
93. *Ibid.*   94. *Ibid.,* p. 225ff.
95. W. Lütgert, *Schöpfung und Offenbarung. Eine Theologie des ersten Artikels,* 1934.
96. *Ibid.,* p. 27.

REACTION TO BARTH'S OFFENSIVE 55

against this, he contends that Reformed theology is *not* Christ-centric but *theological.*[97] He rejects the attempt to base faith in the creator upon faith in the redeemer.[98] On the contrary, redemption is based upon creation. When one has discovered that, he will not attempt an anthropological limitation of religion, but will direct it *theocentrically* upon God. There will then appear a frankness to see *creation* as a manifestation of God.[99]

The *Word* is not the only form of revelation:[100] Creation is revelation . . . [101] "an objective act of God which is real as the will and act of God."[102] Only when this has been recognized can one deal with man's reaction to God's revelation in creation. The *ontological* aspect of this revelation may not be blurred by the *noetic.* "It remains revelation, even when it does not awaken faith in man. Creation in itself is revelation."[103] According to Paul, there is a revelation which precedes the revelation in Christ — viz. the revelation of the power and wisdom of God. Thus Lütgert arrives at the conclusion that faith in the creator is *foundational* to faith in the redeemer. *This* is the point of contact for missions to the heathen world; they can begin with the doctrine of the creation and government of God.[104] The Word of God does not begin with Jesus Christ. More than ever before, we need a theology of the *first* article.

In this reaction we also see the dangers involved in opposing Christomonism. Lütgert starts out from the reality of revelation in creation and then switches over to the *knowledge* of this revelation. The temptation to make this leap does not permit us to overlook the fact that a *leap* has been made. This is most evident in his predilection for the independence of the *first* article. It is difficult to understand how Lütgert would then be able to avoid a natural theology.

---

97. *Ibid.,* p. 28.   98. *Ibid.,* p. 52.   99. *Ibid.,* p. 138.
100. *Ibid.,* p. 140. 101. *Ibid.,* p. 142. 102. *Ibid.,* p. 165.
103. *Ibid.,* p. 165. For him *guilt* is based upon that. Cf. p. 395.
104. *Ibid.,* p. 397.

Lütgert's reaction runs into difficulty in the almost *automatic* transition from revelation in creation to faith in creation, while it is just at that point that an independent and gradual transition may not be made, nor may there be an *independent* priority of the first article over against the second article of the creed.

* * *

There is something fascinating in this whole reaction. It seems sometimes that wherever Christomonism is opposed, the *suction power* of a natural theology is felt.[105] Perhaps it is this that has convinced Barth that he is on the right track with his Christomonism. He can certainly point an accusing finger at many who *began* by pleading for general revelation, but who *ended* by doing injustice to the uniqueness of salvation and the all-inclusive significance of the knowledge of God in Jesus Christ. Is there possibly some *essential necessity* which accounts for the *weakness* of this reaction? Does the danger of natural theology threaten every reaction? Or does the error lie in the *type* of reaction which has been made against Barth?

It is clear that the answer to these questions will be decisive for all the problems of general revelation. It is our conviction, which we wish to make clear at this point, that the reaction has indeed pin-pointed a problem which the Christomonistic view has unjustly neglected.[106] But the *manner* in which this opposition has been expressed, made it unable to overcome the threatening danger of universalism. Again we see the "pendulum movement" in theology! As Barth strongly opposed a universal revelation, so others opposed his Christomonism. The solution to the confusion of these reactions will be possible

---

105. Cf. R. Hermann, *Fragen um den Begriff der natürlichen Theologie*, 1950, p. 16.
106. Cf. also W. Bachmann, *Gottes Ebenbild*, 1938, pp. 20 and 27; E. Gerstenmaier, *Die Kirche und die Schöpfung*, 1938, p. 29; J. J. van Oosterzee, *Christelijke Dogmatiek* I, 1870, pp. 174-180.

only when one tries to avoid the "tension" between the *first* and the *second* articles, and does not confuse revelation with the knowledge of the revelation. We must again make use of the pure light of Scripture which points a clear way to understand the relation between the *universality* and the *particularity* of God's revelation.

The Natural Theology of Rome

CHAPTER IV

The Natural Theology of Rome

BEFORE we discuss the question of the reality of general revelation according to Scripture, it is necessary to get some idea of what is meant by "natural theology," so that we will not lose our way in involved discussions. Only then will one fully understand why the identification of general revelation and natural theology is *an untenable position.*

Natural theology involves *knowledge* of God. From the history of church and theology, we can readily learn what was meant by this knowledge. It is sharply distinguished from that knowledge which is derived from special revelation through Christ and the illumination of the Holy Spirit. Natural theology or knowledge of God was considered possible by another means, *viz.* by way of nature and human reason. The supporters of natural theology do not at all mean to imply that natural knowledge of God is the *only proper* one. Rather, there are two sources of the knowledge of God, and the second source, special revelation, is much *richer* than the other. However, the greater fulness of the second source does not permit one to neglect the first source.

Natural theology does not even pretend to be able to construct a system by means of human nature. It does not pretend to be an *autonomous* theology. Its content is not meant to be a projection of man's inner being nor of that which comes up out of human "nature," but rests basically upon revelation. This revelation, which is the source of natural theology, is not the special revelation in Christ and the Holy Scriptures, but the general revelation in creation, in created reality. It is the foun-

dation of natural knowledge. The products of this revelation
are the "natural" knowledge of God and "natural" morality.
Only in this way, it is said, is one able to do justice to the
varieties of "knowledge" of God (no matter how distorted)
outside of Christianity and special revelation, as well as to the
conceptions of morality and the sense of duty which we still
meet everywhere in life. A knowledge of salvation in Christ or
an illumination of the Spirit are out of the question here. It
is simply a *natural* knowledge which man gets through the
medium of created reality, and therefore is completely different
from the supernatural knowledge of God which is only possible
by means of supernatural special revelation.

*   *   *

Since the Middle Ages, Roman Catholic theology has without a moment's regret defended the right and the possibility
of natural theology. She has not simply used it as a non-es-
sential appendix to her theology, but has made it an organic
part of her system of doctrine. Moreover, it is clear that this
is not simply the hobby of Roman Catholic *theology*, but that
the Roman *church* considers it of great importance. This is at
once apparent in the decisions of the Vatican Council when it
emphasized the natural knowledge of God as a *rational* knowledge and carefully distinguished it from the knowledge of faith.

Even before the Vatican Council, Rome's interest in this
knowledge was clearly displayed in the ecclesiastical struggle
against certain movements which voiced *principial* objections to
natural theology. One is reminded of Rome's conflict with
traditionalism and *ontologism*.

According to traditionalism, knowledge of God depended
entirely upon the *primary revelation* which had once been given
and was later transmitted. Not the power of reason but dependence upon revelation was the way to knowledge. Over
against this traditionalism, Rome maintained that there was a

way from man's reason to God.[1] God's existence can be known with certainty by means of reason.

The conflict with ontologism, which held that man could know God through an *immediate* intuition, was entirely different. Over against this ontologism, Rome maintained the *mediate* character of our knowledge of God.[2] Against the background of these conflicts came the pronouncement of 1870 that "God could be known certainly by the natural light of reason."[3]

It is evident that this mediate knowledge also differs from supernatural faith as to its content. There are *two kinds* of knowledge. Something is added however to the pronouncement quoted above. There is a two-fold order of knowledge[4] in reference to the *principle* of knowledge and the *object* that is known.

As to the knowledge *principle,* there is a knowledge through natural reason and a knowledge through supernatural faith.[5] There is also duality concerning the *object* of knowledge. There are truths which can be known by natural reason, but in addition there are also mysteries hidden in God which can be known only by divine, super-natural revelation. *This* knowledge concerns grace and truth in Jesus Christ. These mysteries exceed the capacity of reason.[6] Indeed, the situation is such that, even if they were revealed and accepted in faith, they would still be covered, as it were with a veil as long as we walk by faith and not by sight.[7]

Rome therefore wants nothing to do with a rationalistic limitation of revelation. But even though the divine mysteries

---

1. H. Denzinger, *Enchiridion Symbolorum, Definitionum et Declarationum de Rebus Fidei et Morum.* Ed. 18-20. Friburgi: Herder, 1932., 1650. Cf. on traditionalism and ontologism, H. Lennerz, *Natürliche Gotteserkenntnis,* 1926. H. de Vos, "Het vraagstuk der natuurlijke theologie," N.T.T. 30e Jrg. 1941.
2. Denzinger, *op. cit.,* 1659.   3. *Ibid.,* 1785.
4. *Ibid.,* 1795. Cf. Heinrich Niebecker, *Wesen und Wirklichkeit der übernatürlichen Offenbarung,* 1940, p. 196.
5. Cf. G.P. Kreling, *De aard der H. Godgeleerdheid,* 1928, p. 4-5.
6. Denzinger, *op. cit.,* 1796.   7. *Ibid.*

are said to be beyond the reach of natural reason, yet this
knowledge of God through the natural light of reason is considered so important that Rome condemns anyone who denies
that we can know the one, only, true God, our creator and
Lord, from created reality by means of reason.[8]

That which the Vatican Council clearly defined had been
generally held by Roman Catholic theologians for centuries. It
seems, then, that there can hardly be any disagreement as to
what Rome means by natural theology: a natural knowledge or
theology derived from the created things *by means of reason*.
It is true, as Bartmann says, that the Vatican Council was
engaged with the *"posse"* (the *possibility* of knowing) and that
it declared "the physical possibility" of this natural knowledge
of God in *principle* only.[9] It did not deny, therefore, that most
men do *not actually* come to knowledge of God by means of a
rational world-and-life view but by another way. Nevertheless,
it still does concern this *physical* possibility, this ability of reason. Whoever denies that is condemned by Rome, and even
Bartmann at a later point simply writes again of the *reality*
of "our natural knowledge of God."[10] It is said that this real
knowledge is *mediate, analogous, inadequate,* and *true.* From
the *possibility,* the ontological structure of reason, the argument simply passes over to the reality of this knowledge, and
Rome emphasizes its significance over against agnosticism,
anti-intellectualism and irrationalism.[11] Only upon the basis
of the reality of this rational knowledge can we understand
why Rome insists so stubbornly upon the "ability" of reason.[12]

The significance of this natural knowledge of God is also
clear from the way in which natural reason arrives at it. According to the Scholastics, there were three ways by which

8. *Ibid.,* 1806, Can. 1.
9. Bartmann, *Lehrbuch der Dogmatik* I, p. 81.
10. *Ibid.,* p. 87.
11. G. P. Kreling, *Het goddelijk geheim in de theologie,* 1939, p. 9, 11.
12. Cf. Henri de Lubac, *De la connaisance de Dieu,* 1948, p. 61. Also Timp,
Bestaat God? p. 32.

this knowledge of God could be attained, viz.: the way of *causality*, *negation* and *eminence*. *From the created things,* we can learn by the natural light of reason that God is the *cause* of all things, and that he is infinitely exalted above all his creatures, and that he is distinguished from them.[13] Think also of the great importance given to the proofs for God's existence. In this we see how the physical ability *passes over into actual* knowledge. Recently some Roman Catholics, under the influence of anti-intellectualism, have expressed displeasure with this positive thesis of Rome. They have tried to show that this way of knowledge does not involve the implication Protestants often suppose. They point out that the Vatican Council did not set forth an independent natural theology. Söhngen, e. g., writes: "According to the Vaticanum, there is no natural theology completely detached from the history of redemption."[14] How does Söhngen arrive at this conclusion? He thinks that it can be deduced from the very text of the Vaticanum itself. He argues that the Council always emphasized the relative or moral *necessity* of divine *supernatural* revelation "even for the natural knowledge of God."[15] Here a problem arises which we may not neglect. The Council declared that whatever knowledge of God could be attained by human reason *as such* was still attainable in man's present state, so that he can know certainly and truly through divine revelation.[16] Söhngen claims that Thomas did not give clear expression to this because of his abstract philosophical conception of nature, but the Vatican Council did give expression to it. Söhngen does recognize, however, that there is a difference between the Reformation and the Roman Catholic views of the natural knowledge of God, but for him this difference lies in the fact that the Reformation maintained the *absolute* necessity of the Word-revelation for our knowledge of the revelation in creation.[17]

13. Bartmann, *op cit.,* p. 88.
14. G. Söhngen, "Natürliche Theologie und Heilsgeschichte" in *Catholica,* 1935, p. 102.
15. *Ibid.*   16. Denzinger, *op. cit.,* 1786.   17. Söhngen, *op. cit.,* p. 104.

When we examine the declaration of the Vatican Council, however, we see that it held that the natural knowledge of God derived from the creation is *made easier* through special revelation, but not that this revelation is *absolutely* necessary. The way to a natural knowledge is, in a concrete situation, hindered by many difficulties, so that supernatural revelation is *morally* or *relatively* necessary. But that does not mean that the Vatican Council did not emphasize that a natural knowledge of God could be had through the natural light of reason (apart from supernatural revelation). The restraining factors which make supernatural revelation relatively necessary are due to the *circumstances,* but *not* to the knowing agent, not to the power or ability of human reason itself. Therefore when Söhngen says: "The Vaticanum did not really maintain the independent ability of man to obtain sure knowledge of God from the works of creation in order to glorify the undisturbed power and beauty of the natural man as he now is,"[18] then we shall have to reply that in any case the natural light of reason in the present situation has nevertheless not been affected. Therefore Bartmann can, from Rome's position, just as rightly underline the *truth* of this knowledge. The light of supernatural revelation may be "morally necessary," but it is precisely that adjective which displays the intentions of the Vaticanum. The sharp lines appear blurred for a moment, but nevertheless they are maintained. *Natural* reason has the ability to know God;[19] it is a physical ability, and . . . "this ability resides in human reason."[20] That the *operation* of this ability is "in certain cases" for some reason hindered or even completely eliminated, does not destroy the basic assertion of reason's ability. The background of this Vatican doctrine is an *ontological analysis* of human nature, the *"anima rationalis."*

Rome's conception of the proofs for the existence of God is also based upon this thesis that natural reason can know God *from* the creatures. It is true that the Vaticanum does not

18. *Ibid.,* p. 107.   19. Timp, *Bestaat God?,* p. 33.   20. *Ibid.*

speak of the probability but of the certainty of knowing God. However, when the modernistic-oath of 1910 referred back to the Vatican Council's declaration of the natural light of reason, to this was added that God, who is knowable by the natural light of reason, "can certainly be known as the cause of all things, and therefore can also be proved."[21]

What is the background of this conception in which natural reason is considered capable of such knowledge? It is clear that a specific anthropology is involved here, an anthropology or view of man, which *lifts* the so-called rational soul *out* of the sin-depraved life of man, and then by way of this non-corrupt reason considers man capable of true knowledge of God. There is, as Kreling characteristically expresses it,[22] an *ecclesiastical* defense of reason, especially over against the modernistic attempt to withdraw God from the understanding. It is true that Rome admits that sin has wounded human nature by the loss of special supernatural gifts, [23] but the physical ability of human reason was neither destroyed nor disturbed, so that reason can still reach God. The nature of the intellect remained intact and so in a certain sense human nature is still *open* for the knowledge of God. Reason operates in the world of created reality and arrives thus at *true,* though incomplete, knowledge of God. That reason can accomplish that much is due to its *structure.* Human reason is rooted in the *soul* which is the *form* of the body. Therefore, there is always a certain dependence upon *matter.* Because of the union of body and soul, it will never be possible for our knowledge to be purely spiritual or intuitive in nature,[24] as is true of the angels. Our intellect must always maintain contact with existing things, and that decisively determines the manner of natural knowledge of God.

From the structure of human nature, specifically of man's reason, it follows that knowledge is dependent upon the oper-

---

21. Denzinger, *op cit.,* 2145. Cf. also 1650. See also Niebecker, *op. cit.,* p. 49.
22. Kreling, *op. cit.,* p. 12.   23. *"Vulneratio naturae."*
24. Timp, *op. cit.,* p. 43.

ation of our senses.[25]   Therefore God, who is "supremely
spirit,"[26] is *least knowable* to us.   There is only one way to a
natural knowledge of God and that is by means of the percep-
tion of the senses of the *created things*.[27]   Here we have the
basis for the proofs of God's existence.

Rome is squarely opposed to Kant who emphatically denied
the possibility of these proofs.   Kant believed their basic error
to be the *transcendent* value which was given to the use of
human reason.   He judged this to be most evident in the cosmological argument.   Here Kant has touched upon a crucial
question for the whole of Roman Catholic theology and apologetics.   "Does this general law of causality lose its validity and
does it deprive human reason of any viewpoint when the cosmic
limits are reached?"[28]   Kant answered this question in the affirmative.   He believed that, where these limits were reached,
further use of reason was simply speculative.   The principle
of causality is valid only within the limits of our experience.[29]
If it were in force *beyond* those limits and even applied to God,
then God as the "first cause" would also be taken up into the
factual chain of experience.   Just this impossibility proves to
Kant that an unwarranted *leap* has been made.

Rome adopts a completely different point of view.   Kant's
criticism   is termed agnostic, and Rome maintains that the
argument from causality is not limited to the extent of our
experience, but is also valid beyond that.   Brocardus Meyer
says of the Scholastics: "Upon good ground they recognized
the transcendent value of the principle of causality."[30]

Experiential reality is the starting point for the proofs for
the existence of God, and from it one "concludes to the exis-

25. Brocardus Meyer, *Katholieke Geloofsverdediging*, 1946, p. 56.
26. *Ibid.*, p. 57.
27. *Ibid.*, p. 59. Cf. Thomas, *Summa Theol.*, P. I, qu. 88 , art. 3, and qu. 12,
art. 12.
28. Brocardus Meyer, *op. cit.*, p. 66.
29. Cf. R. Reininger, *Kant, seine Anhänger und seine Gegner*, 1923, p. 134.
30. Broc. Meyer, *op. cit.*, p. 67.

tence of a first cause which is completely self-existent."[31] *This* is the "common basis for the classic theistic proofs."[32]   In addition to this proof of God as the Prime Mover,[33] a classic illustration of the causality argument is the one which, from the premise that the relation of cause and effect cannot go back infinitely, concludes that there *must* therefore be a *first* cause.

Thus from experiential reality, by means of reason, one arrives at the conclusion that God is the first Cause of all being.[34] The transcendent value of causality makes *natural* knowledge of God possible.

*   *   *

The question now arises *how* and *how far* God is known in this way. We have already seen that this knowledge cannot be adequate because it proceeds through the medium of created reality and is also characterized by it. So, for example, one cannot by means of natural knowledge know that God is triune.[35] The mysteries are entirely hidden from such knowledge. It is apparent therefore, that this is not simply an inadequate knowledge, but that one must really speak of a *partial* knowledge, even in an extremely dualistic way. By means of natural knowledge one knows only *that* part or "aspect" of God which is mediated through creation and relates especially to his *being*. The results of the theistic proofs demonstrate this. By means of these proofs reason comes to recognize the existence of a self-existent being, "which not only expresses the deepest

---

31. *Ibid.*, p. 73.
32. H. Robbers, *Menselijk weten over God en Schepping*, p. 19. Cf. Karl Adam, *Glaube und Glaubenswissenschaft im Katholizismus*, 1923, p. 115.
33. Robbers, *op. cit.*, p. 49.
34. Cf. Broc. Meyer, *op. cit.*, p. 93, 98.   Robbers, *op. cit.*, p. 58,   Also J.B.J. Meyer, *De eerste levensvraag in het intellectualisme van St. Thomas van Aquino en het integraal-realisme van Maurice Blondel*, 1940, p. 282.
35. Thomas Aquinas, *Summa Theol.* I, qu. 32, Art. 1c.

core of God's being, in so far as it is accessible to human understanding, but also the root of his infinite perfections."[36]

This "self-existent being" is the *central point* of the natural knowledge of God. This divine being can be known by the natural light of reason because there is an "analogy of being" between God and man. This analogy of being makes an argument from created reality to the existence of God both possible and meaningful.

Roman Catholic theologians readily acknowledge that this analogy of being, which Barth calls the discovery of the anti-Christ, plays an important role in their system. It is basic to their natural theology and their view of the relation between creator and creature.[37] They want to defend it especially over against Barth in whose criticism they see a reflection of that infinite difference between Creator and creature which rules out all analogy. According to Roman Catholic theologians, the analogy of being does not mean that there is one universal Being under which both God and man are subsumed. Rather, it presupposes a *difference* between Creator and creature. There is a great difference, an "infinite distance,"[38] between God, "the source of being,"[39] and all created beings. But this infinite distance does not eliminate all analogy. There is also "a line of similarity" [40] which God has himself established. God is not a hidden God. The words with which we speak about God are not simply a groping in the darkness of an unapproachable light. There is analogy, in spite of the infinite diversity — an

36. Barth has characterized the RC analogy of being as if God's being and man's being were both subsumed under one general concept of "being" of which both God and man had part. This statement of the position is strongly opposed by Roman Catholic theologians. Cf. W. J. Aalders, *De Analogia entis in het geding*, p. 12ff.: J. J. Louet Feisser, *De strijd tegen de analogia entis in de theologie van Karl Barth*, 1948.
37. Cf. J. Fehr, *Das Offenbarungsproblem in dialektischer und Thomistischer Theologie*, 1939, p. 50. "Upon this principle of the analogy of being rests the whole of our natural knowledge of God."
38. Robbers, *op. cit.*, p. 100.
39. *Ibid.*, p. 100.
40. *Ibid.*

analogy of *being*. "Being and existence are in God, just as well as in the creature."[41]

With that statement one has rejected both agnosticism, which considers God to be unknowable, as well as symbolism, which contends that our words do not touch God's reality.[42] On the basis of the analogy of being, a road is opened to *natural* knowledge. Because of the analogy of being, man, in his natural knowledge, is gripped by the world of created reality. Only in that way is such knowledge possible. This is emphasized so strongly that Robbers even writes that metaphysics and natural theology are not so much "a knowledge of God as a knowledge of created reality in so far as it everywhere points to God as the first principle."[43]

In spite of the measured restraint of this statement, the fact remains that knowledge of this created reality, because it points to God, is and must be called a natural *knowledge* of God. God is known as the first cause, the source and origin of all creatures. The natural light of reason receives this knowledge *apart from* the supernatural revelation, viz. directly *from* the factuality of created reality.

*   *   *

Because of the strong opposition to natural theology, the accent has recently been placed upon its extremely limited significance. It is admitted that reason arrives at a natural knowledge of God, but the limits of this knowledge must be kept clearly in mind. "We know of course *that* God possesses certain perfections (Being, Spirit, Life, etc.), but we do not know *how* he possesses these perfections,"[44] and therefore we do not know God in what applies only to him.[45] Natural knowledge

---

41. *Ibid.,* p. 108.   42. *Ibid.,* pp. 107 ff.   43. *Ibid.,* p. 109.
44. Fehr, *op. cit.* p. 59.
45. *Ibid.,* p. 59.   Therefore according to Fehr, Thomas can also write, "Man's highest knowledge of God is that he knows that he doesn't know God."

of God is therefore "highly indirect, inadequate, dark knowledge,"[46] and can never take the place of the knowledge derived from supernatural revelation. Rather one must recognize "the complete imperfection and insufficiency which belongs to it."[47]

All these reservations do not mean, however, that the natural theology of Rome does not involve "the possibility which the fallen man still possesses" . . . to know God as Creator. Rome engages in a bitter fight for this *ontic* ability of reason.[48]

The official declarations do not make so much of this imperfection and insufficiency, but they do anathematize those who attack the doctrine of the church. It can do nothing else when it still considers this inadequate knowledge to be *true* knowledge. Even if it be true that only Christ reveals to us the true nature of the inner being and life of the Father,[49] nevertheless the natural light produces *true* knowledge. This *ontological* analysis concerns the capacity of human nature for knowledge. Here the knowledge relation between Creator and creature is *ontologically* fixed. It results in knowledge of the formal *aspects* of God's *being,* in an *independent* natural theology of the first article (God as Creator) which has nothing to do with the knowledge of God in the reality of his grace and mercy.

When Christ says, "And this is life eternal, that they should know thee the only true God, and him whom thou didst send, even Jesus Christ,"[50] then according to Rome this does not destroy the fact that there is also *real* and *true* knowledge of God wholly apart from Christ. It is almost inconceivable that the Roman Catholic Church has not been repeatedly shocked by this *empty, abstract,* and *formal* God-concept of her natural theology. What is the significance of this *true* knowledge of God who is here known as the Being "which exists in and of

46. *Ibid.,* p. 60.   47. *Ibid.*
48. Jerome Hamer, *Karl Barth. L'occasionalisme theologique de* Karl Barth, 1949, p. 219.
49. Fehr, *op. cit.,* p. 66.
50. John 17:3.

itself," as "the Prime Mover, first cause, necessary being, the uncaused being, the true and the good, the rational designer, who is his own goal"?[51] How is it possible that such considerations derived from the natural light of reason can be connected with the name, which God himself revealed to Moses when he said: "I am that I am."[52] Can one really be satisfied with this identification of the "natural" conception of "God as *being*" and this covenant name expressing his *faithfulness* to his people? When Moses meets God does that even for a moment concern only the isolated, abstract "being" of God *in itself*, which a natural theology could also reach?

When Brocardus Meyer writes that Protestant theology makes a pretty poor showing in the field of natural theology, and that Protestant criticism of the Scholastic doctrine of God is only "an attempt to hide the poverty of her natural God-concept,"[53] then we ask ourselves if we really have to be ashamed of our Protestant poverty. This is especially so when we note that Roman Catholic apologists set "the religious idea of God" over against "the natural conception of God," and they think that this distinction is an answer to the criticism of Heiler who said that "the God whose existence natural theology proves, is not the living God of mercy. One can therefore speak only of rational proofs for the reality of an Absolute, but not of the proofs for the existence of God."[54]

At this point Roman Catholic theology has never been able to give a satisfactory answer to Reformed critique. In this formal and empty God-concept we see the heart of Rome's natural theology. Dr. de Vogel has attempted an answer. But her attempt only uncovers the impossibility of a natural theology rather than its legitimacy. Over against Barth's reproach for separation in the doctrine of God, she asks: "Who really makes a radical separation between the Creator of heaven and earth and the God of revelation in Christ? The Roman Cath-

51. Broc. Meyer, *op. cit.*, p. 108.
52. *Ibid.*   53. *Ibid.*, p. 109.   54. *Ibid.*, p. 115.

olic church with its doctrine which does not in the least deny
the necessity of revelation (naturally), but which nevertheless
recognizes the validity of the knowledge of God which is natural to man? Or Karl Barth who cancels out this natural
knowledge, declaring it to be 'Baal service,' opposed to revelation and in principle irreconcilable with it?"[55] She calls this
"an impious and false separation when the natural seeking after
God which was implanted in man by the Creator (by whom
else) is cut off from God's work in revelation, in Christ and
in the church."[56]

This criticism does have some significance against Barth
who denies general revelation, but it carries no weight against
Reformed theology. Therefore Dr. de Vogel's reply is no
answer to the Reformation. Rather, her answer is only the
maintenance of the thesis that the *non-depraved reason* is the
means by which to get a preliminary but true knowledge of God
which must be supplemented by supernatural truths of revelation.

Knowledge of God is approached here by an anthropological
analysis which assumes that, by means of his undisturbed reason, man can know the *being* of the true God. Though this
knowledge is inadequate, it is not untrue because even supernatural knowledge is inadequate. By means of thought, one
reaches true knowledge of God which is a "discovery" as the
result of "a natural search" (de Vogel). With this conception
of human reason, it is understandable why Rome so strongly
defends the *true* natural theology, even with its poignant official declarations and anathemas.

* * *

In summary, we can say that Roman Catholic theology involves the relation between man's rational nature and "reality."
The road to a knowledge of God is by way of *logical conclu-*

---

55. C.J. de Vogel, *Ecclesia Catholica,* p. 49.
56. *Ibid.*

sion. This brings us, finally, to the question *whether Rome really acknowledges a revelation of God in this created reality.* This question is answered affirmatively. Reference is frequently made to a revelation of God in nature in distinction from supernatural revelation. Nevertheless, one is *always amazed how little place this revelation idea gets in the exposition of natural theology.*[57] Study of the main idea behind this natural theology makes clear why this is so. Human reason is always placed over against the "fact" of nature. God is not in some way found in nature. Rather, from the fact of nature, no matter how it appears and apart from the question whether it is revelation, reason concludes that nature has a cause, a "first cause."

The idea of revelation does not play a decisive role here. In natural theology the attempt is not made to show *how* God is "revealed" in reality, but reason concludes to the first cause, *viz.* God. This explains why the Roman Catholic argument for a natural knowledge of God often appears to deal with knowledge reached *apart* from revelation. That is also fully consistent because the relation between "abstract rational nature" and reality expresses nothing as to its *nature, except that it has a cause.* The function of human reason is not to investigate revelation but to draw logical conclusions.

This is the reason why many, including some Roman Catholics, have voiced objection to this position. Here we touch upon the background of the Roman Catholic conflict with ontologism. A good example of the difficulties concerning the natural knowledge of God is seen in Max Scheler when he was still a Roman Catholic. In him we see a strong rejection of the causality argument on the one hand, and (closely related to it) a strong accentuation of *revelation* in nature on the other. For him it is not so much a conclusion of reason drawn from a

57. Actually we discover the same true of the Greek-Orthodox theologian Antonius Bairactaris, "Natürliche Offenbarung" *Zeitschrift für Systematischer Theologie,* 14 Jrg. 1937, p. 52.

(no further described) reality about us, but a relation between "natural religion" and "natural revelation."[58]

In order to understand the background of this position, we can begin with Scheler's criticism of the idea that the causality argument is the basis for natural theology. He asks why the proofs for the existence of God, though they are not difficult or complicated, are "yet without power to convince modern man or anyone who has not come to believe in the existence of God previously by way of tradition, faith or some other religious experience."[59]

Why can such "clear proofs," as they are said to be, operate only by means of tradition? The only answer that might possibly be given, says Scheler, is that the proofs are sufficient and clear in themselves, but the sinful *will* of man, who does not want to acknowledge God, is also unwilling to accept the clear testimony of the proofs.[60]

But Scheler rejects this possible answer because *this* relation between "sinful will" and atheism does not fit reality.[61] Therefore the difficulty with the theistic proofs remains for Scheler. He does not want to explain their limited value in the way Kant did, when he denied the validity of the causality argument. The principle of causality does have great value according to Scheler, "as a general, simple and actual principle for the becoming of that reality whose existence is not due to its own essence."[62]

But, and here we reach the heart of Scheler's argument, the reality and validity of the proofs presuppose something besides the logical laws, the principle of causality and the facts of experience, *viz.,* the fact that demonstrative reason is surrounded by the *religious* view of the world. There is a realm of the

58. Max Scheler, *Probleme der Religion* in Vom Ewigen im Menschen, 1923, p. 98.
59. *Ibid.,* p. 297.
60. *Ibid.,* p. 298.
61. *Ibid.,* p. 299ff.
62. *Ibid.,* p. 301.

"ontological being of the divine,"[63] and that region forms the
mediating link between religion and all other rational knowledge." It concerns thus *primarily* "conceptions which are never
to be had apart from the religious sphere of being"[64] Therefore
natural theology cannot result from conclusions drawn (via
causality) from experiential reality. The religious act is completely *unique,* and it can never simply come to expression.
Only when man knows God through this religious act does
that which the proofs aim to demonstrate achieve meaning and
significance.

The religious act concerns "knowledge of being"[65] so that
we do not know God "in the light of the world," but the reverse is true — we know the world *in the light of God.*[66] It
concerns a "knowledge of an *a priori* given content"[67] which is
not innate but which can only be *received.* Natural knowledge
of God does not therefore mean that God is reached simply by a
logical deduction from things, but a "produced experience"
of a wholly different nature. The religious act involves a relationship with an "object" (*Gegenstand*) of "divine personal
form" with *revelation.*[68]

We see now how this is related to Scheler's rejection of the
customary natural theology. It is clear that his view is more
in accord with ontologism than with the natural theology of
Rome. It may be that some seek to avoid the questions which
Scheler has brought to the foreground by referring to his subsequent development in which he disassociates himself more
and more from Rome. But this evolution in Scheler's thought
does not excuse us from taking note of his significant objections to natural theology. This is especially true because
Scheler, by way of his criticism of the old method of natural
theology, has focused attention on the question of *revelation.*
For Scheler, much more than for Rome, the question of general revelation is again in the foreground. For him it is not a

---

63. *Ibid.*, p. 303.   64. *Ibid.*, p. 302.   65. *Ibid.*, p. 167.   66. *Ibid.*, p. 161.
67. *Ibid.*, p. 166.   68. *Ibid.*, p. 257.

question of simple logical deductions of a first cause from an undifferentiated reality, but a question of the *revelation of God in nature*. The relationship between his criticism of rational natural theology and his accent upon revelation is at once evident. "Positive religion and natural religion are not distinguished by the fact that the former rests upon revelation while the latter is based upon spontaneous rational knowledge, completely independent of the religious act,"[69] but the essential difference between natural and positive religion is based "upon the nature and manner of revelation, i.e., whether this revelation is general, symbolically mediated through the constant basic factors of the inner and outer world of history and nature, attainable in the religious act everywhere and at any time by all; or whether it follows and is given through the special exalted union with God of certain persons."[70] Here then, general revelation is again recognized *rather than simply a relation between reason and reality*. According to Scheler it is absurd "to prove reality or existence."[71] *To find God* is something completely different from proving God.[72] Only after one has found God can he speak of proofs, but then only as "information" (*Machweis*). It is true that Paul acknowledges that the artist can be known from his works, but only later was the erroneous conclusion drawn that this meant "a scientific rational knowledge of God."[73] Over against this Scheler maintains that the whole creation does bear traces or "fingerprints of God" its maker, but this "is an assertion which becomes true only and exclusively of the perceivable matter, when the religious world-view brings this to the non-religious facts as an absolutely new and positive phenomenon."[74] Even the expressions, "traces," "fingerprints," and "working-character," point to something completely different from "some general causal argument drawn from pre-religious permanent facts of a pro-

69.. *Ibid.*, p. 258.   70. *Ibid.*   71. *Ibid.*, p. 265.   72. *Ibid.*, p. 267.
73. *Ibid.*, p. 289.   74. *Ibid.*, p. 290.

fane world and life view."[75]   Scheler thinks the basic error of
the traditional natural theology is that it tries to conclude to
that which is already possessed from a completely different
source."[76] Only religious language speaks of the heavens declaring the glory of God and of the traces and footsteps of God
implanted in it. There is on the part of things "a significant,
meaningful rising up above their own causal being" [77] and man
can only seek to understand and repeat this objectivity in reality. In this way we see things *in God's light.* It was always
understood in this way until Thomas changed this *in lumine*
into a *causal per lumen* and thus the theistic proofs of natural
theology arose.[78] Religion deals with the "self-communication"
of the object (*Gegenstand*)[79] upon which the religious act is
directed and with the *evidence* by which this given is made
known to our consciousness. Therefore it does not simply concern the *That* (*Dasein*) but the *How* (*Sosein*) and the significance of this *How* can lead to certainty only by means
of evidence.[80] This self-communication points to a natural revelation of God "by means of which man's rational spirit is ac-
tively instructed in the essence and meaning of the Creator's
work.[81] Thus Scheler dares to speak of *revelation, i.e.* to say,
"that if the absolute being becomes a divinely qualified object
by shining out and through to an empirical object of relative
being, it is for the first time by this set off from all other *Ge-
genstände* of relative existence."[82] Just as a certain window of
a house is distinguished from the other windows when a person
looks through it to the outside, so too the finite becomes special
when it symbolizes the absolute. The religious act is always
correlated to "a being revealed, a self-communication of one-
self." The argument from causality goes *from* effect *to* cause
and "the first cause in no way puts itself into the effect; one
cannot simply see the effect of which it is the cause."[83] But

---

75. *Ibid.*, p. 291.   76. *Ibid.*, p. 295.   77. *Ibid.*, p. 295.   78. *Ibid.*, p. 311.
79. *Ibid.*, p. 327.   80. *Ibid.*, p. 328.   81. *Ibid.*, p. 345.   82. *Ibid.*, p. 103.
83. *Ibid.*, p. 105.

the religious act is different, for here "the creatureliness of the creature appears at once as an imprinted phenomenal trademark."[84] Indeed, "it points to the creator in a symbolical way and it 'mirrors' him in a one-sided, inadequate manner." Phenomenally the work of art expresses something of the spirit of the artist.[85] Therefore Scheler speaks of "a presence of God in the creatures."[86]

In all of these expressions, one can readily see that the main lines of Scheler's phenomenology have been applied to religion. Above all, especially Roman Catholics can point out how the tendencies involved in this phenomenology finally led Scheler to break with the Roman Catholic church.[87] We believe that these observations are correct.[88]

Nevertheless, Scheler has again emphasized a problem which touches the weakness of Roman Catholic theology with its theistic proofs. It is the question of a revelation in nature.

Scheler has correctly observed that the causality argument did not actually *presuppose* revelation. It is certainly true that in Roman Catholic theology (here natural theology) God's revelation in nature does *not* function as such. What does function is simply the *fact* of this reality which via causality leads to the first cause. At the same time it must be said that the problem indicated by Scheler has been ignored by Rome. It is true that in Roman Catholic theology we often do find the concept of revelation expressed in relation to nature. Karl Adam, e.g., in a discussion of the natural knowledge of God, says that God has freely revealed himself in this world, which is a "form of his gracious self-revelation."[89] He also says that its difference from supernatural revelation lies only in the *form* of revelation. Even in nature it is the personal God's "desire to be revealed" in the visible world.[90]

84. *Ibid.*   85. Ibid., p. 106.   86. *Ibid.*, p. 107.
87. M. Scheler, *Die Stellung des Menschen im Kosmos*, 1928.
88. Cf. Hafkesbrink, *"Das Problem des religiösen Gegenstandes bei Max Scheler."* Z. für syst. Theol. 82 Jrg. 1930.
89. Adam, *Glaube und Glaubensschaft im Katholizismus*, p. 61.
90. *Ibid.*, p. 62.

Things are "a *mirror* through which God wishes to be known and contemplated, even if imperfectly transparent." Adam *here* agrees with Scheler and writes, "the fact that we can discover God in the essential form of the world is not due first of all to the world but to God's displaying himself in the world."[91] Adam even criticizes Scheler's illustration of the window and reproves him for destroying the concept of "natural revelation." It is not simply the looking through a window, but of God revealing himself *in* things, "for since things do not of themselves, by their own meaning content, declare anything about God; rather it is God himself as revealer who enlightens the things of nature, and thus immediately discloses himself. Therefore things themselves are not God's revelation but only the condition and occasion for the immediate revelation proceeding from God."[92] In this way Adam comes to the idea of a *reflection* of God in created reality. This view of revelation, of course, influences the idea of natural theology. If natural revelation comes to us in this way, there must be "a certain congeniality with the pure spirituality of God if these broken rays are to be caught up in creation."[93] Blessed are the pure of heart, declares Adam at this point. Consistently he therefore adds that natural revelation does not primarily captivate and fill the impersonal, practical, cold mind, but rather its source of activity, viz. the warm, living *heart*.[94] Natural revelation, therefore, does not in the first place present being — but values data. And if knowing God is not *preceded* by first seeking and finding Him in love[95] then *this* natural knowledge will not stand in the test since "it is not based upon and motivated by *the sum total of personal experiences,* nor has it any connection with original, effectual experience of value, or with elemental psychical activity, but it is based solely upon impersonal, logical evidence apart from and outside of the soul's experience."[96]

---

91. *Ibid.,* p. 62.   92. *Ibid.,* p. 63.   93. *Ibid.,* p. 68.
94. *Ibid.,* p. 69.   95. *Ibid.,* p. 70.   96. *Ibid.,* p. 71.

We have now seen the profound tensions within the natural theology of Rome. It is perfectly clear that both Scheler and Adam reject that which Rome has officially accepted. The Roman Catholic method of the analogy of being, the primacy of the intellect and the primary significance of the causality argument are attacked at their very root even though an attempt is made, by Adam especially, to reconcile it with the Vatican Council through an unacceptable interpretation. Here also recourse is taken from the abstract "reason" to man's *"heart"* upon the basis of which the search is made for the *actual* revelation of God in his works.

But this is certainly *not* in agreement with Rome's natural theology. For it is based upon the relationship of *"reason-reality,"* and therefore in principle has *no* need of God's revelation. It is striking that the objections to natural theology (as result of causal conclusions) are raised chiefly by those who have been strongly influenced by *phenomenology.* That is understandable because phenomenology wanted to direct itself, not simply to the fact of reality, from which a causal argument could be formed, but to the character and nature of this *reality itself.* Over against critical idealism, all emphasis is put upon the *givenness* of reality. Upon the basis of this givenness, this *self-unfolding* of reality, they came to combine this reality with God revealing himself *in* it. It must be admitted that the phenomenology of religion involves many dangerous tendencies and is in error as well as is ordinary natural theology. In the phenomenology of religion, Scheler and others came to a view of reality in which the dangers of pantheism were not absent and the development of Scheler's thought shows how acute these dangers can become. In spite of the dangers,[97] we must not forget that the attempt was made to do justice to the idea of revelation. The question of revelation was again considered, while in the official Roman Catholic theology it was

---

97. Scheler, *Die Stellung des Menschen im Kosmos,* 1930, p. 105ff. Cf. J. Nota, *Max Scheler. Een worstelen om het wezen van de mens,* 1947,

practically discussed only in the sphere of *supernatural revelation*.

The whole movement had little effect upon Rome's natural theology. Rome maintained the old natural-rational knowledge as declared by the Vatican Council and felt that it had good Scriptural basis for doing so. In the decisive canon of the Vatican Council reference was made to Romans 1:20. It is remarkable that in Article II, the Belgic Confession also refers to Romans 1:20. This situation reflects the urgency and the seriousness of *an appeal to Scripture*. It could rightly be said that if one understands the background of this appeal, in this two-fold appeal to Scripture, the *heart* of the conflict concerning natural theology is seen.

Is the Revelation of Christ Exclusive?

CHAPTER V

Is the Revelation of Christ Exclusive?

S O FAR we have considered some of the aspects of the discussion concerning the general revelation of God. As we now consider more directly and positively the general revelation of God, we are fully conscious of the fact that we are constantly surrounded by numerous dangers, and especially by one danger, *viz.* that we are speaking of revelation but that we make this revelation of God subject of our subjective schemes and conceptions of our preference by which the fulness of revelation is limited and misjudged. It is by no means hypothetical that man constructs a revelation-concept which actually is nothing but a projection of his own subjectivity. More than once the Christian idea of revelation has been disqualified as such a subjective, human projection. And although it is obvious that such a psychological analysis of the revelation-concept is the result of enmity against God's revelation itself, still we shall have to be continually on our guard against this very real danger, knowing the history of human thinking.

That is the reason why at the beginning of our discussion concerning God's revelation we took a stand of far-reaching consequences. Again and again the attempt has been made, exactly at this point of the way of contemplation, to produce a certain foundation with respect to the discussion of God's revelation. They wished to avoid that this discussion created a subjective impression and they tried to make it rationally transparent why exactly here and thus revelation could be spoken of. Such an attempt, however, is always doomed to failure, because the very nature of God's revelation excludes

the possibility to listen to still another revelation of God outside
of and beyond the former which would afford it foundation
and reliability. The point at issue in the *Deus dixit* is always
a final pronouncement, which is at the same time a primary,
foundation-acknowledging pronouncement. It is not possible
to give a foundation to this revelation because it is itself foundation. There is, therefore, only one way left for all reflection
on revelation, *viz.* to listen to God's revelation itself. This has
frequently been referred to as a vicious circle: in order to answer the question "What is revelation?" . . . . . an appeal is
made to revelation itself. However, that which is called "cir-
cle-reasoning" here, belongs to the essence of God's revelation, which comes to us sovereignly and omnipotently and
which does not wait until it has received an unconditional
guarantee from elsewhere on the basis of an instance outside
of revelation. This searching for a still deeper foundation is
in itself already a misjudgment of God's speaking, because
this speaking of God is thus considered *insufficient* and no
guarantee *in itself*.

It is, to the contrary, the marvel of faith that it unquestion-
ably knows for certain to hear the revelation of God, and
every believer knows that this certainty and the hearing of
the voice of the Lord do not emerge from one's own reasonable insight or from the intuitions of one's own heart, but are
the results of the irresistible power of the work of the Spirit.
This has more than once been referred to as the "defencelessness" of faith, which *rests,* here and now, in this revelation.
By this may be meant that rationalistic apologetics are not able
to furnish proof that a certain instance evidences true revelation but another does not. However, it is not advisable to
speak of "defencelessness" here because this is quite something else than not being able to furnish proof. When in the
Old Testament the true prophecy struggles with the false, then
there is the possibility that the moment may arrive that this
stupendous struggle for the prophetic revelation is being placed

into *God's* hands, but this can hardly be called "defencelessness" because faith's defence lies exactly in faith's certainty that waits for God's action in history.[1] But that the reasonable mind, which wishes to search for the revelation of God *outside of revelation* and thus wishes to determine it, cannot furnish proof must absolutely be maintained, whereas faith, which is certain, may boast of its riches instead of lament its poverty.

Thus the Church has in faith confessed to have recognized and listened to the Lord's voice in Holy Scripture. She was conscious of the fact that there were also other so-called book-religions, and that on the basis of this phenomenon frequently the attempt has been made to prove God's revelation relative. The entire problem concerning the absoluteness of God's revelation presents itself in its gigantic dimensions when the holy book is considered a religious-historic phenomenon.[2] Faith cannot refute this relativism with a rational argument by which the revealing nature of Scripture is "proven" as is done with regard to the Koran or the Book of Mormon, but solely with the profession, "Thy Word is a lamp unto my feet, and a light unto my path." For this reason it is possible for the Church to speak of God's revelation only on the basis of God's Word in which she finds her norm and source for all her discussion of revelation. And also the question whether we may speak of a *general* revelation in the works of God's hands can be answered only in the light of this burning lamp. The point at issue simply cannot be a subjective and, as it were, self-evident appreciation of the gifts and powers and beauty of nature, which we, by intuition, or feeling, or via our consciousness of dependency, in a particular way relate to God. Thus we would

---

1. Cf. the eloquent example from Jer. 28, in the conflict between Jeremiah and Hananiah, where we read after Hananiah's testimony ("Thus says the Lord"), "And the prophet Jeremiah went his way."

2. H. W. Obbink, *Het heilige boek als godsdiensthistorisch verschijnsel*, 1940.

at best arrive at a constructed idea of revelation, but not at the reality of revelation itself.

* * *

The problem as to how to approach God's revelation has lately become the topic of discussion, especially e. g., by Rudolph Bultmann who called special attention to the problem of the so-called "pre-conception" of revelation. He says that our inquiry concerning what the New Testament understands by revelation "is directed by a certain conception of the idea of revelation."[3] Already *by this question* we picture something in our minds, so that the idea "revelation" is not just an "x" to us. We have already a "pre-conception" of revelation. Bultmann proceeds from the assumption that this "pre-conception" consists in "the discovering of that which is veiled, and the revealing of that which is hidden" (p. 5), and such in a twofold sense, *viz.* as imparting of *knowledge,* by which something that is unknown to us becomes known, *and* as a *taking place,* which places us in a new situation. This "pre-conception" must pass the test of the criticism of the New Testament in order to possibly be corrected by it. On the basis of this test Bultmann arrives at a certain fixation of the idea of revelation and he concludes that the point of issue concerning revelation is not — as is the opinion of Protestant orthodoxy — imparting of *knowledge,* but a *taking place,* which penetrates the limitation of man's life (p. 18). According to him revelation in the first place gives *life.* In the New Testament death is considered "simply as the boundary of man" (p. 21). Revelation, which as the life breaks through this border, is an "event that abolishes death" (p. 22), which takes place in the *"factum"* Jesus Christ (p. 25). In *him* the *life* was manifested (I John 1:2). "Revelation is not clarification or communication, but a fact" (p. 29), an event which is proclaimed and thus enters

---

3. R. Bultmann, *Der Begriff der Offenbarung im N. T.,* 1929, p. 5.

into our lives. This proclamation of revelation, which itself belongs to revelation (p. 29), includes a *knowing*, but this knowing is "always a knowing of myself" (p. 41).

These conceptions reveal a typically philosophic schematization to which the conception of revelation is made to apply. There is every indication that the Heideggerian categories have occasioned this fixation of the idea of revelation, which is especially concentrated upon the anthropologic vision on the "limitedness of the human existence."

This is quite evident when Bultmann comes to the conclusion, "The knowing of God is in the first place man's knowing of himself, of his limitedness, and God operates as the power which penetrates this limitedness of man and thus elevates him to his actual self, to his substantiality."[4] By means of the category of the "limitedness" Bultmann arrives at the *actual* conception of revelation. This appears to be what he considers the real "pre-conception." The impression is created that the "pre-conception" (knowing *or* taking place) is corrected on the basis of the New Testament. But actually there is no correction whatsoever, because he imagines to find in the New Testament that which he considers the *actual* "pre-conception." Thus revelation in the end becomes nothing but the reflection of the human "self-conception," by virtue of which man arrives at his "substantiality."[5]

On the basis of this conception Bultmann considers revelation exclusively as the grace of Christ in the "situation of the crisis"[6] in which the limitedness of our life, because of sin and

4. R. Bultmann, *Die Frage der natürlichen Offenbarung*. In, *Offenbarung und Heilsgeschehen*, 1941, p. 9.

5. Cf. also Th. L. Haitjema, *Dogmatiek als apologie*, 1948, p. 39, and Bultmann, *Das Evangelium des Johannes*, 1950, p. 194, where he says that Jesus promises the believer as 'life,' that "which he, (the believer), misled and misunderstanding, vaguely yet strongly, desires, viz. the real existence, which he receives in the illumination of the definite self-understanding."

6. Bultmann, *Jesus*, p. 49f.

death, is broken through. "He who searches for still other revelations besides the revelation in Christ, has never taken God's thoughts seriously nor fathomed the depth of his own existence."[7]

Whenever there is mention of a revelation of God in nature and history, then this is essentially not revelation concerning God, because nature and history keep us *within our boundaries.* . . . "The constant revelation of God in nature and history is that it teaches us that we just don't have revelation and that we, in whatever we are and have, are insignificant before God."[8]

It is obvious that thus on the basis of philosophical premises of modern thought the revelation of God is made void. We are dealing with an evident, subjectivistic interpretation of revelation which can only be carried out with some semblance of logic when one's attitude as to the pronouncements of Scripture is very critical.[9]

*   *   *

This example of serious schematization urges us that much more to consider the question, What does Scripture itself say of God's revelation? Does it indeed justify the Christo-monistic conception of revelation: Christ alone reveals God in an absolutely exclusive sense? This question is therefore of such decisive importance because this "Christ only" resounds very strongly through the entire Scripture and also in the Reformation, which found the road back to the Scriptures again and thus formed a bulwark against the attack upon the

7. Bultmann, *Die Frage,* etc., p. 22.
8. Cf., among other things, Bultmann's explanations concerning the "eschatology" of the Gospel of John, the futura-texts of which do not fit in with his argument concerning the crisis. This, however does not create a problem for him. "In any event, however, verses 28f. (*shall* hear and *shall* proceed) are the addition of an editor who wishes to make the dubious statements of v. 24f conform traditional eschatology" (*Das Evang. des Johannes,* p. 196).
9. Cf. Bultmann, *Die Eschatol. des Johann. Evangeliums, Zwischen der Zeiten,* 1926.

sovereign salvation of the Lord. Is a closer examination indeed necessary when we recall the impressive tone of the *"sola fide, solus Christus, sola gratia"?* Did the Reformation not exactly in these *"particulae exclusivae"* express its deepest tendencies? This "Christ only" functioned in several directions, *viz.* against the merit of good works, against merits of saints, and against the pope's vicariate. Is the term "Christo-monism" in itself unacceptable? The Heidelberg Catechism says that no salvation whatsoever is to be sought or found in *any other* than Christ (Q. 29); it speaks of the "only" Deliverer and Savior, of the "complete" Savior in whom we have *all things* necessary to our salvation (Q. 30). It says of Christ, whom we therefore alone must *seek,* that He "has fully revealed to us the secret counsel and will of God concerning our redemption" (Q. 31), and that *He* is our only High Priest. All these pronouncements clearly depict that the revealed salvation in Christ is very exclusive. To recognize and acknowledge this "exclusiveness" makes it possible "to learn rightly to know the *only* true God, to trust in Him *alone,* to submit to Him *alone,* and to expect all good things from Him *only"* (Q. 94). We might here — if the word were not overcharged already, and if it would not create all kinds of misunderstanding — speak of *theo*-monism and *Christo*-monism and thereby mean nothing else but that which the Church had in mind with the adoration of the Lamb which is slain.

This, however, does not represent a true picture of the actual present-day discussion. The pivotal question is, *whether we have the right to simply conclude from the exclusive salvation in Christ to the exclusive revelation in Christ.* Exactly with respect to such "conclusions" we may not reason as though *now* our intellect can dispense with the lamp of Scripture. If it ever is imperative to turn to Scripture, certainly it is *in this respect.* It has indeed been asserted that this conclusion from the exclusive salvation in Christ to the exclusive revelation is *religiously necessary.* And on the basis of the exclusive salvation in Christ the question has been asked whether it would make sense to look for still another kind of revelation. Should the fulness and depth of this "Christ only" not fully satisfy and occupy us? Does not any one, who desires or seeks *more* revelation, receive *less?* Does not the "Christ only" of the Reformation lead us to the exclusive amazement at the revelation of God *in the flesh?* Is it not *a priori* impossible ever to assimilate the *singularity* of this revelation as a unit in the *plurality* of *more* revelations?

* * *

The apparently very strong and suggestive power of these questions may not prevent us from again searching the *Scriptures.* He who does so will soon discover that Holy Scripture speaks of God's revelation in various ways. A great variety of words are employed to designate this act of divine revelation and all kinds of theories have been connected with it. Among several other words there are two notable words in Scripture which both may be translated by "revelation," *viz. apokaluptein* and *phaneroun.*[10] Again and again a search has been made for the *actual* word for *revelation* in Scripture. Also an attempt has been made to differentiate between the two words just mentioned. One thing is certain, however, that the difference between both words has nothing to do with general and special revelation. The New Testament shows us that the word *phaneroun* indeed is used in connection with creation (Rom. 1:19, 20), but also for the revelation of salvation in Jesus Christ. When Paul in Romans 16:25f. speaks of his gospel and the preaching of Christ, then he uses in that connection

---

10. Among the other words in the N. T. we mention: *dēloō, gnōrizō, laleō, deiknumi.* This last word is usually translated "to show," but it often has the meaning of "to reveal," cf. John 10:32; 14:8. In Rev. 1:1 we read, "The revelation (*apokalupsis*) of Jesus Christ, which God gave unto him, to shew (*deiknumi*) unto his servants." Cf. Kittel, *Theol. W. B.* II, p. 27f., "In Acts 1:24 this word is used in the prayer for God's intervention: 'Shew whether of the two thou hast chosen.' "

IS REVELATION OF CHRIST EXCLUSIVE? 95

both words, "according to the revelation (*apokalupsis*) of the mystery, which was kept secret since the world began, but now is made manifest (*phaneroun*)." We may not conclude from the word *phaneroun* in Romans 1 that it has a special connection with general revelation, since Paul uses the very same word in the well-known expression of I Tim. 3:16, "God was manifest (*phaneroun*) in the flesh."[11]

More than once, indeed, the attempt has been made to point out a difference between the two words and this difference was put in such a way that the problem concerning revelation became acute. Oepke agrees that these two words seem to be completely identical because the usage of them, for example in Eph. 3:5, and Col. 1:26 indicates the same "revelation of the mystery."[12] However, this is not sufficient, according to him. He examines the statistics of the usage of the word in the New Testament, which show that in the synoptic gospels *phaneroun* appears only in Mark 4:22, [13] and further not in Galatians, Philippians, Thessalonians, James and Peter; on the other hand, often in the Gospel of John, I John, II Corinthians, Colossians, and the Pastoral Epistles. *Apokaluptein*, however, appears often in the synoptic gospels, the epistles of Paul, and I Peter, but never with John and in Colossians. Oepke concludes from these statistics that *apokaluptein* originally has a *jewish-primitive-christian* color and that *phaneroun* shows more of a *gnostic* shade.[14]

When we wonder what is meant by this differentiation and especially with this "gnostic" color, we are told that the gnosis considers that which is seen and perceived by the knowl-

---

11. Cf. also John 17:6, "I have manifested (*phaneroun*) thy name" and II Tim. 1:10 "now made manifest (*phaneroun*) by the appearing of our Savior Jesus Christ."
12. Eph. 3:5, the mystery of Christ . . . "as it is now revealed (*apokaluptein*) unto his holy apostles and prophets by the Spirit"; Col 1:26, "*now* is made manifest (*phaneroun*)."
13. Except at the end of Mark, which, according to him, is not authentic. Moreover, the parallel texts to Mark 4:22 in Matthew and Luke have also *apokaluptein.*
14. Kittel, *Th. W. B.,* s.v., *apokaluptein.*

edge of revelation, as principally "belonging to this world" and "accessible to knowledge," whereas *apokaluptein* refers to that which does not belong to this world and which is not accessible to man, and which can be revealed only by an act of God's will. The contrast between *phaneroun* and *apokaluptein* is, according to this theory, this: we have the disposal of the *phaneroun* in its reality, but never of the *apokalupsis*. Whatever is *phaneroun* is there as a *fact* in the actual reality, which we can approach, find, and reach in a direct relationship of knowledge, so that Oepke comes to the conclusion that we are *not* dealing with the *actual,* strictly biblical concept of revelation in *phaneroun* but we are in *apokaluptein*.

Consistently reasoning, this viewpoint should lead to the assumption that only where *apokaluptein* is mentioned, revelation in its fullest sense is meant. For *this* certainly belongs to truly divine revelation — if it is to retain its significance — that God reveals himself *sovereignly* and *omnipotently*. If this is being taken away from the *phaneroun* then it can hardly be called revelation any longer, because then there is only a reality left, which belongs to this world and of which man has the disposal in free knowledge. Oepke does state that the contents and quality of the word *apokaluptein* are shared by its synonyms, but the bases for this assertion are nowhere evident and *cannot* become evident because this whole argument is based on the assumption of the 'gnostic color' of the *phaneroun*. There is, however, in the entire New Testament no evidence whatsoever[15] of any real difference between *phaneroun* and *apokaluptein,* in connection with the *subject* of this revelation, *viz.* the free and sovereign God. It is very clear that wherever *phaneroun* is mentioned, a sovereign *act* of God is meant. We are not simply facing there a *transparent being-evident,* which can

---

15. Cf. the sharp criticism by J. de Zwaan of Oepke's theories: *Openbaring en exegese in het N.T.* In: *Vox Theologica,* 1940, p. 178. De Zwaan calls Oepke's differentiating "pseudo-problems."

be seen, but the being-evident is the *result,* the effect, of *God's revealing himself.* This shows that Oepke's contrast between having the disposal of the *phaneroun* and not having the disposal of the *apokaluptein* is entirely without any foundation. There is indeed no such thing as simply having revelation at our disposal. Flesh and blood have not revealed it unto Peter, but the Father in heaven (*apokaluptein*), Matt. 16:17. But the same holds true whenever *phaneroun* is mentioned (cf. Rom. 1:17 and 3:21). This, of course, does not mean that there is no possibility of a shade of difference in meaning between the two words. According to Bavinck it is well nigh impossible to prove a constant and consistent difference between the usage of the two words in the New Testament, but it is possible to show some shade of meaning.[16] The word *apokaluptein* indicates, according to him, the removal of a cover, a wrapping, by which an object had been hidden. This indicates the removal of an obstruction, which creates an obstacle to *knowledge, viz.* the obstacle of the *"mystery"* and of the "inaccessibility" so that *apokalupsis* may be taken in the sense of *unveiling.* The *phaneroun* indicates more the revelation with respect to its positive aspect, *viz.* above and beyond the removal of the covering.[17] This shows us that we need not assume any contrast on the basis of the usage of the words since *by* the removal of the covering the revealed object becomes visible and public. That is why Paul in Eph. 3:5 and Col. 1:26 can use *apokaluptein* and *phaneroun* alternately, although both texts mean the taking away of the mystery. At stake in both words are two inseparably related *aspects* of the one reality of divine revelation.

---

16. Bavinck, *Gereformeerde Dogmatiek I,* p. 295. Thus also W. Elert, *Der Christl. Glaube,* 1940, p. 163, and J. Riemens, *Het begrip der Openbaring in het Christendom* 1905, p. 8f.

17. In John 9:3 we read concerning the man who was blind from his birth that his blindness had a purpose, viz. "that the work of God should be made manifest in him" (*phaneroun*).

It is furthermore important to note that "to reveal" in Scripture does not always denote a *divine* act. Because *apokaluptein* means the removal of a covering, this word can also serve with respect to intercosmic relationships, namely this: between mystery and revelation. It is love which covers a multitude of sins and hides them (I Peter 4:8; James 5:20). And just as love exercises a hiding and covering function, so it is also possible for something *to reveal itself*. Thus Scripture speaks of every man's work *being made manifest* (I Cor. 3:13 — *phaneroun*), for the *day* shall declare it (*deloun*), the day shall reveal (*apokaluptein*) it with fire. The *thoughts* of many hearts are *revealed* (Luke 2:35 — *apokaluptein*). We even learn concerning the antichrist, that he, the man of sin, must be revealed (II Thess. 2: 3, 6, 8 — all three verses have the word *apokaluptein*). The idea of revelation, therefore, may also generally be described as "to unveil, uncover, make visible, something which is veiled or covered up."[18] There is not one special, sacred word denoting God's revealing activity. The words of Scripture, also when they direct our attention to the powerful, sovereign working of God, are gauged to the comprehensibility which is the objective of God's revealing himself. Therefore, it is, of course, absolutely incorrect to construct a conception of revelation on the basis of this general employment of words, which would be able to subsume all these forms of "to reveal (itself)." It is absolutely impossible to deduce the meaning of divine revelation from the word itself. It is even impossible to operate with the scheme "revelation" and "mystery," as though *this* would explain who God, who reveals himself, is. The Scriptural employment of the word, which denotes a transcending of the inaccessible mystery, can be understood only in the reality of God's revelation. Then the point of issue is no longer the comprehending of an act of revelation "as such," or the nature of revelation in itself (the antichrist must reveal himself also) but *he,* who sovereignly and all-powerfully

---

18. Kittel s.v.

comes to us in his revelation. The same thing may be noted when we recall that Scripture continuously mentions God's speaking, again a word that is also said of *creatural* subjects.[19] Also in this respect it is not possible to arrive at a conclusion who this "speaking" God is on the basis of the general idea of "to speak." It is true, however, that the idea "to speak" is generally used to call our attention to the sovereign speaking of the Word of God.

There is not one word in Scripture, which would keep us — by the word as such — to a special action of revelation. That is the reason why we ought to proceed very carefully when speaking of a "conception of revelation." By numerous words, which are gauged to our *understanding* of these words, Scripture points our attention to God's revelation. Therefore *apokaluptein* is not *more* the "actual" word for revelation than God's *speaking*. Scripture always points to God's active revealing of himself as an all-powerful reality, which may be expressed as a transcending of the mystery, as a *speaking* or *showing* or *making known*. Not without foundation DeZwaan states, "every act of God which directly or indirectly concerns man is 'revelation' in a New Testament sense,"[20] and he correctly criticises Oepke's definition which is based on the statistics that "revelation in New Testament sense is, in short, the self-revelation of the Father of Jesus Christ to mankind." The issue here is not the problem of Christo-monism as yet but a rashly defining of the idea of revelation. Exactly because the issue at stake in God's revelation is the revelation of the mystery, a *modus* of revelation, which is implied only in *his* omnipotence, we may not yield to the desire to arrive in a simplistic manner to one New Testament word for revelation

---

19. This holds true also for the word "to reveal" in the O.T. (*galah*) because it is also used with regard to what people "reveal," relate, as in I Sam. 20:2, "Behold, my father will do nothing either great or small, but that he will shew it me: and why should my father hide this thing from me?"

20. J. de Zwaan, quoted article *Vox Theol.*, 1940. p. 169.

as the only actual one. How broad and wide Scripture speaks
of God's revealing activity!

We learn that the arm of the Lord (Isa. 53:1; John 12:38),
the Son of man (Luke 17:30), the righteousness of God (Rom.
1:17), the wrath of God (Rom. 1:18), the grace (I Peter
1:13), and the mystery of Christ (Eph. 3:3) are revealed.

The point of the whole idea is that something which first
was hidden now becomes distinguishable and known. It is impossible to construct a *contrast* between God's Word and
God's deed, between "knowing" and "taking place." With respect to a viewpoint as Bultmann's we wonder whether the
result of the "biblical theology" is a reverting to a *separation*
between Word-revelation and deed-revelation. Does Scripture
not speak far more freely concerning God's coming to man, his
doing and speaking, and his self-revelation? Everywhere we
learn of God's revealing activity but besides and above that also from his Word, which comes to the prophets as a calling
Word. Thus we find, for instance with Samuel, the calling
Word of God recorded against the background of the mystery
of God. The Word of the Lord had not yet been revealed to
Samuel until God called Samuel.

God's Word is the opposite of his mystery and offsets the
latter. In those days the Word of God was dear, precious;
there was no open vision (I Sam. 3:1). When God's revelation is heard then a reverent listening responds with, "Speak,
for thy servant heareth!" Israel's light of salvation is contained
in this gracious speaking. Therefore, in connection with the
historic circumstances under which it appears, this revelation of
God is pluri-form. It is an *act* of God, but at the same time a
Word, which *makes known* that which is necessary to know
this God. The representation of revelation as a "taking place"
over against a "knowing" minimizes the greatness of the Scriptural revelation of God. We nowhere find any under-valuating
of this beneficial "knowing" imparted by revelation, because
it is not simply an intellectual knowing of a system of truths

but the knowing of *his* grace and *his* judgment. The things which he reveals and speaks in the ears of men are deep and secret (Dan. 2:22), in order that they may *know* and acknowledge *him* (I Sam. 9:15; 20:2, 12; 22:8, 17).

This revelation is sovereign with respect to choosing the means. It cannot be demanded but only accepted as a present. God himself only can take the mystery away. He *can* do it and *does* do it. He appears as the dayspring from on high (Luke 1:78). "Out of Zion, the perfection of beauty, God hath shined" (Ps. 50:2). He is known and seen and served only by *faith*. His acts do not take place in secrecy. Only the *understanding* of revelation can become a problem.

* * *

On the basis of the numerous Scriptural data it cannot be denied that within the revelation God *himself* comes to us. He himself dwells in the inaccessible light and thus, revealing himself, he comes to the world. No *a prioristic* schematization whatsoever is therefore able to ignore this revelation and make limitations or mark borders. Only faith, which penetrates schematism, finds rest in the reality of revelation. For, this faith is not of a *creative* but only of a *receptive* and *attentive* nature. It rests in the *"Deus dixit."*

This sheds light on the conception that "only *in the incarnation* God *himself* comes to us and that we, therefore, only in this respect are dealing with real, actual revelation." It is obvious that we are dealing here with a certain dogmatic reflection. Scripture does not state such a thing at all. To such a conception can one arrive only when speaking of abstract, indicative, *and* actual revelation. The Christo-monistic conception of revelation does so because it considers Jesus Christ exclusively as the revelation, as that revelation of God by which time, so to speak, stands still in order to be fulfilled with God's eternity, "the superhistoric event of God's revelation,"[21] not just simply an ambassador of God, but "God himself" (p. 232), the revelation by which God becomes "historic."[22]

This only is revelation, *real and actual* revelation, as a "rending of God's secret."[23] All the other things are *grouped* around this, are *participating with* it in a certain way, but are still not revelation in the *real* sense of the Word: God *himself*, in the form of the flesh.

The consistent conclusion from this conception must be, then, that there is not only no revealing activity of God in nature and history but neither can there be any real revelation of God under the Old Covenant. Usually a "participation" of God's revelation by the Old Covenant is mentioned — as a foreshadow — but in the light of the uniqueness of revelation this can never mean that also under the Old Covenant there was *real, actual* revelation of God. On the basis of this "God himself" the Christo-monistic conception of revelation cannot recognize any *other* revelation than the one in the incarnated Word. In this connection the distinction between an Old Testament prophet and Christ has thus been expressed, that the prophet *has* the Word but the Son is the Word.[24] Anyone who thus, on the basis of his *a prioristic* conception of revelation differentiates, inevitably ends up with devaluating or denying the revealing quality and aspect of Old Testament prophecy. When Brunner says, "that is the reason why the revelation by the prophets cannot be final," he immediately makes a jump and continues, "it is not yet real revelation but only a foreshadow of revelation. A prophet *has* the Word,

21. Barth, *Prolegomena*, 1927, p. 230.
22. *Ibid.*, p. 233, cf. Barth., *Weihnacht* 1934.
23. Barth, *Weihnacht* 1934, p. 10.
24. E. Brunner, *Der Mittler*, 1927, p. 197. Cf. also R. Otto, *Das Heilige*, 1925, p. 199, who pictures a prophet as one, "who possesses the Spirit as the power of the 'inner Voice' and of divination and, by means of both, as religious power of expression." Quite different from a prophet is he, "who, both by his person and by performance and achievement, becomes the object of divination of the holy person who makes his appearance." "Such a person is more than prophet. He is the Son."

but he *is* not the Word."[25] According to Brunner this constitutes his *limited* authority [26] because "the prophet himself is not the scene where revelation takes place." Observe the procedure in this reasoning. Because of a narrow conception of revelation the Old Testament revelation is under-valued on the basis of revelation being once-and-for-all, but still with an *appearance* of being Scriptural: "the prophethood is 'Messianic' " but the prophet *cannot* be the focal point of revelation. It is true, Scripture does say that the Lord cannot do anything unless he "revealeth his secret unto his servants the prophets," (Amos 3:7) but this *cannot* be *real* revelation in the full sense of the word.

It must be noted how entirely differently this dogmatic conception of revelation speaks of God's revelation than does Scripture, because it does not give a synthesis of the words and ideas of revelation as Scripture has them, but all revelation is Christologically — or better still — Jesu-centrically limited.[27] *Only* this is considered real revelation if it proceeds from God himself as *reconciliation,* and if it is *absolutely once-and-for-all.* In this conception there is no room for any *plurality* nor for any *history* of revelation. For, only in the incarnation, God himself has entered into the flesh, i, e. into our world.

* * *

It is obvious that this "once-and-for-all" of revelation has nothing to do with the "once" from the epistle to the Hebrews, because there the issue is that the sacrifice of the cross

---

25. Brunner, *ibid.,* p. 197; cf. Brunner, *Dogmatik* I, 1946, p. 25f.

26. Such ideas can be maintained only by means of abstractions such as, "the prophet himself, as a man, has no authority" (Brunner, *ibid.,* p. 198) and, over against this, "no one has authority but God, who speaks, himself." Considered in the light of the history of salvation these are nothing but abstractions when we think of Scripture: "the word of the Lord came unto me" (Jer. 1:4, 7, 9, etc.: 2:1) and: "The *Lord speaketh.*"

27. Cf. Brunner *ibid.,* p. 8, "Essentially revelation is (as it is once-and-for-all) that which either does not take place at all or that which can take place only once."

is unrepeatable. He who tampers with that minimizes the blessed power of this sacrifice by which he has perfected for ever them that are sanctified (Heb. 10:14; cf. 9:28). It is true, we read moreover (Heb. 9:26) that Christ now once, at the end of the ages, has appeared to put away sin by his sacrifice, but this "once" refers to Christ's sacrifice being final, conclusive, and all-embracing, in contrast with the Old Testament sacrifices. The conclusion that the revelation of God himself is "once-and-for-all" in the sense as discussed above, on the basis of the exclusivity of salvation in Christ, cannot be deduced from this "once" from Hebrews. Exactly this epistle, in which "once" has such a prominent place stresses the great significance of the *Old Testament revelation*. When picturing the figure of the high priest the author [28] says that the Holy Ghost signified this (Heb. 9:8), "that the way into the holiest of all was not yet made manifest, while as the first tabernacle was yet standing." And then a word follows in which our present discussion of revelation plays such an important role, *viz.* "figure"; "which was a figure for the time then present."[29] But this figure is not just simply *human* witness but exactly this figure, this symbol, contained God's revelation of that which was not yet *actually* present in the Old Testament sacrificial rites, *viz.* the *open* road.

In this connection there is still another expression of this epistle which is very remarkable, because it clearly evidences again how freely Scripture speaks of God's revelation. We have in mind the opening sentence of this epistle, "God, who at sundry times and in divers manners spake in time past unto the fathers by the prophets, hath in these last days spoken unto us by his Son" (Heb. 1:1, 2). The very striking aspect of this statement is, that it appears (at the beginning!) in the epistle which leaves no stone unturned to show that the

---

28. Heb. 9:8: here the word *dēloō* is used, one of the words for *revelation* in Scripture, besides *apokaluptein* and *phaneroun*.
29. Heb. 9:9; *parabolē*.

absolute and exclusive salvation is *in Christ*. This exclusiveness of salvation apparently does not at all conflict with the fact that God's speaking in and by His Son is mentioned together with God's *earlier* speaking "in divers manners." The vision of the unique salvation in Christ, *the* High Priest, is no occasion whatsoever to devaluate God's speaking and revelation in time past.[30] To the contrary, God's speaking is seen in its broad and varied scope: at *sundry* times and in *divers* manners. It is pluriform over a long historic period, a historic multifarious activity of God, which is placed *next to* "God's speaking" by the Son, and this apparently does not in the least minimize and weaken Christ Jesus' import, to the author's estimation.[31] This is possible because God's speaking "in times past" *indicated* God's "speaking" through the Son.[32] In these last days, i.e. in the definitive, conclusive phase of God's salvation on earth, God spoke through his *Son*. The difference between the former and latter speaking of God is not that the former was less trustworthy or would less contain the nature of *actual revelation*. All such inferences are completely ruled out. Grosheide correctly states that we find in Heb. 1:1 "that the revelation under the Old Covenant was not inferior (cf. I Peter 1:11), but that the

---

30. Cf. Q. and A. 19 of the Heidelberg Catechism, "Whence do you know this? From the holy gospel, which God Himself first revealed in Paradise, afterwards published by the holy patriarchs and prophets, and foreshadowed by the sacrifices and other ceremonies of the law; and lastly fulfilled by His only begotten Son."

31. On Heb. 1:1, cf. Jac. J. Muller, *Progressive Revelation,* in The Evangelical Quarterly, Oct. 1934, who does justice to both the historic variety of God's speaking and God's conclusive speaking in and by Christ Jesus: "Apparently Christ (in the quoted passage from Hebrews) is put on the same line with the prophets as a personal instrument for the revelation of God, but He is also essentially other than they," (p. 376). Also: "Jesus Christ is at the same time the consummation and the personal fulfillment of what was foreshadowed under the old covenant," (p. 377). "All the revelations, under both covenants, bring us the one unspeakable gift, Christ, the Son of God, the Logos of the Father." (p. 379).

32. Cf. Muller, *ibid.,* p. 379, "Just as a sentence consists of many words, but has only one meaning, so the revelation of God under both covenants, in law and gospel, has only one meaning: Jesus Christ."

prophets are under the Son."[33]   Exactly this constitutes the
possibility and the meaning of this *placing next* to each other
in Heb. 1:1 that revelation under the Old Covenant is not
considered a thing by itself next to and apart from the revelation in Christ in the last days. Heb. 1:1 shows us that the
New Testament can still speak in such an unproblematical
way.   This is possible because God's deeds of revelation are
not limited, nor are they ever mentioned as though God's
revelation commences with the historical Jesus.   The fact
that every speaking of God points to Christ and that the *light*
of God's revelation *fully* arose in him, is something entirely
different from revelation *commencing* with him.   Asserting
the latter is forcing the Scriptural data into an *a prioristic*
scheme.   The core of this scheme is this "God himself," and
it is our firm conviction that this idea is connected with the
dialectic conception of the trinity and with the satisfaction-
doctrine of Karl Barth (God in our stead).   We cannot discuss this aspect of this problem now.   But in our opinion
one thing is clear, namely, that this dialectical speaking of
"once-and-for-all" reveals a tenacity which in Scripture itself is *nowhere* to be found, because we observe everywhere
in Scripture God's revealing voice, God's Word entering
into the world, God's revealing activity in the history of His
people, and in the appearances of the Lord.   It is absolutely
contrary to Scripture to deny the *real* characteristics of revelation in these things.   It is the Spirit of the Lord who in the
process of history and of historical revelation governs everything.   "The Spirit of the Lord spake by me, and his word
was in my tongue" (II Sam. 23:2).   Scripture's unbiased
speaking is most evident (besides in Heb. 1:1) in I Peter
1:11, where Peter is dealing with the salvation of God in
Jesus Christ, with love towards and faith in him, and with
the salvation which is found in him.   "Of which salvation,"
thus he goes on, "the prophets have enquired and searched

33. F. W. Grosheide, *Comm. on Hebrews*, p. 64.

diligently, who prophesied of the grace that should come unto you, searching what, or what manner of time the Spirit of Christ which was in them did signify, when it testified beforehand the sufferings of Christ, and the glory that should follow." The Old Testament revelation of Christ truly pointed to Christ. The Spirit of Christ testified *beforehand*.[34] The *significance and meaning* of Old Testament prophecy lies, by the guidance of the Spirit, in the historicity of Christ's suffering and glory. And it is in this text that we read of the revelation (*apokaluptein*) to these prophets, "Unto whom it was *revealed,* that not unto themselves, but unto us they did minister the things, which are now reported unto you" (I Peter 1:12).

* * *

All this is a warning to us not to limit and define God's revealing voice and activity on the basis of the incarnation and the *kenosis* of Philippians 2. This had been done on the basis of the exclusivity of the salvation in Christ and the adherents of this theory did not want to classify this revelation under a broadened "type"-conception of revelation, of which the revelation in Christ would be a certain "form." But thus sight was lost of the fact that Scripture places God's revelation in Christ in the broad and historic framework of God's acts of revelation. For this reason Scripture never makes God's revelation conditional on the *nature* of God's revelation in the humiliation and *kenosis* of Christ. He who does this forgets that the incarnation of the word became "necessary" *on the basis of the lost condition of the world.* Throughout the history of the church and theology the idea arose here and there that the Son of God would have taken upon himself the very nature of man even if the world had not fallen away in sin from God. It may be possible to construe an idea of revelation on the basis of such an abstract

---

34. Cf. Gal. 3:8, "And the scripture, foreseeing," etc.

hypothesis (which Scripture does not warrant at all) and accept this, then, as the "incarnation." But anyone, considering in the light of Scripture the incarnation as God's act, as the *giving* of his Son, that whosoever believeth in him should not perish, but have everlasting life (John 3:16), will not and may not attempt to define the *modus* of God's revelation on the basis of the *modus* of His *reconciling* and *gracious* acting *in Jesus Christ*. We cannot contemplate upon this unique drama of incarnation, cross, and resurrection, but in connection with *guilt* and our *lost condition*. We may not limit the conception of revelation because of the incarnation for this reason, that we cannot speak in any other way of revelation — because of the uniqueness of Christ's revelation — than seeing it as an incomparable act of God and as a holy, divine answer to man's *guilt*. It is not out of a desire to *broaden* the aspects of revelation in our lives and in the world that we reject the Christo-monistic conception of revelation, but we do so because, on the basis of the uniqueness of Christ's birth, suffering, death and resurrection, the vision must remain open towards the whole of God's deeds of revelation and God himself. Only this explains, in our opinion, the manner in which Scripture speaks of the Word, of revelation, of God's speaking, and of his proclamation. If we but avoid misunderstandings we might say that Scripture does not in the Christo-monistic sense consider God's revelation Christo-centric, but *trinitarian*.

This explains why we frequently come across words which very *concretely* speak of revelation. Thus we read in one of Christ's discourses, "he that loveth me shall be loved of my Father, and I will love him, and will manifest myself to him" (John 14:21, 22; cf. John 21:1, 14). The point at issue in this statement is not the *"factum"* Jesus Christ, but a concrete, real act of revelation. And, moreover, we read in the *Revelation* of John, "Revelation of Jesus Christ, which God gave unto him, to show unto his servants things which must shortly come to pass," (Rev. 1:1), which denotes that Jesus Christ is the recipient of revelation. This fact can hardly be given a place in the Christo-monistic scheme, but it does fit the entire Scriptural witness. Scripture is able — according to the very words of Christ — to point out to us that no man knoweth who the Father is, but the Son, and he to whom the Son will reveal him; but also, that no man knoweth who the *Son* is but the *Father* (Luke 10:22).

The revelation in Christ, therefore, can be placed next to the multifarious speaking of God in times past by Hebrews 1:1 because Scripture never restricts God's activity to the Christologic. Scripture, therefore, always clearly indicates that the *guilt* of God's people is based upon the misjudgment of the reality of God's revelation. This is the background of the alarming prophetic preaching which calls heaven and earth as witnesses against Judah and Jerusalem, which have transgressed against the Lord, "The ox knoweth his owner, and the ass his master's crib: But Israel doth not know, my people doth not consider" (Isa. 1:3). Jeremiah contrasts God's deeds of revelation for and in God's people with the reaction of the people and the "priests" who "said not, Where is the Lord? and they that handle the law knew me not: the pastors also transgressed against me, and the prophets prophesied by Baal" (Jer. 2:8). The hypothesis of all prophetism is the *reality* of God's revelation.

Exactly because of the sovereignty of God's revelation in history we may not schematize the modalities of this revelation. The adherents of the Christo-monistic idea of revelation were inclined to do this, and this frequently caused them to connect in a curious manner revelation with mystery, God's power with weakness, God's majesty which was hidden under the cloak of the flesh. The *kenosis,* Christ's "emptying of himself" was made the *structure* of revelation, and thus, it was believed, this stumbling-block in Holy Scripture could be explained and understood. But this *kenosis*-theory, which by its apparent consistent defining of the idea of revelation had a suggestive influence on many, does not do justice to God's revealing voice. God's speaking under the Old Covenant pointed to Christ and by giving heed to this speaking it imparted the wealth of the salvation of the Lord. God's speaking points to the mystery of the fulness of time. We learn of the revelation of this mystery, "hid from ages" but *now* revealed (Rom. 16:25. Cf. Col. 1:28; Eph. 3:5). This "now" indicates the historic fact of *this* revelation of God in its reconciling and saving power. And especially the expression, "revelation of the mystery, which was kept secret since the world began, but now is made manifest" signifies the very special nature of *this* revelation in Christ.

We must be careful, however, not to draw all kinds of speculative conclusions from this "silence." We might come to the conclusion — if we isolate the word from the context of Scripture — that we are dealing here with a "new" revelation in the sense that in the ages past nothing whatever had been known of God's dealings which now became actuality in Jesus Christ.

It is certainly not Paul's intention to state *such a thing*. There is a tremendous gulf between the wonderment which fills Paul in this doxology and Marcion's gospel of the "strange" God. The entire epistle of Paul to the Romans is *most closely connected* with God's revelation in the Old Covenant. But Paul's expressions are indeed extremely *strong* and *penetrating*. In Col. 1:26 we do not read "kept secret" but *hid*, "the mystery which hath been hid from ages, but now is made manifest."[35] Paul wishes to call attention to the unsearchable mystery which *now* has become reality and which has been made part of the preaching, and the richness of

---

35. In Eph. 3:5 we read that the mystery of Christ in the time of former generations *was not made known* unto the sons of men. Here the mystery of Christ is considered in connection with the fact that the heathen are co-heirs of the promise in Christ Jesus.

which is known to the heathen. The point at issue is the
"now" of this revelation. This reminds us of Christ's statement, "But blessed are your eyes, for they see: and your
ears, for they hear. For verily, I say unto you, That many
prophets and righteous men have desired to see those things
which ye see, and have not seen them; and to hear those
things which ye hear, and have not heard them."[36]

All this clearly evidences the uniqueness of that which in
Christ became manifest.[37] The phraseology which Scripture
in this respect employs is so strong and doxologic that it cannot be doubted that a conception of revelation which wants to
be Scriptural cannot and may not undervaluate this unique
revelation. But in the history of revelation as Scripture describes it there is no sign of such undervaluation. To the contrary, the entire history of revelation *emphasizes* the exclusivity of this abundance of revelation. However, we shall
have to object to any conception of revelation which pro-
claims the *modus* of the revelation of Christ to the *modus* of
God's revelation and so limits the latter to the revelation in
Christ. It has the appearance that thus this revelation is hon-
ored for its incomparable nature, but actually it is disconnected from its historic relationships by denying, on the basis of

---

36. Matt. 13:16, 17, cf. H. N. Ridderbos (*Korte Verklaring*), "He refers to the great O.T. future expecters."

37. Cf., among other things, John 6:32f., where manna *and* Christ as
bread from heaven are contrasted. Christ says, "Moses gave you not the
bread from heaven; but my Father giveth you the true bread from heaven.
For the bread of God is he which cometh down from heaven, and giveth
life unto the world. And Jesus said unto them, I am the bread of life."
This statement does not contain an undervaluation of manna but it does
point out the *true* bread, whereas manna is the *symbol* of the bread of life.
(Grosheide. *Comm. John I*, p. 437). This statement attacks that of the
Jews, by which they showed they set more value to what God performed
in the desert (manna), than to what Jesus was doing then (Grosheide,
p. 434, commenting on John 6:31). Christ's statement concerning the bread
of life does not deny revelation under the Old Covenant, but it does point
out the finality of God's revelation in himself (cf. *katabainein*, John
6:38, 51, 58). The Jews reject the revelation in Christ and thus they cannot understand the meaning of Old Testament revelation either.

the incarnation, that all other revelation can be *actual* revelation, because we do not see "God himself" in it.

* * *

The issue at stake in all these discussions was not specifically the "general" revelation. We have considered the Christo-monistic conception of revelation in as far as it raises questions in connection with God's revelation in the Old Covenant. All this, however, is indirectly also of importance to the problem with which we are concerned. Here we come to a decision of great import. *The principal attack against the profession of general revelation came namely from the adherents of Christo-monism.* This monism denies all revelation in actual sense outside of the historic Christ and recognizes only "witness" and "indications" which as such indeed are connected with *the* revelation but still *are* not revelation. Since this in principle applies to the Old Covenant it must apply in far greater measure to the realm outside of the special revelation in Christ (and in Israel). We may ignore the question whether it is consistent when Brunner's view, which is strongly Christo-monistic and excludes prophetism from actual revelation, still emphatically defends the *revelation* of creation over against Barth.[38] It is sufficient to point out that, in our opinion, Christo-monism's opposition excludes *every* form of revelation outside of Jesus, because the

---

38. This tension is quite evident in Brunner's dogmatics (I, 1946, p. 19ff). He speaks of a "plurality of revelation-forms" in the Old Covenant (p. 19), furthermore of a "revelation which precedes all history" (p. 20) and of a "revelation-form of the apostolic witness" (p. 21). The church — according to Brunner — has experienced the revelation power of the apostolic word so strongly that she "simply considered it as God's word" (p. 22). But this implied a misunderstanding, "namely that God's revelation was identical with a human word from God," whereas the revelation of Christ exceeds this: incarnation. To call the New Testament the Word of God, however, is correct again, inasmuch as it "indicates the form of revelation" (p. 22). So the problem is solved with revelation and "form" of revelation.

"God himself" manifest in the flesh has no plurality by virtue of its very nature. We do well to keep in mind the basic motive of Christologic monism lest we employ it against the profession of general revelation. For the battle extends much further than against general revelation and concerns God's revelation under the Old Covenant just as much. And all this against the background of the absolute "once-and-for-all."

* * *

This contains warnings for anyone who concerns himself with general revelation in our day. He can be sure that soon the suspicion will fall on this contemplation that it indicates a flight from the "once-for-all" of the revelation in Christ and a turning to an irrational appeal to data in nature or history, which are being haloed with divinity. We may not let such a suspicion scare us off, especially since we know that the revelation in the Old Covenant is also at stake. But if we are not scared and wish to listen to Scripture without an *a prioristic* scheme of revelation, then we shall still have to be very careful. We shall especially have to know *in concreto how* Scripture speaks of the revelation of the mystery of Christ and in this connection of the "Christ only" and of the exclusivity of his salvation; of Christ as *the* Door, *the* Way, *the* Truth, and *the* Life.

He who does not listen to and believe this message any more will get lost in the "generality" of revelation in which the voices *then* will fade into utterly lonesome silence. Also in the history of theology may be observed something like a judgment. The exclusivity of salvation is truly exclusive. Whoever is offended because of this salvation *in* Christ and therefore searches for wider perspectives and thus for other revelations besides Christ, will finally grope around in utter darkness. In times like we are living in we can everywhere detect the pretension of "revelation," of the unveiling of the world's mystery, and of the "mysteries" of life.   In such times it is imperative to fully realize *what* we are looking for when contemplating general revelation.

Only then shall we be able to successfully reject the Christo-monistic idea of revelation, when from the beginning to the end the uncontradictable word of the Lord himself keeps echoing, *"No man cometh to the Father but by me."*

The "Nature Psalms"

CHAPTER VI

The "Nature Psalms"

U P UNTIL NOW we have examined the various aspects of the controversy concerning the profession of general revelation and every time we arrived at the pivotal question which dominated every discussion: Is there, besides a special revelation in Christ, also a more *general* revealing activity of God? Now that we wish concretely to direct our attention to the pronouncements of Holy Scripture, we are confronted with a peculiar problem. For when Reformed theology differentiated between general and special revelation, it always proceeded from the position that Holy Scripture itself belonged to the special revelation. This already fixes the question in a certain direction: Does the special revelation in Holy Scripture teach us anything concerning *general* revelation?

He who thinks in terms of Christo-monistic categories will, *a priori,* be inclined to answer this question in the negative, for, if in Scripture God's word of salvation comes to us, then we may expect that this will be indeed and completely a word of God's salvation and that this will witness to Christ. Does Christ Himself not say, "Search the scriptures; for they are they which testify of me" (John 5:39)? Can we, then, expect that Scripture will direct us to still.another revelation, to a more *general* one by which God *also* comes to us?

The apparently logical nature of this question may not prevent us, however, from listening to Scripture itself, for, if God's revelation comes to us in and by Holy Scripture, then we will have to listen again and again to the concrete words of

117

Scripture. Only thus can the puny and obscure deliberations of our minds be conquered. When we now wish to take this road of examining Scripture, it immediately strikes us that, at first glance, quantitively few passages seem to come into consideration for the discussion concerning general revelation. Barth, as we have learned, once spoke of a "main line" and a "sideline" in Holy Scripture and he arrived at this designation because the "main line," according to him, obviously dealt with God's revelation in Jesus Christ. Is the point at issue in Scripture not the message of God's grace, and is this not given to us for instruction, for reproof, for correction and for doctrine in *righteousness,* so that the man of God may be perfect, thoroughly furnished unto all good works? (II Tim. 3:16, 17). And are the Scriptures, of which Paul is speaking here, not able to make wise unto salvation? (II Tim. 3:15). Is it imaginable, then, that this Scripture calls our attention — to the revelation! — to still *other* things in the world besides *this* salvation? And whereas revelation wishes to convey knowledge, is it plausible, then, that Scripture would want to call us to any other knowledge besides the one which *is life eternal?* (John 17:3). Must we not necessarily arrive at the conclusion that this knowledge, in any case, will be of a *supplementary* nature?

* * *

Neither is the one, who is of the opinion that we cannot only speak of a revelation in Jesus Christ but also under the Old Covenant and thus not subscribe to the consistent Christo-monistic vision, always ready at all times to accept a revelation in the reality outside of the reality of *salvation.* He may accept a revelation with respect to Israel's history of salvation, because it points toward the revelation of salvation through Christ. But is it not an unwarranted jump to go still further and speak of revelation in *nature, history* and *man's life* "in general"? Will this not distract the attention and will it not lead to a "philosophy of life" *outside* of faith?

It need not surprise us that in the controversy concerning general revelation there have been emphasized especially those passages of Holy Scripture which place nature in a certain relationship to God. By this we do not mean at all that the point at issue in general revelation is "nature," as though this general revelation were a sort of *nature*-revelation.[1] We are of the opinion that this is not the case at all. But it is understandable indeed that the problem of "nature" has been frequently connected with general revelation and discussed in connection with the so-called *"nature psalms."*

Indeed, it cannot be denied that in Holy Scripture we meet with a peculiar interest in "nature" as a divinely created reality. It will not do to determine some quantitive-statistic results and to come to the conclusion, on the basis thereof, that Holy Scripture pays only moderate attention to nature and that the full emphasis — except for a few exceptions — does not fall on "nature" but on "grace," because the manner in which Scripture speaks of nature certainly calls for our attention. It cannot be denied that in numerous passages on nature we discern a *doxological* tone and whenever Scripture sounds a doxology we surrender every desire to figure with quantities and statistics.

*   *   *

There is no need for a lengthy argument to show that Scripture speaks differently of "nature" than many who — for whatever reason it may be — laud and glorify nature *in itself*. Moreover, many who wanted to see more in nature than nature only, have tried to find God in nature in a complete or partial identification, in pantheism or panentheism. To how many has the way (back) to nature not automatically

---

1. *Cf.* Chapter XI.

been — to their idea — the way to God, who, as the mysterious origin and immanent power of the entire realm of nature, could as it were, directly be traced, by which nature itself — because of its fascinating and multifarious aspects — then became the *form of God's revelation?* We are thinking of the very illustrative example from the pen of Goethe who once wrote, "If anyone ask me, if it is in my nature to render adoration and honor to Christ, then I say: yes! I bow before him as the divine revelation of the highest principle of morality." But he immediately added, "If anyone asks me, whether it is in my nature to adore the *sun,* then I say again: yes! because she, too, is a revelation of the highest, nay, the most powerful, which we, human beings, may observe. I adore in her the light and the power of God by which we all live, move, and are, and all plants and animals with us."[2] It is obvious, that Scripture does not know of such a nature-religion which disregards all revelation.

We could call this — as in any nature-religion — the self-evidence of the nature-revelation. God "appears," as it were, clearly through nature in a way which everyone easily detects. This way it could hardly be said that revelation is an *act of God* because thus nature is more or less *identified* with God. At different times in history nature has been identified as the "place, the theater" of revelation, and "God" as the "primary motive" of nature, and mention was made of the divine earth with its inexhaustible, living dynamics, and its overwhelming creative power. This way there is no such thing as any real *transcendence,* nor a truly sovereign, transcendent *revelation*

2. Concerning Goethe's natural religion, see Kurt Leese, *Natürliche Religion und Christlicher Glaube. Eine theologische Neuorientierung,* 1936, p. 34. Goethe has said that everything he discovered in the pluriformity of nature, "revealed to him the deep-glowing, holy life of nature; how I embraced all this with my warm heart, how I filled myself with this overflowing fulness as though I were a god, and the glorious forms of the infinite universe moved in my soul and filled it with life" (Leese, p. 35); cf. also other samples from nature-religion and mysticism with Leese.

of God. At best, mention was made of a deity which was "apparent" or "evident." Revelation thus became, as it were, a constant and self-evident "quality" of nature. These different forms of natural religion can be found not only outside of the realm of theology. We hear an identical note in Scholten, the father of modern theology, when he writes, "God's activity, therefore, is not supernatural but *natural,* for the simple reason that *nature* is the word used by science to designate the collectivity of all operations in her realm. God's activity, therefore, is one and the same as nature's operation, because it is the collectivity of God's operations."[3] The point at issue in pantheism, according to Van Mourik, is "the idea of God, who reveals and expresses himself in the sum total of what is and takes place in the universe, and who unfolds his being in the visible reality."[4] It is true, he does not want to identify God with the universe (p. 315) and he is of the opinion that theism frequently but incorrectly accuses pantheism thereof, but he does mention an immanence which can hardly be differentiated from an identification. This pantheism indeed uses the word "revelation" since God reveals himself in "everything" but it is obvious that this "immanence"[5] actually does away with all *real* revelation as a *deed of God.*

The only thing that is left is a logical and actual "evidence." There is no room for a sovereign, divine deed of revelation in any form of pantheism, whatsoever. This "evidence" therefore, does not correspond to faith but to the "feeling" of man's unity and relationship with this "all" of which he is an integral part.[6] This pantheism in the aesthetic nature-religion can lead to adoration of the sun, moon or stars, and of the entire earth in its orderings as the divine mother of all things. The nature-

3. J. H. Scholten, *Supranaturalisme,* pp. 5-7
4. M. C. van Mourik Broekman, *De Vrijzinnige Godsidee,* p. 178.
5. R. G. G., s. v. *Pantheismus,* p. 885.
6. K. Leese, p. 29.

mysticism, the "cosmic feeling"[7] has crowded out all transcendent revelation. A "general" revelation in nature is still mentioned, but this "generality" sounds very antithetically in comparison with the revelation of the living, mighty God, who reveals himself *freely* and *sovereignly.*

The evidence in natural religion becomes a penetrating light which automatically beams forth from men's eyes. Therefore, there cannot be such a thing as a "mystery." All this is far removed from what Scripture teaches us concerning God's sovereign operation from the mystery and inaccessibility *to* the revelation. To the contrary: He himself shines *through* all things and anyone can see and find him in a *direct* "contact" with "nature." Thus considered, one has God at his disposal, because he simply has to reveal himself. He just cannot hide his face but simply must lift it up upon the world. Thus in all nature-religion and nature-mysticism the *reality* of sovereign revelation is at stake.

* * *

When asked how this pantheistic natural religion came about, we may answer, that nature has always had an extremely fascinating and suggestive attraction. Man descries in nature, with her superior power, birth and death; with her vegetative power and fertility, the power of gods, which manifest themselves in this nature before our astounded eyes. This kind of natural religion has a far greater sense of *manifestation* and *revelation* than does Goethe's aesthetic natural religion. But this attraction of nature, with her fascinating *and* terrifying aspects, leads to idolatry, because sight is lost of the creatureliness of nature. The connection between nature and "god" may be expressed in all kinds of ways. "God" may even be *localized,* as we find in the Old Testament, in the idea of *mountain gods.* The Syrians, preparing themselves to the bat-

7. *Ibid.,* p. 38.

tle against Israel, said, "The Lord is God of the hills, but he is
not God of the valleys," and the answer of the man of God is,
"therefore will I deliver all this great multitude into thine
hand, and ye shall know that I am the Lord" (I Kings 20:28).

Van Gelderen points out that the Arameans consider Jehovah as an ordinary mountain god, "a personified quantity
of natural power."[8] In contrast to this the *Lord* becomes manifest, for whom there is no *separate* relationship with respect
to the mountains, because he is the Creator of heaven and
earth. The prophet who announces the victory of Israel, "here
opposes the gods of nature." He is "the God of the entire realm
of nature."[9] But this is an entirely different conception from
the one of the Arameans. The difference is not simply *quantitative* (the *mountains*, or all things) but *qualitative*. He is
the Creator, to whom also the mountains belong,[10] but in the
light of his universal power as Creator, all things are revealed
in their *absolute creatureliness*. Everything which is able to
impress us deeply partakes of *this* creatureliness. All variations
of nature do not cancel the common denominator: *creature*.
All "gods," being projections of the human mind, are radically
unmasked and all identification between God and nature, or
one of her phenomena, give way for the appearance of the Lord,
who forms the mountains and creates the wind (Amos 4:13),
and for whom the mighty mountains tremble and the hills
melt away. The earth rises up for him, the world and all that
dwell therein (Nahum 1:5). Here all suggestion is spent in
the face of God's revelation. Here the fear, which nature with
her depths can evoke, is covered by the glory of the *Creator*.
This is the joy of faith, that it recognizes *pure* creatureliness.

---

8. C. van Gelderen, *Koningen, Korte Verklaring II,* p. 252.

9. *Ibid.,* p. 252.

10. *Cf.,* "For every beast of the forest is mine, and the cattle upon a
thousand hills. I know all the fowls of the mountains: and the wild beasts
of the field are mine" (Psalm 50: 10, 11).

and that it witnesses the downfall of the gods, which manifest themselves in the relentless powers of nature.

This is the Scriptural view on nature and it shows us the enormous prophetic opposition among Israel against anything which may seduce God's people to some kind of nature-religion, whereby fear and uncertainty will threaten the quiet and peace from Jehovah, the Creator, upon his people. We think particularly of the *Baal worship* which was especially native in Canaan and from there became a great temptation to God's people. This Baal worship is decidedly of a "natural" nature. Whether Baal is considered strictly a local nature god, or whether he is considered more a universal deity, at all times it is nature itself, which, in connection with Baal, is the central object. These Baals "have their origin in the natural phenomena of their region, in vegetative and animal life, and in the powers of springs and streams, of thunderstorms and heat of the sun,[11] which strengthen their position." Buber has pointed out that, at times, the imported Baal worship in Israel did not necessarily mean that Jehovah was no longer wanted. The local nature of the ancient Baal worship allowed calling upon Baal on account of certain interests. God's revelation received a place beside Baal's. For this reason the prophets force a *choice*: either Jehovah or Baal! This dilemma hit the nature-religion in the *core*. "The slogan 'Jehovah against Baal' aims to shake the religious foundation of the western-Semitic agriculture."[12] The point at issue in the battle against this Baal worship is nature and her *creatureliness* and *in* this the belief in the Creator. Elijah's battle on Carmel concerns Jehovah, the God of salvation, and at the same time *rain* and *life* in the creaturely nature. Elijah shows, on the basis of the irrefutable facts of God's deeds, that there is no *revelation* in the Baal worship. Here the pro-

11. Eichrodt, *Theology des Alten Testaments*, I. p. 99.
12. M. Buber. *Het Geloof van Israël*, In: *Godsdiensten der Wereld*, I, 1948 p. 210.

phetic irony is very meaningful: Baal either sleeps or is on a journey! It is exactly in the realm of nature and the needy life of the creature, both men and animals, that this decisive battle is fought. Here is a decisive moment of far-reaching consequences. "The Baals' secret has been snatched away from the fields and given back to the rightful Owner."[13] It is the secret of creatureliness in the most absolute sense, as becomes clear from the withered land under the scorching sun and when the withering is terminated exclusively by a *deed* of God from heaven.

We find in the entire Old Testament the border-line between God and creature sharply drawn, especially in the polemics against heathendom. There is in the entire realm of nature not a single secret, as far as prophetism is concerned, which finds its origin and existence in nature itself. The mystery of nature, her meaning and reality, consist in her *creatureliness*. Because here — exactly in the midst of the revelation of the salvation of God — decisive matters are at stake; prophecy is able to take up the weapon of sharp irony in the description of and fight against the "idols," as in Isaiah 40 and other places (Isa. 40:18f.; cf. Ps. 135). But the irony is filled with seriousness and admonition, "They shall be turned back, they shall be greatly ashamed, that trust in graven images, that say to the molten images, Ye are our gods. Hear ye deaf; and look, ye blind, that ye may see" (Isa. 42:17, 18). The message of the transcendent loftiness of Jehovah is inseparably connected with the salvation of God. Considered in this light all things and all men are alike, in spite of all differences; alike in *creatureliness*, "Behold, the nations are as a drop of a bucket, and are counted as the small dust of the balance: behold, he taketh up the isles as a very little thing. All nations before him are as nothing and they are counted to him less than nothing, and vanity. To whom

---

13. *Ibid.*, p. 210.

then will ye liken God? or what likeness will ye compare unto him?" This "nothing" and this "vanity" should not be taken up as though inferring an acosmistic interpretation of the world, and as though there may be no interest in this "nothing" and this "vanity." Such a modern, nihilistic conception of life is *alien* to Israel's prophetism, *i.e.* to God's revelation. In nihilism man alienates from the significance of things because of his alienation from God's revelation, whereby the light of God no longer enlightens his eyes. With Isaiah the "nothingness" and "vanity" of all things and nations implies the preaching of the majesty of Israel's God, Creator of heaven and earth. On the basis of this preaching *this* "nothing" and *this* "vanity" (compared to *him*) receive their *meaning in their creatureliness.* In the same chapter in which Isaiah speaks of this "nothing" and this "vanity" Israel is called upon to lift up its eyes to the stars God has made, and which he calls by name, so that not one is being missed (Isa. 40:26). And under the nocturnal heavens echoes the comfort of God's salvation upon Israel, from the *Creator* of the ends of the earth, who gives power to the faint and increases strength to those that have no might.[14]

It is not necessary to point out that in the entire Old Testament this creatureliness is taught and kept in mind in connection with the salvation of the Lord. Here many mysteries *and* horrors make way for his light that penetrates everything: "It is he that buildeth his stories in the heaven, and has found his troop in the earth; he that calleth for the waters of the sea, and poureth them out upon the face of the earth: The Lord is his name" (Amos 9:6). He who understands the meaning and the consequences of this teaching could ask himself the question, whether, on the basis of this absolute and radical creatureliness, then every thought of a divine revelation in nature is not out of the question. For, if we

---

14. Isa. 40:28, 29; cf. the analogy of the multitude of stars and the seed of Abraham, in Gen. 15:5.

think of the different forms of nature-religion, then the idea of a manifestation of God in nature again seems to lead to a total or partial *deification* of nature. The "mysteries" and "depths" of nature return again! Nature again becomes mysterious, whereas she is "only" creaturely in all aspects of her scope. It is one of the most peculiar things of Scripture that it, in spite of, nay, *in* the teaching of the absolute creatureliness, recites those hymns which are usually called *"nature psalms"* and that they pay such "attention" to nature, that all kinds of modern nature-religion frequently quoted and appealed to such passages of Scripture. These "nature psalms" are so remarkable, that they deserve all our attention, the more so, since we can hardly speak of a *strange* "sideline" at this point. For, this so-called "sideline" apparently confronts us with the *heart* of religion: *the adoration.*

* * *

As we listen to these psalms on nature, one thing is immediately clear, that here nothing is detracted from the teaching of creatureliness which is so evident in the entire Scripture. To the contrary: all "things" and the entire realm of nature remain "un-deified" and are considered *as creature,* over against all glorification of nature. Moreover, nowhere is evidence of a concentrated attention for "nature" *as such,* for an abstract, substantified nature.

But that does not in the least imply that nature does not have a place within the scope of God's Word.

We find this interest in nature, which is considered as a creature of God's hand, in several psalms.

"O Lord our Lord, how excellent is thy name in all the earth! who hast set thy glory above the heavens. When I consider thy heavens, the work of thy fingers, the moon and the stars, which thou hast ordained; What is man, that thou art mindful of him? and the son of man" (Psalm 8:1-4).

"The heavens declare the glory of God, and the firmament sheweth his handywork" (Ps. 19:1). The poet of psalms *hears* the Lord's voice upon the waters, "the God of glory thundereth, the Lord is upon many waters. His voice is powerful and full of majesty and breaketh the cedars of Lebanon. It devideth the flames of fire and shaketh the wilderness. It maketh the hinds to calve" (Ps. 29:3-7f.). We hear how God is clothed with majesty and strength, so that the world is established, that it cannot be moved (Ps. 93:1f). Psalm 104 is full of the ecstasy concerning the majesty of God's power: "O Lord, how manifold are thy works! in wisdom hast thou made them all: the earth is full of thy riches" (Ps. 104:24). "The glory of the Lord shall endure for ever: the Lord shall rejoice in His works" (Ps. 104:31). Thus the poet, after having observed nature, comes to the adoration: "I will sing unto the Lord as long as I live: I will sing praise to my God while I have my being" (Ps. 104:33). These are only a few passages from Israel's songs relative to nature, and the question arises, What does this special attention for the cosmic mean *in the realm of the salvation of the Lord?*

Because *this* is unconditionally evident, that nature is not seen isolated from the salvation of the God of Israel. With the psalms on nature we touch úpon Israel's psalmodies and upon the songs of praise of *the Lord's people.* This always evidences a relationship to the revelation of God's salvation upon earth. The topic in Psalm 8 is God's handiwork in nature and it contains Christologic perspectives of which we frequently hear in the New Testament (Matt. 21:16; Heb. 2:6f.). Psalm 19 deals with nature, but also with the *law* of the Lord; Psalm 29 deals with God's *temple* in which he is worshipped; Psalm 93 with nature *and the holiness of God's house;* Psalm 104 with nature *and* the breach which sin struck through life (Psalm 104:35). The curious thing about all these psalms consists exactly in this, that these poets

do not feel a tension or dualism between these — so to speak
— *cosmic* and *soteriologic* aspects. This is most evident in
Psalms 65 and 147. Psalm 65 is usually not counted with the
so-called nature psalms, but this psalm, however, does not
only speak of stillness (Dutch verse 2 has: "the song of praise
is in stillness to thee") prayer, guilt, and reconciliation, in short,
of the house and salvation of God, but it sings also of God's
power over the ends of the earth, seas and mountains, and
the bounty of his blessing, with which he crowns the year of
his goodness (Dutch version of verse 11). This psalm begins with the song of praise to God in Zion without at the
end specifically and explicitly returning back to Zion. His
last glance rests upon the pastures: "they are clothed with
flocks; the valleys also are covered over with corn; they shout
for joy, they also sing" (Ps. 65:13).

We hear the sound of the song of reconciliation and *at
the same time* the enraptured eyes are fastened upon God's
handiwork. "The congregation, assembled in the temple, sees
this and shouts for joy. Her song joins the song of creation."[15]

This harmony is still more striking in Psalm 147. Here
the graciousness of the Lord, (Dutch has in verse 1: for *he* is
lovely" — see the RSV — whereas the KJ has, "for *it* is pleas-
ant") Israel's God, is praised. He builds *Jerusalem,* and
gathers together the outcasts of *Israel;* He heals the broken in
heart and binds up their wounds (Ps. 147:1, 2). And then,
all of a sudden, the topic is changed, "He telleth the number
of the stars; he calleth them all by their names. *Great* is our
Lord, and of great power" (Ps. 147:5).

A little further we observe the contrast between *meekness*
and *pride.* God's salvation upon his people comes in view again
(verse 6). He lifts up the *meek* . . . . Sing unto the Lord with
thanksgiving, who . . . . covereth the heaven with clouds, who

---

15. Valeton, *De Psalmen II.* p. 162.

prepareth rain for the earth.   The words concerning nature, *and* those concerning God's salvation, stumble, as it were, over each other and overtake each other in playful haste. We learn of God's good pleasure in those that fear him (verse 11), then again we hear about *Jerusalem* and *Zion,* and then again about *snow, ice* and *his cold* (verse 16f), while the psalm ends with the salvation that, by way of election, manifested in the revelation of his Word, comes to *Jacob* (verse 19f). It will be very difficult to catch this harmony of the psalms by differentiating between "sideline" and "mainline," or between core and periphery, or between primary and secondary. These differences are obviously alien to the psalmists, as they do not at all feel themselves far removed from the salvation of the Lord in their *harvest songs,* but are very conscious of being *in the midst of it.*[16] It will be difficult to maintain — also quantitatively! — that the interest in nature in Psalm 104 is secondary or peripheric.[17] Not in one respect does there appear to be a contrast between the cosmic and soteriologic aspect. Frequently this has been thus construed, motivated by a so-called anti-metaphysic inclination, in order to expel the cosmic as the "non-soteriologic" from theology and the service of God. But the result was — with an appeal to the salvation of God! — an anthropocentric belittlement of the works of God's hands and of his *glory.* Do not misunderstand us: the anthropocentric belittlement does *not* consist in the soteriologic — if anything be theocentric, it is the reconciliation — but herein, that *on the basis* of the soteriologic, the revelation of God in his handiwork is, if not denied, then certainly pushed to the *background.* Thus the glory of the Lord is being belittled and minimized, whereas exactly the "nature psalm," Psalm 104 especially, praises God's *wisdom* (Ps. 104:24), his glory (v. 31), the joy in him (v. 34), and ends with, "Bless

16. See Psalm 65:1 (Dutch Version), "Stillness belongs unto *Thee, a song of praise,* O God, in Zion," in connection with verse 5f.
17. *Cf.* A. van Deursen, *De Achtergrond der Psalmen,* p. 114f.

thou the Lord, O my soul. Hallelujah!" (v. 35). Hans Rust correctly writes that the psalmists do not emphasize the aesthetic aspect of nature *as such*, but that does not give him the right to add that the nature psalms "do not speak at all of a revelation of God in nature."[18] Scripture speaks more unbiasedly, "O Lord our Lord, how excellent is *thy name in all the earth!* who hast *set* thy glory above the heavens" (Psalm 8:1). His glory is above the earth and heaven (Ps. 148:13); "thou art clothed with honor and majesty!" (Ps. 104:1).

This harmony and this outlook, this *insight*, can only be thus explained that man *in* and *by* the salvation of God is *delivered* from the tenacity of the egocentric and commences to sing of the *glory of God*. It is this salvation that opens doors and windows toward God's handiwork, and God's majesty above heaven and earth is beside, and immediately connected with, the *horn*, which God has exalted for his people (Ps. 148:13, 14). Here nature is no longer separated and dissolved from her creatureliness and not elevated to an idol, but known — as creature — with the stamp of her Maker. And that is the reason why there is no tension in the nature psalms between the salvation of the Lord and the glory of God upon his works.

It is wholly justified when again and again it is emphasized that it is *Israel* that sings these psalms. In this emphasis the characteristic principle is distinguished which in all correct *evaluation* of creation is of decisive importance. The thing which is needed here is *eyes* which are able to see and discover. And there are those that seeing, do *not* see. *Israel* does hear the voice of God in nature and in the thunderstorm. Israel does *see* him when he covers himself with light as with a garment and rides on the clouds as his chariot, and walks on the wings of the wind (Ps. 104:2, 3). This understanding, and seeing, and hearing, is possible only in the communion with him, in the enlightening of the eyes by the salvation of God,

18. H. Rust, *Ueber die Naturpsalmen. Ev. Theol.,* 1938, p. 68.

and by the Word of the Lord. But this seeing and hearing is *not* a *projection* of the believing subject, but an actual *finding*, and *seeing*, and *hearing!* Here nothing is "read into," [19] but it is only an *understanding* of the *reality* of revelation.

That this fact could become a topic of discussion is a sign of the times. A deep concern developed with respect to an *independent* theology of nature, a second source of revelation beside the one source from which salvation flowed to us. It was pointed out that especially since the *Aufklärung* the expression "nature psalms" came into general use.[20] It was feared that *via* the acceptance of the idea of the nature psalms, natural theology would be next! But this false problematic position of the *Aufklärung* may never — even not indirectly — be applied to what Scripture says. It is clear from the history of mankind what can be construed from and of nature. The natural heart of man lays hold on nature and tries to force her into his own schemes and superior power: nature as such, which may become an idol. We may listen to the "harmony of the spheres," as Pythagoras, and still not understand God's revelation in nature.[21] However, it is also possible that there be a correlation between the knowledge of faith and God's revelation. Then, in principle, all friction between the cosmic and soteriologic is conquered, which is a prophecy of the glory to come. But it is also possible that there be a breach between the revelation of God's glory upon his works and the knowledge which deteriorated into misjudgment. But we may not come to the conclusion, on the basis of our misjudgment and the errors of the human heart, that God is hidden. He, who identifies the ontic aspect of the problem of knowledge with the noetic aspect, subjectivates revelation and takes away man's responsibility. He only makes the darkness of man's thinking still greater and instead of the undeification of nature by Israel's prophetism, this problem presents itself to man in a dark world in which God's lamps

---

19. Barth, *K. D. II*, 1. 123, 126; cf. Chapter XI.
20. Rust, *Evang. Theol.*, 1938, p. 67.   21. *Ibid.*, p. 68.

have been extinguished. And even a Christo-monistic conception of revelation cannot halt the damage any longer, because this Christo-centric view can no longer conquer the dangers of anthropo-centrism.

We could almost call the situation *dramatic*. In the 19th century, nature became, *via* positivism and materialism, just "nature" as such; the closed world of mechanical causality. Nature was isolated from God. The faith in a speaking God faded away. It was believed that we had *exceeded* Psalms 19 and 104 in knowledge regarding nature and that we had stripped her of her secrets. Under the influence of nature, thus become transparent, theology withdrew more and more to the realm of *inner* experience, which would remain unthreatened and could be maintained, to which, then, corresponded, as for instance Herrmann has it, "the inner life of Jesus." Theology became "Christo-centric" and lost sight of God's great handiwork and of his wisdom, which the psalms praised. In spite of all kinds of changes in theology we still are in the midst of *this* process of development. The 20th century, with its terrifying aspects in the realms of nature, culture, and history, has caused God to be still more "hidden" for many. Present-day theology reflects this situation in a peculiar manner. It was tossed to and fro in the unscriptural dilemma of the cosmologic and the soteriologic. Already the 19th century knew such a problematic situation in Christology, when Harnack wrote his history of dogmatics, and, on the basis of the limited salvation of his theology, criticizingly amputated the history of dogma. This evoked some reaction here and there, but was not carried through. The old line of thinking was continued in the Christo-monistic conception of revelation. In all fairness it must be acknowledged, that the dangers of a substantified appeal to a "second" independent source of knowledge of God played an important role and discouraged uncompromising, biblical thinking. But the friction between creation and salvation *must* be recognized as unbiblical fiction. On the basis of the Bible we .

can say that the whole of eschatology is linked up with this. The dangers of natural religion, in whatever old or new form, may never seduce us to understand and sing no longer the song of Israel. That will be possible only when the salvation of God enlightens our eyes by the *revelation of the Word*. Only thus is nature no competitor with respect to the knowledge of salvation. No one comes to the Father but by *Christ,* but neither to the understanding of the works of his hands. But in his *light* we see the light of creation, and Israel's psalms remain forever elevated above the state of "primitivity," which modern thinking supposedly has outgrown. And on the basis of God's salvation we shall not isolate the knowledge of the works of his hands, the power and majesty, the wisdom and glory of God from his love, grace, and mercy. For the harmony of God's attributes is manifested in the knowledge of the salvation of God in Jesus Christ. And because of this knowledge we praise him in all his works and through the window of salvation we look forward to his coming, when his glory will be upon his works and when God's salvation will fill the new heaven and the new earth. In that future the earth will be full of the knowledge of the Lord, as the waters cover the sea (Isa. 11:9). Because of *this* knowledge the greatness of being *creature* will be placed in the full light of eternal restoration. "Thou art worthy, O Lord, to receive glory and honor and power: for thou hast created all things, and for thy pleasure they are and were created" (Rev. 4:11).

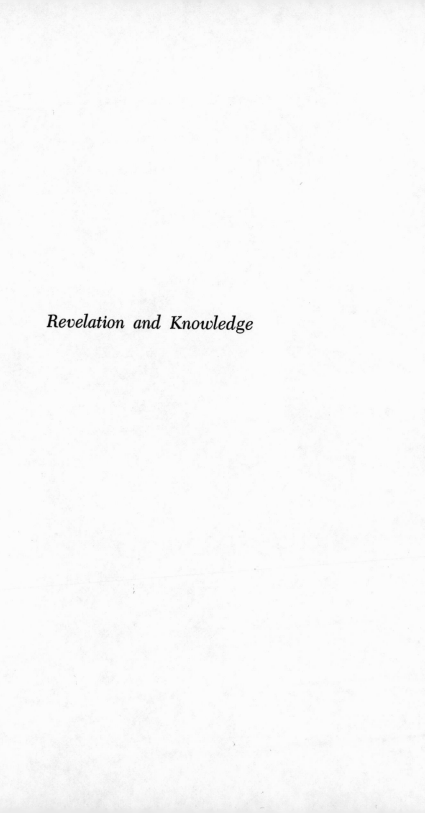

Revelation and Knowledge

CHAPTER VII

Revelation and Knowledge

T HE SCRIPTURES are concerned much with knowledge, but almost exclusively with man's knowledge of God through faith in Jesus Christ. This is the knowledge of salvation and the forgiveness of sins. The so-called "nature psalms" present us with this kind of knowledge. They are the songs of Israel, the songs of the people of God. And the knowledge coming to expression in these songs of nature is the knowledge of the heart. That is to say, the knowledge of the "nature psalms" is faith knowledge. The *Creator* of heaven and earth is adored even as the *Redeemer* of Israel is praised: for Israel the two are identical. Hence, it is impossible to appeal to the "nature psalms" on behalf of a natural theology.

There is, however, still another avenue from which the Scriptures approach the relation between the revelation of God in nature and human knowledge. The revelation is directed to Israel, but through Israel to the world. The heathen sometimes come within the perspective of divine revelation. This presents a problem when we recall the biblical antithesis between the people of God and the Gentiles. This antithesis gets sharp focus in the doctrine of divine election. "He sheweth his word unto Jacob, his statutes and his judgments unto Israel. He hath not dealt so with any nation: and as for his judgments, they have not known them" (Ps. 147:19, 20). Amos also speaks of God's specific choice: "You only have I known of all the families of the earth" (Amos 3:2). What is the real place of the heathen in this choice of Israel and the rejection of others? This is a real problem because even with an absolutistic affirmation of the antithesis it cannot be said that the heathen are totally free of divine concern. Granted that they do not possess the Torah, they are still not wholly shut off from divine revelation. Not only is the salvation of Israel channeled outward to the world, not only are the peoples of the world included in the future of the covenant (Ps. 65, 67, 87), but in a very specific sense they are within the scope of the divine revelation. But in what sense? That is the crucial question.

The subject is broached only incidentally in Scripture. It is not surprising that the theological discussions of the subject revolve around a few select passages. The two main portions of Scripture around which the discussions center are Romans 1 and Acts 17. Here we encounter clearly a teaching concerning the relationship between the divine revelation and the heathen's knowledge of God. "For the invisible things of him from the creation of the world are clearly seen, being understood by the things that are made, even his eternal power and Godhead; so that they are without excuse; Because that, when they knew God, they glorified him not as God, neither were thankful; but became vain in their imaginations, and their foolish heart was darkened" (Rom. 1:20, 21). If this were the only passage in Scripture which spoke of the Gentile's knowledge of God it would be enough to pose a thorny question in Christian theology. It is the more difficult in the light of what Paul says immediately preceding the passage just quoted: "Because that which may be known of God is manifest in them; for God hath shewed it unto them."

The question deals with the *nature* of this revelation and this knowledge. What does Paul mean when he says that the heathen are without excuse because God's revelation was shown to them? What significance has it that they indeed knew him, though they neither thanked him nor glorified him? What is the meaning of the statement that they knew him and yet were darkened in their hearts? These are some of the questions which we must face.

There is still another question, however, which forces itself ahead of these. It is a question that touches the harmony of the Scriptures. It has been argued that Paul speaks otherwise of the pagan knowledge of God in Romans 1 than he does elsewhere. If so, there is a hint of deviation by Paul from his own prior stand on heathendom's knowledge of God. Romans 1 is really foreign to Paul's main line. The real Pauline doctrine is that the heathen *do not know God at all.* It is in this vein that he speaks of the pagans "who knew not God" (I Thess. 4:5) and of the divine vengeance upon "them that know not God" (II Thess. 1:8). It is thus that he writes to the Galatians that "not knowing God, ye were in bondage to them that by nature are no gods" (Gal. 4:8). Paul often speaks of the Gentiles who "know not God." This would appear to be Paul's typical view of the Gentile's spiritual capacities. It is here that Paul seems most in line with the Old Testament perspective. "Pour out thy wrath upon the nations that know thee not" prays Asaph (Ps. 97:6. Cf. also Job 18:31 and Jer. 10:25). The Old Testament categorically puts the antithesis between Israel and the Gentiles as between those who do and those who do not know God. We may compare this with what Paul says about the ignorance of the heathen: they are estranged from the life of God by the ignorance that is *in* them. That is, their ignorance is not an accident in their lives; it is constitutional (Eph. 4:18. Cf. I Pet. 1:14 and Acts 17:30). The picture is bleak: emptiness of mind, ignorance, estrangement. The darkness is sharply contrasted with the light of the Gospel: "But ye did not so learn Christ" (Eph. 4:20).

The antithesis is just as sharp when Paul speaks in I Corinthians 1 of the contrast between wisdom and foolishness. The world in her wisdom did not know the wisdom of God (I Cor. 1:20). Paul alludes to a sentence of Isaiah when he says: "I will destroy the wisdom of the wise, and the discernment of the discerning will I bring to nought" (I Cor. 1:19). The world could not reach God through its wisdom. It did not know him.

Is this not the decisive and really radical conversion: from the ignorance of God to the true knowledge of God in the countenance of Jesus Christ? The believers did not know him at all formerly; they know him truly now (Gal. 4:8, 9). Is it not here that Paul is in tune with other inspired writers — with John, for instance, who writes that the world did not know the Word (John 1:20)? Is it not the knowledge of God which alone gives life (John 17:3) and is not obedience to the commandments of God the first principle of the knowledge of God (I John 2:3-5)?[1] Opposite this life and knowledge lies death in sins and transgressions (Eph. 2:1, 2).

It is hardly likely that Paul means to suggest in Romans 1 a compromise; there is surely no intermediate point between knowledge and ignorance or between life and death. Is there then a heterogeneity within Paul's thought?[2] Is Paul somewhat less radical and somber in Romans 1? Is it that here heathen are not unqualifiedly heathen? Do the heathen according to Romans 1 and 2 have more knowledge than the heathen according to Galatians or Thessalonians? In Romans 1 we read that the heathen know God, and in Romans 2 that they do by nature what the law commands. Is this not a different picture of the heathen than that given us by Paul when he rebuked the hysterical crowd of Lystra which wanted to worship Paul and Barnabas: "ye should turn from these vain things unto a living God, who made the heaven and the earth and the sea, and all that in them is" (Acts 14:15)? Here

---

1. "And hereby we know that we know him, if we keep his commandments." Cf. I John 3:6, "Whosoever sinneth hath not seen him, neither knoweth him."

2. This has been suggested by J. Dupont, *La Connaissance religieuse dans les épîtres de Saint Paul,* 1949, p. 21.

the heathen are not reminded of their knowledge of God; they are told to turn from their emptiness.[3]

These and other passages from Paul have often been used to show that there is and can be no point of contact with the heathen for the preaching of the Gospel. In the sermon on the Areopagus, it may seem as though Paul is appealing to the religious sensitivity of the heathen, but actually he is only making a methodological adjustment to the pagan mind. He came to better senses — in view of the small success of the sermon — and went back to the direct, antithetical preaching of salvation in Christ. It is possible, according to this, to discern two methods of approach in Paul's teaching: one which assumes a radical antithesis and another which assumes the presence of a point of contact. In the former, the salvation of God is placed head-on against the vanity and darkness of heathendom. In the later method, which assumes a point of contact, there is an appeal to a religious sub-structure already present in heathendom.

Actually, there is nothing in Scripture that gives any material for support of such a dualism in Paul's teaching. The argument needs the notion that Paul was disappointed after Athens. Actually, he never had any illusions about the readiness of the heathen heart to accept his message. Even when he used the direct method, he awakened opposition and rejection. Paul surely knew that limited acceptance of his message could not be charged to his *method*. The Gospel of the Cross is a stumbling block to the Jews and foolishness to the Greeks. Very soon after the Athens sermon, Paul preached to the Jews that Jesus was the Christ and there too aroused opposition and blasphemy (Acts 18:5, 6). Moreover, Paul preached the resurrection to the Athenians, which was the very reason why the Epicureans and Stoics wanted to hear more: "He seemeth to be a setter forth of strange gods; because he preached Jesus and the resurrection" (Acts 17:18). At Athens, too, Paul urged

---

3. Cf. I Thess. 1:9, "...how ye turned unto God from idols, to serve a living and true God."

conversion, for God was coming with judgment "by the man whom he hath ordained; whereof he hath given assurance unto all men, in that he hath raised him from the dead" (Acts 17:31). It was precisely this sort of sermon which placed the truth of God antithetically before the ignorance of his pagan hearers that aroused definite opposition. It was the resurrection at which they began to mock (Acts 17:32).

It seems clear, then, that Paul did not attempt a new experiment with a different method of preaching on the Areopagus. Nevertheless, the fact remains that he found a way of approach through the altar to the unknown God. Moreover, when he spoke of having our being in God, he referred back to the pagan poet (Acts 17:28). It seems difficult to deny the use of a point of contact here, a fact which appears to water down the life/death, either/or, knowledge/ignorance duality of other parts of Scripture. In consideration of this, we should recall that Paul himself was provoked in spirit when he saw the city filled with idols (Acts 17:16). Soon he urged the Athenians to be converted from all these idols and he warned them of divine judgment (Acts 17:30).

It is nonetheless undeniable that Paul does not set off immediately and directly on this antithetical approach. He begins his sermon with: "I perceive that in all things ye are very religious" (Acts 17:22). It has been said that even here Paul is attacking the paganism of the city, but he evidently is not. The word Paul uses does not imply sanction of the religion of the city, but neither does it imply criticism. He makes note of the religious tenor of the people with no hint of approbation or disapprobation. Paul does not intend to carry on a noncommital conversation; but he does maintain the freedom to attack the religiosity of the Athenians at his own moment and in his own way. He woos their attention; he knows that faith cometh by hearing, and a hearing is what he seeks. Hence, the mention of their religiousness. He was himself for no instant neutral; and it was just his clear position that allowed him to chose his method.

From the acknowledgment of the Athenians' religiousness, Paul goes on to speak of the altar that he had seen to the unknown God. Their unusual respect for deities is marked in that they leave not even the unknown deity unworshipped. There was a strange paradox here. Worship assumes at least some knowledge, at least of the existence of the god. Paul makes use of this contradiction: "What therefore ye worship in ignorance, this I set forth unto you" (Acts 17:23). He comes to grips with the pseudo-religion of the Athenians by way of this altar. He does not mean to complete what they already possess of true religion. On the contrary, what the Athenians acknowledge as ignorance has a far deeper meaning for Paul. He makes contact with the Greek mind by way of the altar and the unknown god; but his point of contact is the ignorance of the Greeks. And he sees this ignorance more profoundly than the Athenians' own acknowledgment of it would agree to. He calls the Athenians to conversion from this ignorance; to them it is a sign of real religion.

One might ask how the Athenians ever came to the idea of building an altar to a god of whom they were ignorant. This is in itself a most interesting question in the history of religion, though one of which we can hardly speak with certainty. We actually know only that Paul preached him whom they did not know. There is no hint here of a point of contact in the sense of a preparation for grace, as though the Athenians were already on the way to true knowledge of God.

Yet, Acts 17 is always included in any discussion of the point of contact. This is especially to be accounted for by what follows, where Paul weaves a few heathen citations into his argument. "For in him we live, and move, and have our being; as certain even of your own poets have said; for we are also his offspring" (Acts 17:28). Without doubt, the whole sentence is a citation. How does Paul come to say of his own

Gospel that it is "as even" certain heathen poets have spoken? It should be said that he does not give ground for saying that there is a common ground between the heathen religiousness and the Gospel. Yet, that he gives the citation is remarkable. The phrase "even as" does not suggest, we are sure, that Paul thinks the thoughts of the pagan poets to be identical with the deepest intent of his own Gospel. Paul understands the background of the citation and makes no attempt to idealize it. And yet he cites the words. This is to be explained only in connection with the fact that the heathen poets have distorted the truth of God. Heathendom lives off this truth; it distorts it and opposes it, but without this truth there would be no false religiousness. This should not be confused with the idea that false religion contains *elements* of the truth and gets its strength from those elements. This kind of quantitative analysis neglects the nature of the distortion carried on by false religion. Pseudo-religion witnesses to the truth of God in its apostasy. When the living God is forgotten, false gods of one's own are created. Where the status of man as the *image* of God is denied, that status is transposed in the heathen mind to one of *kinship* with God. In all this there is no reapproachment with the true religion and the true faith. Here, too, comes a call to radical conversion. Still, in this pseudo-religiosity heathendom witnesses to the revelation of God in the works of his hands. Heathendom is not an autogenerated creation of religious people, poets, or philosophers. Heathendom is dependent on the revelation of God even in its distortion of the creaturely reality which reveals *his* power. This is how it is that pagan poets find words and thoughts which are parallel with the words and thoughts of divine revelation. Far from providing a common principle on which to build a natural theology, the parallel witnesses to a basic conflict; and in this it witnesses indirectly to the true revelation of God.

We must also reject the distinction between form and content in this context. Form and content are not to be separated, as though paganism were something formally true though content-wise erroneous. Nevertheless, a pagan could say, with his own implied interpretation, exactly what Paul would say, with a biblical intent, that "we are his offspring." After this superficial agreement, Paul begins to speak antithetically. In the face of the pseudo-religion, he uses the thought of God's offspring to reject all forms of idolatry: "Being then the offspring of God, we ought not to think that the Godhead is like unto gold, or silver, graven by art and device of man" (Acts 17:29). From there, he launches into the necessity of conversion, now that the time of God's toleration of ignorance is past (Acts 17:30).

Thus is there full agreement between Paul's characterization of heathendom as ignorant of God and his speech on the Areopagus. Ever with Paul, the call to faith is a matter of radical conversion from ignorance of God. There is no knowledge of God that lies interspersed in heathen religions which is later incorporated into the body of faith. The antithesis looms large in every encounter with heathendom. It is directed, however, against the maligning that heathendom does to the revealed truth of God in nature and it calls for conversion to the revelation of God in Christ. This is why heathen, pseudo-religious life is inexcusable. It is not an independent phenomenon; it is a life of wrestling with God's revelation from which, try as it might, it cannot free itself.

* * *

An earnest inquiry into the first chapter of Romans makes it impossible to maintain the notion that it brings to light another type of mind than is apparent in other epistles. Paul is not moved by a great respect for heathen knowledge to give us an exposition of how far it succeeds in knowing God. He does not point us to a bright light shining in heathendom even apart from Christ. Indeed, to the contrary, he begins his argument by referring to the wrath of God which is revealed from heaven "against all ungodliness and unrighteousness of

men, who hinder the truth in unrighteousness" (Rom. 1:18).
Paul talks of darkness and foolishness, of the terrible things
heathendom has done with the revelation which has come to
it (Rom. 1:1-23·). The encounter between divine revelation
and human existence has issued in the worst sort of idolatry.
This in turn has occasioned the judgment of God in the divine
giving-over of human beings to their own lusts. The judgment
of God consisted in his letting men loose to their own desires "for that they exchanged the truth of God for a lie, and
worshipped and served the creature rather than the Creator"
(Rom. 1:24).

There is surely no contradiction here with Galatians, Thessalonians, or I Corinthians. Rather, they are all of the same
inspired stamp. The vanity of heathendom is a main theme of
Paul's argument here as elsewhere. Not only in I Corinthians
does Paul expose the wisdom of the world as having been made
foolishness by God (I Cor. 1:20). In Romans 1 we read:
"Professing themselves to be wise, they became fools." This
is so clear that it is denied by no commentator, Reformed or
Roman Catholic. Thomas Aquinas, for instance, makes much
in his comments on Romans 1 of guilt and punishment, wrath
and judgment.[4] But with closer observation, there appear
many differences in the manner with which these various elements are understood within the entire framework of Romans
1. For instance, we are told that, in spite of the negative tendency of much of Paul's argument and notwithstanding the
somber conclusion of the chapter, there is also a positive note
to be heard. For, it is asked, does not Paul associate the fall
of heathendom into progressively intensified error with a certain truth and a kind of knowledge?[5]

4. Cf. Kaplan Fahsel. *Des Heiligen Thomas von Aquin Kommentar zum Römerbrief,* 1927, pp. 52 ff.

5. "In the Epistle to the Romans, Paul seems to admit the coexistence, among the heathen, of truth and injustice," the appearance of a "co-exist-ence monstrueuse." Dupont, *La connaissance religieuse dan les épitres de Saint Paul,* 1949, pp. 29 f.

With this we meet one of the most important questions in the relation between revelation and knowledge. To get an insight into the only proper solution, it is necessary to be convinced that Romans 1 does not sacrifice anything of the radical antithesis between *knowing* and *not knowing* as it is taught throughout Scripture. That is, the knowledge of the heathen in Romans 1 is not the least in contradiction with the ignorance of the heathen of which Paul speaks in other letters. In other epistles, Paul is concerned to say that there is no halfway stop between the idolatry, foolishness, and darkness of heathendom and the knowledge of God. A man can leave the one for the other only by way of conversion as by the passage from life to death. This, too, is the only way of escape from the wrath of God. The Christians of Thessalonica, who have made this passage, are reminded to anticipate Jesus Christ's revelation from heaven: "even Jesus, who delivereth us from the wrath to come" (I Thess. 1:10). There comes into the picture here a fellowship with Christ, in which the wrath makes room for the love of God. In the face of this kind of knowledge, heathendom can be characterized only as a radical ignorance, a thoroughgoing nescience. This knowledge in the fellowship of Christ, which at the same time is eternal life (John 17:3), is presented so clearly in its full luster and glory by the Scriptures that it is impossible to suppose that Paul would intrude a tension by teaching in Romans 1 a knowledge of God amongst the heathen that contradicts the exclusiveness of the knowledge of God in Christ.

Romans 1 approaches heathendom from another perspective than do the other passages of which we have spoken. This chapter is not dealing with a true and reliable knowledge which is comparable with, though perhaps *less* true and reliable than, the knowledge of God in Christ. It deals rather with a "knowledge" that points to an inescapable confrontation with the revelation of God in his works, to a truth that encounters man[6] and elicits the reaction of his vain understanding. The heathen do not escape the divine revelation. That which is knowable in respect to God is revealed amongst them. The light of revelation shines into their existence as a revelation of his eternal power and divinity — though they "refused to have God in their knowledge."

Paul is profoundly convinced of the clarity and the irrefutibility of this revelation. It is, indeed, so evident and so clear that he speaks of the heathen as knowing God. This indicates a fundamental relation between heathendom and revelation which cannot be negated. Romans 1 is good material for the confession of general revelation. But one must take care of how he uses it. This "knowledge" can never be isolated from the prevailing theme of Romans 1 — the wrath of God. The history of theology parades before us numerous attempts to isolate it from the context.

It is only with such kidnapping of the phrase from its context that it can be used to support a natural theology. Such a natural theology is defended by the Vatican Council which appeals to Romans 1 in defense against heretics.[7] The Vatican Council theoretically recognized the existence of Romans 1:18 (the wrath of God) and Romans 1:24ff (the judgment of God), but went ahead nevertheless confidently to the thesis of the natural light of human reason by which man is able to know God, be it incompletely. Paul's portrait of this "knowing" man is quite different. It does not reveal the clear color of true knowledge, but is murky with vanity and foolishness. Paul's picture (the glory of the incorruptible God is exchanged for the likeness of an image of corruptible man, and of birds, and

---

6. H. Kraemer speaks of man's "indestructible relatedness to God." He adds, in respect to the point of contact: "To deny it is virtually to deny the humanity of man." *The Christian Message in a Non-Christian World*, 1938, p. 130.

7. Cf. the way in which Lagrange assumes the self-evidence of the identity of Romans 1:20 with the conclusion of the Vatican Council. "The Apostle's thought is really very simple. It is repristinated by the Vatican Council." M. J. Lagrange, Saint Paul, *Epître aux Romains*, 1916, p. 24.

four-footed beasts, and creeping things) is wholly other than that of the Roman Catholic picture (the knowledge of first causes, of God the unmoved mover).

How is it possible to discern in Romans 1 a natural power of the human reason which already has been able to achieve a partial knowledge of God? Paul indeed speaks of the understanding, but of that same understanding (*nous*) he says elsewhere: the heathen walk in "the vanity of their mind, being darkened in their understanding" (Eph. 4:17). This is for Paul the upshot of the "natural light of reason." We saw previously that for Roman theology as for Barth, general revelation and natural theology are practically identical. But for Paul the important thing is the break between the revelation of God and the reaction of man to that revelation. What the "natural light of reason" has done with revelation is what Israel did when she exchanged her gods and when the people "changed their glory for that which doth not profit" (Jer. 2:11).

It is not permissible to separate the "knowing God" of Romans 1 from the dark matter of the "exchange of gods." For this "knowledge," this being confronted with the revelation of God, with his eternal power and divinity, is degenerated and exchanged for what calls forth the judgment of God. While Rome is occupied with Romans 1:20 to lay there the foundation for the proofs of the existence of God, Paul is already concerned with the exchange of gods and with the holding under of the truth in unrighteousness by the heathen. Paul is not interested at all in observing nature as that from which the natural light of reason draws conclusions about the first cause. He is full of the revelation of the living God. "Because that which is known of God is manifest in them; for God manifested it unto them" (Rom. 1:19). Since the beginning of creation, divine revelation shines forth to man. What cannot be seen, viz., his eternal power and divinity, is perceived with the understanding.

Again, we stumble upon a much discussed question. It has to do with the *noumena kathoratai* clause. Does Paul observe the "being clearly seen and mentally perceived" as a fact or is it a condition: "if one thinks back"? Greijdanus says that the participle has a conditional sense, suggesting a provision: as, whenever they are perceived with the mind. The conditional element, however, must never be used in order to negate the "knowing" of verse 21. It is true, nevertheless, that Paul is not attempting to pose a positive thesis regarding the true knowledge of the heathen. He is concerned only with the revelation which is directed toward "being clearly seen" and "perceived." There is a relation between this revelation and the human subject. Man can never remove himself so far from divine revelation that the light of revelation no longer shines upon his life. But what does man do with this revelation, how does he react to his encounter with this revelation, to his "knowing" of God in this revelation? This knowledge which results from his inability to escape the overpowering clarity of God's revelation is, in Greijdanus's words, "not a right knowing which leads to recognition, as the verses subsequent to this one make clear, but only a superficial notation. It touches his consciousness and is active there, but issues in no true knowledge which reveals itself in true service of God." This knowledge is far from being a conclusion *via causalitatis* to the *prima causa*. This fact appears not only from what is said about the vain reasonings, but also from verse 28: "And even as they refused to have God in their knowledge, God gave them up to a reprobate mind." There is contact with revelation, but a contact which fails to lead to a true knowledge and acknowledgement. There is no static fund of knowledge on which a natural theology can be built; Paul is concerned only with the divine revelation which is changed, rendered vain, and distorted, as it is encountered by the natural man. This does not and must not lead us to deny the revelation. For Paul is convinced of the significance of it. He sees an irresolvable connection between this divine revelation and the guilt of man: "that they may be without excuse."

There is no possibility of excuse for their ignorance, as though they had lived outside of revelation. There is only reason for a complaint on the part of God, for they have known him in the irrefutability of his revelation which they have, nonetheless, refuted. They are not non-religious men. On the contrary, they produced their own idols. In their production appears the reality of the revelation of God which has reached and encountered men. Heathendom is understandable phenomenologically only from the viewpoint of divine revelation. From this perspective it is seen that man even in his most extreme aberations does not release himself from God's revelation. We do not find a self-sustained "understanding" that maintains itself in the face of a storm of idolatry blowing in the human heart. Man is immediately in action against this revelation. This action has often called for the discussion of the *sensus divinitatis*. The *sensus divinitatis* is an accompanying result, an effect of the power and perceptibility of the glory of God. But it does not lead to a natural theology as though it itself were a partial knowledge of God. Rather, it bursts out in a many-sided heathendom and a multiformed idolatry.

* * *

It would be grossly inaccurate, however, to conclude from all this that general revelation is of no significance. Such a sweeping negativism would be as objectionable as a natural theology. Paul emphasizes that there is a connection between revelation and guilt. In Romans 1:20 it is not clear whether Paul means to say that guilt is a result ("so that they are without excuse") of the revelation or whether he means that the revelation is purposed ("that they might be without excuse") to leave them guilty. Both ideas probably lie in Paul's mind. At any rate, the argument of Romans 1 is open to no misunderstanding. Paul reveals no special interest in what the heathen "knows" apart from the revelation of God in Christ. But he does wish to point out what man has done and does with the clear revelation that comes to him. There was a "seeing" and a "knowing" by way of a superficial observation of reality; and this reality carries clear traces of its Creator. But what Paul is concerned with in all this is the human reaction. The human understanding does not gaze tranquil and undisturbed upon God's revelation. It reacts to the revelation in opposition. For the *heart* is darkened and brutish of understanding.

Enlightenment is necessary, without which the divine revelation cannot be recognized *as* revelation. Paul says that "the god of this world hath blinded the minds of the unbelieving, that the light of the gospel of the glory of Christ, who is the image of God, should not dawn upon them" (II Cor. 4:4). The gospel shines as a light, but the eyes of the unbelieving are blind. In Romans 1:20 ff. we see that the eyes of the heathen are blind to the appearance of the glory of God over the works of his hands. Yet, life is not left undisturbed by the power of divine revelation. The *sensus divinitatis* is not an organ of the knowledge of God which transcends the corruption of human nature; it is an unavoidable impression left on man by the prevailing power of God. It is especially Calvin who translated the language of Scripture accurately on this point. He said that the human mind possesses some sense of a Deity, so that "no man might shelter himself under the pretext of ignorance."[8] All men have a sense of religion, and there is "no nation so barbarous, no race so savage as not to be firmly persuaded of the being of a God."[9] But Calvin is far from going on from here to construct a natural theology. He goes on rather to say that the idolatry of the heathen is an excellent proof of the universality of the

8. Calvin, *Institutes,* I, iii, 1.
9. *Ibid.*

religious sense. The "representations" God gives of himself are clear enough, but "their conceptions of him are formed, not according to the representations he gives of himself, but by the inventions of their own presumptuous imaginations."[10]

Calvin makes bold, as does Paul, to speak of blindness and vanity. The fruits of their foolishness lead to a worship of "the creature of their own distempered imaginations, wherefore the apostle pronounces a vague and unsettled notion concerning the Deity to be ignorance of God."[11] The kernel of religion bears sour fruit. And thus Calvin concludes that, though the prayer of despair shows that heathen are not altogether ignorant of God, "what ought to have appeared before had been suppressed by obstinacy."[12] He uses the illustration of a man in sleep. A thousand things can occur round about a man in sleep, but he is oblivious of all of them. In this way Calvin can reject a natural theology and still confess the reality of general revelation. Only by distinguishing between general revelation and natural theology can we do justice to the message of Scripture.[13]

What we have seen in Calvin is likewise taught in the Reformed confessions. On one side, Article II of the Belgic Confession teaches us of God's revelation in creation, preservation and divine government. And on the other hand, it is confessed in Article XIV that man is "become wicked, perverse, and corrupt in all his ways." He has lost "all his excellent gifts which he had received from God, and retained only small remains thereof, which, however, are sufficient to leave man without excuse; for all the light which is in us is changed into darkness." In the Canons of Dordt we are taught that man "by his own free will, forfeited these excellent gifts; and in the place thereof became involved in blindness of mind, hor-

---

10. *Ibid.*, iv, 1.   11. *Ibid.*, 3.   12. *Ibid.*, 4.
13. Cf. the remark of Calvin on Acts 14:17. "But faith is not conceived by the bare beholding of the heaven and earth, but by the hearing of the word."

rible darkness, vanity, and perverseness of judgment." The
Canons also teach that there remains in man after the fall "the
glimmering of natural light, whereby he retains some knowledge of God, of natural things, and of the difference between
good and evil, and shows some regard for virtue and for good
outward behavior." But they immediately proceed to say:
"But so far is this light of nature from being sufficient to bring
him to a saving knowledge of God and to true conversion that
he is incapable of using it aright even in things natural and
civil. Nay further, this light, such as it is, man in various
ways renders wholly polluted, and hinders in unrighteousness,
by doing which he becomes inexcusable before God."[14]

This would lose its thrust if Barth should be correct in interpreting the phrase "becomes inexcusable" as meaning
"inexcusable in the light of Golgotha." Barth's christological
exegesis closes off the possibility of revelation through creation.
The constructive part of Barth's exegesis is additional proof
for the connections we have already noted in Romans 1. But
his exegesis is more the result of an *a priori* view of revelation
than of an unprejudiced reading of the text itself. Paul simply
is not talking about the cross of Golgotha, but about God's
eternal power and majesty. To conclude from Romans 1 that
the heathen know God now in the light of the cross even though
they have not as yet realized this knowledge subjectively is to
force a notion of revelation upon the Scriptures. Barth's exegesis is isolated from the stream of the history of exposition.

* * *

We are now in a position to go further into the general significance of what Paul writes in Romans 1. The first thing of
crucial importance that confronts us in connection with
Romans 1 is the question of false religion. Do the false religions present us with a complete darkness that has fallen

14. *Canons of Dordt,* III and IV, 1.

upon human existence, with an ignorance of which nothing more can be said than that it is non-knowing? Or is there in Scripture the suggestion of a connection between false religions and the reality of general revelation? If so, is it proper to speak of the *complete* ignorance of heathendom and of the so-called absoluteness of Christianity? Is false religion wholly false, all lies, or has it, at least in its high moments, partnership in elements of the truth of God?

Ever since the nineteenth century intense study has been given to the religious depth and pluriformity of the non-Christian religions. With the study appears an apparent tendency to accent the merits of these religions. The question rises as to whether we have possibly done injustice to the great variety of religious phenomena in the world by branding them all with the one mark of false religion. Söderblom says that he can prove that God exists by the history of religions. What does he mean? Is there reason to re-open the question of the antithesis between the Christian and the non-Christian religions? Is that antithesis as absolute as we have always thought? The study of the false religions has led many to conclude that the term "false religion" often suggests little more than the haughtiness and intolerance of super-naturalism, which boasts in the exclusivism of the Christian religion. Furthermore, it is said that the categorical rejection of the non-Christian religions was the result of an ignorance of the depth and richness of these religions. The newer researches into the history of religions, it is said, have proven that the so-called false religions do not present less worthy, but only other forms of religion.

We may here recall the older studies that sought to get at the "essence of religion." The science of comparative religions was searching for an essence that was common to all religions and which was the connecting link between them all. The attempt was to get beyond the peculiar and idiomatic of each religion to the essence, the universal of all religions. The peculiarities of each religion were seen as special forms of the

common essence. Coupled with this study often went a profound doubt as to the legitimacy of the claims of Christianity
to exclusiveness. The study itself was in part a symptom of a
growing relativism. The presumption was that religion is an
important disposition of the human spirit and that there was
good reason to get beneath the manifestations of this "apparent" disposition as they appear at many times and among
many peoples. Many refused to begin the study with any presuppositions as to the exclusiveness of revealed supernaturalism. Troeltsch, for example, rejects what he sees as a "forced
isolation of one's own religion from foreign religions because
of the exclusiveness of supernaturalism."[15] Such isolation has
become impossible, according to Troeltsch, in the light of the
interweaving of Christian and non-Christian religious phenomena, an interweaving that has been revealed in the sacred
documents of the world's religions. With supernaturalism set
aside, it is possible to search out the essence and basic truth
of religions.

One of the forms in which this search was carried on is
contained in the theory of the religious *a priori*, developed by
Troeltsch among others. The task of the science of religion,
according to this theory, was to demonstrate the existence of
"an *a priori* law of religious ideation rooted in the universal
human reason."[16] It does not concern itself with the actual
existence of the object of religious worship, but only with the
"rational necessity" to form religious ideas. Troeltsch believes
that the essence of the religious *a priori* is to be found in the
universal human reason. All notions of reality and especially
all values are drawn from an absolute rational Substance as
source and norm.[17] What motivates Troeltsch is fairly clear.
He will not concede that the many religious phenomena of the
world present a chaotic jumble of unrelated reality. He is seeking a certain uniformity or rationality in the whole world reli-

15. E. Troeltsch. *Gesammelte Schriften*, II, 477.
16. *Ibid.*, p. 494.   17. *Ibid.*

gious picture. There is, he thinks, an *a priori* law of consciousness which expresses itself in the actuality of the religious life.[18]
It is not, as positivism contends, that the world's religions
are only a stream of phenomena without order or regularity.
On the contrary, there is an *a priori* law present in all religions, and one must take this into account if he would understand the essence of religion. There is a normative aspect to
the religious *a priori* which makes it possible for us to make
a judgment of religion in its apparent chaotic multiformity, as
well as to see the whole picture in some perspective. Thus, the
science of religion seeks after a law of human consciousness
which would take its place along with the logical, ethical and
aesthetical *a priori* in the human mind. There may be nothing
in all this said about the reality or unreality of the "object" of
religious thought, but that is irrelevant to the significance of
the subjective religious *a priori*.

Thus, we come to the impasse presented by the theory of
religious *a priori*. Originally, Troeltsch wished to arrive at a
theory of religious knowledge by way of analytical psychology,
and thus be in a position to raise and answer the question of the
truth and validity of religious knowledge as well. Now the last
word in the theory of religious knowledge is not truth, but the
compulsion of the understanding toward religion by humanity's
religious *a priori*. The law found in analyzing human religion is
not a law that functions as a norm for religion, but a law that
arises from the religious human subject. The so-called law of
religion and the religious *a priori* of humanity have to do with
the "centralized organization" of the consciousness. Humanity
has religion. That is a *law* of the normal consciousness. The
religious *a priori* actualizes itself in religion. Thus, revelation
is edged slowly into the shadow of the necessity of the religious
a priori which is lodged in the human consciousness. The
regularity of religion is recognized, but is wholly subjec-

---

18. E. Troeltsch *Psychologie und Erkenntnistheorie in der Religionswissenschaft*, p. 17.

tivized. A certain order is discovered in the great medley of religious phenomena, an order actually rooted in the consciousness of the religious subject. It need not surprise us that the theory of the religious *a priori* leads to the rejection of the absoluteness of Christianity. For in Christianity the norm for faith is laid exclusively in the normativity of revelation.

* * *

Another view of religion which observes a kind of universality in the world of religions, but which makes quite another judgment on it, is that of Karl Barth. He has reacted violently against almost every theory of the psychology of religion and religious historicism. His reason is that they all seriously impugn the absoluteness of revelation. Far from paying honor to human religion, Barth speaks of religion as unbelief. Revelation is the abolition (*Aufhebung*) of religion. Barth does not want to think of the value of religion from the viewpoint of man and especially not as the expression of the life and activity of man on his way toward God. Religion is, rather, "an affair, yea rather, *the* affair of the godless man."[19] All religion is cut off sharply from faith. Religion is nothing but the attempt to know God by way of man's own abilities, an attempt that is unmasked by revelation as resistance to revelation and grace. It forms an enterprise of man by which he encroaches with his own means and power upon what God wills to do and does in His revelation.[20]

What man achieves thereby is, however, never the knowledge of God, but only a fiction that has nothing to do with reality. This is why there is no point of contact between revelation and religion. "Revelation does not attach itself to an already existent and active religion of man; it contradicts human

19. K. Barth, *Kirchliche Dogmatik*, I, 2, p. 327. *Cf. The Epistle to the Romans*, London, 1933, p. 246: "Through religion we perceive that men have rebelled against God and that their rebellion is a rebellion of slaves." 20. *Ibid.*, p. 329.

religion as human religion previously contradicted it; it abolishes human religion as human religion previously abolished it."[21] There is thus no continuous line between religion and revelation; the line from religion is broken off by revelation. In short, revelation is the *Crisis* of all religion.

This applies, according to Barth, not only to the non-Christian but also to the Christian religion. In the characterization of religion as unbelief, the distinction between Christian and non-Christian religions is "consciously left out of consideration."[22] But Barth does insist on speaking of the Christian religion as the true religion. Though the Christian religion as such also falls under the category of unbelief, it still can be called the true religion. This is possible only as it is the religion of the *justificatio impii*, the *sola fide, sola gratia*, as it is religion of true faith.[23] In the context of true faith, religion is no longer a human disposition, but a disavowal of all human capability; it is thus true religion in the *event* of the grace of God in Jesus Christ.

Barth sees human religion as the darkness of the human heart. To admire religion as a worthy expression of the best of humanity, as an important part of the spiritual life of man, or as the manifestation of a universal religious *a priori* is to take religion from the sphere of faith and place it in the sphere of the natural world and to replace what is specifically Christian with something universal in humanity. It places religion in man and thus makes man religious; in this way "revelation becomes a historical confirmation of religion by which man, without revelation as well as with it, can know himself and thus know God."[24] Religion is then no longer understood by means of revelation, but revelation is understood by way of religion. Since natural religion is the religion of fallen man, it accounts for the normalcy of unbelief, of resistance to revelation and grace. Religion is not a chaos, but a human enterprise, a directed activity resting on human capabilities. The great var-

21. *Ibid.*   22. *Ibid.*, p. 357.   23. *Ibid.*, p. 362.   24. *Ibid.*, p. 315.

iation found in religions does not change the one direction of all religion. If man would believe, he would listen rather than speak; he would let something be given him instead of insisting on taking something. "Because religion is snatching at God, it is opposed to revelation and is the concentrated expression of human unbelief."[25] Only as the normalcy of this "snatching" is broken and conquered by the concrete and actual revelation, is the Christian religion the true religion. The tendency to create God in man's own image, as occurred in the idol worship of the Old Testament, lies in all religions, for in religion lives the religious man. And what this religious man creates is nothing but the mirrored image of what he himself is and has.

When we compare Barth's and Troeltsch's views of religion we see that both have noted a certain order, regularity, or necessity in human religion. According to Troeltsch this regularity is the regularity of human consciousness with its religious *a priori* alongside of other *a priori*'s. According to Barth it is the regularity of the unbelief of the religious man. Barth speaks of a "certain, final un-necessity." History and the phenomenology of religion prove that the religious consciousness is not bound by an absolute necessity and that the creations of gods by man can cease. But as a man gives himself to the way of unbelief, the regularity appears — the normalcy of idolatry.

*   *   *

It is now a common conviction that the religions of the world do not present a disconnected and chaotic variety in which there is no perceivable unity. This conviction has had a marked influence on the classifications that scholars have drawn in the religions. The lack of agreement as to these classifications is interesting in itself. Someone has even termed this confusion an "emergency situation" in the science of com-

25. *Ibid.*, p. 330.

parative religions.[26] There is a general conviction of a certain
regularity, but it has proven exceedingly difficult to arrive at
a further pin-pointing of that regularity. Parallels are discovered in the forms of expression that different religions use.
Similar problems come to the attention of students of different religions. Scholars have sought the "common elements
which come through various religions." They have also
looked for the "primitive religious phenomena," which might
form the origin of the parallels discovered everywhere. In
short, "the duty of comparative science of the history of religions consists also in the working out of a typology."[27]
The difficulty with this lies in the fact that either one discovers in the evident regularity nothing more than note-
worthy parallels and analogies and then stops with this observation or he becomes concerned with the origin or cause of
the regularity. Only in the latter instance does the problem of
the regularity of phenomena in religions become a serious
one. For here we encounter the matter of normativity. Since
this normativity is left out of the discussion as a rule — even
when "law" is spoken of — an empirical analysis was about
as far as the classification ever got. It is indeed impossible
to go further as long as one goes to work as a neutral without
bringing the real problem of norm, the problem posed by
revelation, into account. Thus, though one may recognize a
regularity, he falls back into a chaotic religious irrationality,
by which at most he can arrive at an inexplicable similarity
of religious activity. Even if one does not go along with
Troeltsch's theory of the religious *a priori,* he comes to

---

26. H. Frick, *Vergleichende Religionswissenschaft.* 1928, p. 10. He recalls
how Söderblom came upon the idea of handling the pagan religions according to the accidental order in which Israel and Christianity came into contact with them. He says that this points up the "evident flaw of every
generally recognized typology." All systems of the science of religion
give only "glimpses through the jungle of the history of religions."
Ibid., p. 11.

27. *Ibid.,* p. 18.

ascribe religion as a universal phenomenon to the normality of the human consciousness.

It is therefore of acute importance to realize that we can speak significantly of "regularity" in religions of the world only from the vantage point of the Holy Scriptures. For here we do not find an observation of various striking analogies and similarities of structural phenomena. We encounter the normativity of the revelation of God. Every religion is a reaction to divine revelation. This is what Paul indicates in Romans 1. For this reason it is impossible to understand this reaction rightly when revelation is left out of view. The observed regularity among the religions of the world is understandable only from the fact that man cannot escape the revelation of God. True, indeed, he can misconstrue, avoid, exchange and pervert it. But in all this, religion is not independent of revelation, but rather, a reaction, an answer, a resistance to, and a defense against revelation. All human life is estranged from the life and the glory of God, but that does not mean that man has escaped the revelation of God.

According to Paul this is precisely what has not happened. The dynamic persistance of religion also underscores the fact that man is ever confronted by revelation. In this lies the source of the "regularity" in the religions. It is not identifiable with obedience, but with disobedience; as disobedience it is normative in its misconstrual of divine revelation. This is clear from the way in which this disobedience manifests itself in the world of religion. Man is and remains man confronted with the reality of God's revelation, confronted with the sovereign working of God in nature, in history, and in human existence. He is confronted with the reality of God who is never far from any one of us and who never allows himself to be without witness in creaturely reality. Barth, to this day, is shocked by the notion of this kind of confrontation; according to him it must lead us either to a positive or to a negative notion of a point of contact. Though it is true that he too perceives a certain regularity in all religions, namely that of unbelief, he is unable to understand and to explain it in relation to revelation.

Barth is consistently opposed to the idea of the normality of the religious *a priori* as posed by Troeltsch. He concludes that the subjective pole of the divine-human relationship is a condition of lostness. But this notion of lostness occasions a constant flow of question marks that are never cleared away in Barth's dogmatics. For instance, the creation of man in the image of God plays no significant role in Barth's understanding of the false religions. Fear of anthropology, that it may become an entrance for natural theology, exercises a large influence on him. For this reason the regularity of religious phenomena remains for him a question shrouded in mist. He points to various passages of Scripture and associates himself again and again with Calvin's explanation of idolatry, but the regularity of religious phenomena provides him more of an occasion for a vicious attack on the religious humanity than an opportunity to see it in connection with revelation as normative. This is why it never becomes clear in Barth why fallen and lost man still goes on and must go on in the way of religion. Barth qualifies religion as unbelief, but he cannot make clear why this unbelief should manifest itself in the form of religion. Ultimately this lacuna can be accounted for by Barth's own christological anthropology.

Man in his sin and lostness is actually no longer "the real man" according to Barth. Sin is "not a possibility, but the ontological impossibility of human existence."[28] To be human is, considered from christology, to be together with God. To *be* in sin and in godlessness is to exist contrary to our human existence; it is an attack on the existence of one's own

28. Barth, *Kirchliche Dogmatik*, III/2, p. 162.

creatureliness.[29] "Yes, it is his existence as man which is brought into question with every occurrence of sin."[30] De Graaf correctly summarizes Barth's sentiments by saying: "The man who walks in sinful contradiction to his origin and destiny, we may not call a real man; he has denied his reality and falls into nothingness, into chaos, into nonsense, into the impossibility."[31] Only thus can Barth's view of fallen man be understood. The problem of the real man and the revelation of God can no longer be considered here as it is in the Scriptures. According to the Bible it is precisely the real man who is confronted with divine revelation, even man in his lostness. Only in connection with this real humanity and its God-given capabilities can it be said that man is not cut off from the revelation of God. The power of the revelation goes out to this real man as the image-bearer of God.

Thus, man in his encounter with divine revelation can only react. His life is *never* neutral human existence; it is antithetical human existence. His life is a flight from God and therewith a struggle with the living God. Barth's conception of a "certain, last non-necessity" is in contradition with the permanent confrontation of man with God's revelation. Hence, his characterization of the universal element of all religions as unbelief is a distortion. Unbelief in the form of religion is suspended in mid-air because Barth has not seen that unbelief can have a correlation only with revelation and can be understood and explained only by way of the normativity of the revelation of God. Only as this is understood will it be possible to get beyond a mere empirical observation of the regularity in the multiform phenomena of religions to a profound understanding of religions in relationship to the normativity of the divine revelation; for it is only divine

---

29. *Ibid.*
30. *Ibid.*
31. J. De Graaf, *De anthropologie in de moderne Russische wijsgerige theologie*, 1949, p. 149.

revelation which takes away from every religion its assumed
character of an autonomous creation *sans* norm.

* * *

There is a third way, besides and over against those of
Troeltsch and Barth, governed neither by the religious *a
priori* idea nor by the idea of man's descent into nothingness.
Kuyper in his own day stated the real problem of the manifest regularity in the religions of the world. The tremendous
stream of theories coming from the researches of the science
of religion common to his time is mirrored in Kuyper's thinking. He complained that the older theology failed to give
proper encyclopedic place to the subject of elenctics and hence
thwarted its development. When confronted with non-Christian religions, theologians usually were content merely to consider them antithetically. Their neglect came back to haunt
them when, in the nineteenth century, the science of religion
concentrated intensely on the non-Christian religions, and
placed them side by side with Christianity rather than con-
trovert them. Kuyper pointed to the enrichment of our knowledge of the non-Christian religions brought about by such
study. "What often seemed to be pure fantasy and fable and
play is now seen to be a well ordered, thought-through, and
practically organized whole that was coordinated with the
natural, be it corrupted, form of the religious life."[32] Therefore, theology could no longer ignore the non-Christian religions. The specifically theological study of elenctics, which
would have special practical significance for missions would
have to be given its rightful place. It would be necessary to
understand the false religions accurately in order to find the
point of contact, the point where we as Christians are one
with the people of a given false religion. "We must understand the false religions and see how the natural inclinations

32. A. Kuyper, *Encyclopaedie der Heilige Godgeleerdheid,* III, 447.

of the *sensus divinitatis,* which offered the point of contact for our own conversion, groped in false religions for the satisfaction of the yearnings of the heart of people, strange to us but in principal much the same as ourselves."[33] We have to do with the real man, be it the pagan man. With that man we possess a common point of departure; it is a common sinfulness which causes him and us to go astray. "Thus there arises on one side a consciousness of being fellows with the heathen. There is a similarity of the human heart, a heart with the same *sensus divinitatis* corrupted by the same sin. We are by nature pagans as are they, and were rescued only by the same grace that can be their share also."[34] This does not abolish the antithesis at all. It is at this point that Kuyper poses the Christian religion as the only absolutely true religion in the face of all the other religions. But the other religions in their multiform manifestations are not isolated from one another. Kuyper discovers as do others a certain regularity, and sees in this the connection between all the false religions. The apparent separateness falls away as soon as we view all religions together as the necessary products of the apostasy to which the natural knowledge of God in the sinner must come when left to itself. The common point of departure for all false religions lies, according to Kuyper, in man's corrupted natural knowledge of God. This forms *the* motif of false religion. The regularity in religion manifests itself as the result of religion being a reaction to the revelation of God, a reaction defined by disobedience and apostasy. What Kuyper calls the natural knowledge of God is quite other than what Rome understands by this term. In Rome's natural theology we have to do with a true knowledge which is obtained by the natural light of reason. In the natural knowledge of God, or the *sensus divinitatis,* we have to do with the reaction of man to God's revelation. This reaction can never be accurately described without an awareness

---

33. *Ibid.,* p. 449.   34. *Ibid.*

that it holds the truth in unrighteousness. So does Kuyper view the so-called natural knowledge of God which is manifested in the false religions, be it in various ways and in connection with many different historical circumstances. False religion is an anomaly in endless variations all growing geneologically from the same root. Elenctics can teach us the truth about false religion when•it not only observes and chronicles the givens of the history of religions, but explains them in such a way that every form of false religion is seen as necessary for that people holding it.[35] We must, in other words, understand every particular phenomenon of religion as necessary, given its origin. The perversion of man's natural knowledge of God plus a given people's natural disposition and history produce a particular kind of false religion.

It should be added that Kuyper wants to take account of not only the negative element of the disturbance of man's natural knowledge of God through sin, but also the positive element of common grace present among the pagan peoples. In this connection he points to the paradise tradition and the influences of the Old and New Testaments. But it is of most importance that Kuyper did not arrive at this view of false religions by way of one or another neutral anthropology, but by way of the Scriptures. In the matter of elenctics he speaks of the abiding apostolic program of Romans 1. This is further illumined by the fact that he speaks elsewhere of the discovery of the *law* of paganism.[36] The seed of religion is still remnant in the fallen sinner, thanks to common grace, and there is no form of apostasy conceivable that is so low and so corrupt that it cannot be traced to this same *semen religionis*.

It is surely clear from all this that Kuyper does not mean to say by his use of the term natural knowledge of God that it forms a stairway to grace or a preparation for conversion. His view is sharply defined when he writes that "without

---

35. *Ibid.*, p. 154.   36. *Ibid.*, II, 259.

natural theology there is no more possibility of an Abba, Father than the worship of Moloch."[37]   Directly following this he adds a protest against the attempt to narrow the distance between this Abba, Father and the worship of Moloch by means of a gradually advancing process from the latter to the former. In the larger context of Kuyper's thought it is impossible to suppose that Kuyper capitulates to a natural theology in the sense of a theology of nature that is placed adjacent to supernatural theology. Kuyper sees in pseudo-religion an anomaly, degeneration, disturbance, apostasy. He is concerned with the structure of paganism. "Christianity and paganism are related to each other as the plus and minus quantities of the same series."[38]   Kuyper's view has nothing in common with a rationalistic understanding of natural theology; it deals with man in his relationship to God, to God's revelation against the background of the unity of the human race and the preservation of human existence. It deals with real man in his human existence, unable to escape the normativity of revelation and revolting in apostasy against the living God only within the circle of this normativity.

Kuyper poses a problem of high order as to Romans 1. We have in the so-called regularity of religious phenomena not simply a form of causality because of which everything runs in a regular causal order, but the normativity to which all reaction to divine revelation is bound. This same idea has been worked out by Dooyeweerd. With Dooyeweerd we find a concentration on the apostate character of faith; false religions constitute an apostasy in the "subject, the direction,

<hr/>

37. *Ibid.*, p. 254.
38. *Ibid.*, p. 255. Cf. also, *ibid.*, his statement: "From this it should be clear that natural theology is not taken here in the sense of the end of the seventeenth century when men drew up a system of several truths to form a natural theology alongside the supernatural. To us the natural theology is not a system; it is the very knowledge of God which remains in the sinner and is still within his reach." In another place Kuyper recalls that even the Devil has a natural theology; he believes and trembles.

and the content of faith."[39]   He too notes the regularity.
Apostate faith is not a subjective arbitrariness; it remains
bound to law. Dooyeweerd consciously follows the line of
Kuyper. False religion is not a chaotic phenomenon; it goes
consistently down the way of devolution, of corruption and
estrangement from the true nature of faith. We could, then,
speak in a certain sense of a point of contact. But not of a
point of contact that forms a "pre" to grace or conversion or
a "pre" in the sense of a disposition to believe. "The activity of apostate faith as such offers us no point of contact
for the development of the Christian faith. First the religious
root of human existence itself must be reversed if faith is going
to be a usable organ for hearing the Word of God."[40]   This
radical reversal of the direction of faith is impossible for fallen
human nature.

The *semen religionis* is preserved by God in the human
heart. This does not relieve the darkness, but it does help
explain how it is that religions still arise in a fallen world
and how it is possible that these false religions bear a marked
semblance of order. Only thus is the whole process of devolution in the apostate natural knowledge of God explicable in
its necessary structure.

* * *

It is necessary to remark with some emphasis that what
Kuyper calls the "apostolic program" according to Romans 1
may never be an occasion for a simplicistic schematizing of
the false religions. We cannot suppose that a few generalizing qualifications can explain the phenomenon of false religion. We meet such schematizations too often in the science
of religion to escape the total unsatisfactoriness of them.
How often has not a common essence of religion been pro-

---

39. H. Dooyeweerd, *Wijsbegeerte der Wetsidee*, II, p. 236.
40. *Ibid.*, p. 239.

posed with which the various particular religions were measured? The apostolic program of Romans 1 surely does not
lead to such over-simplification. This can be observed in the
fact that Paul himself never generalizes. More often than not
he emphasizes the pluriformity in the perverting of God's
revelation; "they have changed the glory of the uncorruptible
God into an image made like to corruptible man, and to birds,
and fourfooted beasts, and creeping things" (Rom. 1:23).
Within the circle of the normativity that is given with the
norm of revelation there is a world full of variation. This
variation is due to many factors in the life of men and peoples
in very different circumstances and times of history. Dooyeweerd in particular has pointed out these variations and has
warned against a naive approach to the phenomenon of the
false religions. He rejects the method by which students
search for a primitive faith of the natural reason from which
the various religions are higher or lower forms of development. The development of false religion is a conjunction of
what he calls "the exercise of the activity of faith in an apostate direction," which exercise is defined in character by
the type of the civilization of a given people. The forms in
which the exchanging of God for gods according to Romans
1 manifests itself is closely associated with the entire life of a
people in a given historical stadia of development. Dooyeweerd makes it clear that if one does not snatch faith away
from the totality of human life he can be spared the danger of
generalizing and schematizing the false religions. For, seeing
faith in its human and historical context, we see how much the
development of a people, its civilization's milieu, and the level
of its knowledge and view of nature can influence the nature
of the perversion of the truth of God.

How else would the perversion manifest itself in a period of
primitive views of nature than as a vision of nature full of
mysterious powers, and in a period of mechanical views of na-

ture than as a theory of an enclosed world of mechanically governed reality? For this reason the research into false religions must have as broad and serious a character as possible; and never must a single fact suffer violence. The apostolic program renders such a research in no wise superfluous, but rather offers a stimulus to the most rigorous analysis. It is only this kind of analysis that can build a dam against the flood of theories about the common essence of religion, especially those arrived at without too much concern for the great variety of facts in the phenomena of religion. Van der Leeuw recalls somewhere a definition of religion as a relation of man to personal beings of a higher order. He adds that there are many religions which this definition does not fit. Then he warns against forming too easy an idea of what man understands by God. He further cautions against deducing general theory from that idea. This may illustrate the limitations of generalities. The regularity which is present in the variations among the false religions does not release us from the task of studying the complicated associations of religious life.

One may now raise the question whether with the recognition of the pluriformity of the false religions we have also not brought in a generalization via the apostolic program, viz., that of exchanging and perverting. But this motif is not a generalization. For we have in this a fundamental perspective of God's revelation which touches on the fundamental relation of man to that divine revelation. This fundamental aspect of revelation, this normativity, this circle of regularity within the apparent chaotic variety can help us avoid all simple generalizing. In this way we do not come to the normality of a religious *a priori,* nor to a constant and inherent "natural religion," but to the picture of the real man with his searching and groping, with his apostasy and lostness, with his homesickness and idolatry, with his altars and his sacrifices. And in all this we come to the reality of man, the man who is without excuse, because he lives in the midst of a permanent confrontation with the living God. To this man, with his religious depth and his pantheon of gods comes the Gospel with its call to conversion as a call from death to life. The call breaks through the demonic process of exchanging God for gods and of perverting the truth of God, so that the benighted heart may be enlightened and the eyes opened to the God who is never far from us all.

Revelation and Fulfillment of the Law

CHAPTER VIII

Revelation and Fulfillment of the Law

THE PROBLEM of general revelation and of natural theology
has not only frequently been connected with Romans 1,
but also with Romans 2. This need not surprise us because the
point at issue is the "knowledge" of God's law. This chapter
especially has played a role in connection with the ideas of so-
called *natural morality* and *natural righteousness*. The verses
particularly in question are Rom. 2:12-16 and especially verses 14 and 15. "For when the Gentiles, which have not the
law, do by nature the things contained in the law, these, having
not the law, are a law unto themselves: Which show the work
of the law written in their hearts, their conscience also bearing
witness, and their thoughts the mean while accusing or else ex-
cusing one another."

It has always struck the attention that Paul is speaking here
of those who are *outside of* and *without* the special revelation
in Christ. Of them it is said that they are a law *unto themselves*
and that *by nature* they do that which the law commands. The
work of the law is somehow written *in their hearts* and their
conscience performs a special function in their lives.

On the basis of these words the conclusion has been drawn
that there is not only a natural *knowledge of God* (Rom. 1)
but also a natural *morality*. This confronts us directly with the
question whether we are not facing a contradiction regarding
what Scripture teaches elsewhere concerning the *total depravity*
of the human heart. Is there also not a discrepancy between
Romans 2 and other statements from Paul when he says that
the inclination of the flesh is enmity against God, "for it is not

subject to the law of God, neither indeed can be. So then they that are in the flesh cannot please God" (Rom. 8:7, 8)? Are not, according to Paul, the works of the flesh: adultery, uncleanness, licentiousness, and idolatry? (Gal. 5:18f). How can Paul in Romans 2 express himself so "relatively favorably" concerning heathendom? We moreover recall that Paul said in Romans 1 about the reprehensible inclination to do the unseemly (Rom. 1:28), whereas they not only do such things but they also have pleasure in those who do them (Rom. 1:32).

"Natural" morality?

In order to obtain a clear insight into what Paul is driving at, it is first of all necessary to consider the context. In Romans 2:1ff. the apostle said that Jew as well as Gentile — "no man, whosoever thou art" — are inexcusable. God's judgment is righteous and will recompense everyone according to his deeds (Rom. 2:6) : be he Greek or Jew (Rom. 2:9). In Romans 1 it became evident that the Gentile fell under the wrath of God. But — God's judgment includes also the Jew. The latter indeed fancies *to be able* to escape and *to have* escaped God's judgment and to be in a position to judge and condemn others. But — according to Paul — he, too, is, in spite of his law, subject to the judgment of God because he does the very same things. Paul launches his sharp rebuke at the Jew who prides himself and relies on the law (Rom. 2:17f) and even upon God whose will he knows. They consider themselves leaders of the blind, a light unto them that walk in darkness, because in the law they possess the body of knowledge and truth (Rom. 2:20). Paul sharply refutes this self-esteem. Both Jew and Gentile are subject to God's judgment. There seems to be a great distinction between them: the Jews do have the law of Moses, the Gentiles do *not*. However, this distinction which the Jews so readily bring to bear when judging heathendom does by no means justify them. To be sure, Paul does not deny Israel's specific privilege (Rom. 9:4, 5; cf. Eph. 2:12), but he who boasts himself of it understands neither the privilege nor the seriousness of God's judgment.

In this connection now Paul says several things about these Gentiles who were so far separated from the Jews and who, in a word, do *not* have Moses' law and are "lawless." There is no doubt that it really concerns *heathen*. At times it has been thought that Christian Gentiles were meant, but the arguments to prove this are so insufficient that this exegesis is obviously the result of the tendency to avoid certain problems of Romans 2. This was deduced from what Paul says about the work of the law, which was written *in the hearts,* and in this connection Jeremiah 31 was quoted where we read about the New Covenant (Jer. 31:33; cf. Heb. 8:10) "I will put my law in their inward parts, and write it in their hearts."[1] But Paul obviously speaks here about those who do *not* have the law and *by' nature* do that which the law commands, expressions which Paul certainly does not use to show that this is the fulfillment of the law through the Holy Ghost. Is it not the heathen only of whom it can be said that they do not have the law of God, the *Torah?*[2]

Only thus can we understand why Paul refutes the Jewish boast and pretension and calls their attention to the Gentiles who do not have the Jewish law and nevertheless may do the work of the law which is written in their hearts. Paul is after an argument against the Jews' self-exaltation.

And thus — exactly because of the connection — the question becomes crucial. What does Paul mean by these words and is he really praising gentile "natural morality"? What does Althaus mean when he writes, "Paul has also something else to say of heathendom besides what he says in chapter 1:18-32."?[3]

Frequently a straightforward recognition and appreciation of the "natural morality" has been inferred from Paul's words.

---

1. K. Barth, *K. D. I.* pp. 2, 332.   2. P. Althaus, *Römerbrief,* p. 21.
3. P. Althaus, *ibid.,* p. 21.

In the writings of Althaus, who attacked Barth's offensive so sharply, is this very evident. "There is a natural inclination towards the good which refers to a law of nature. God has written in the hearts of the Gentiles that which the law of Moses demands. They do not have the holy Book of the Law but the writing is in their hearts. This is evidenced not only by their conduct but moreover by their conscience, which after the deed says, 'this was right' or 'this was wrong.' "[4] Any careful reader will have to admit that this rendition of Paul's words is tendentious. A considerable shifting or change of meaning has taken place. In the first place, Althaus puts *Scripture* in their hearts whereas Paul speaks of the *law*. Moreover, Paul does not say that the law but the *work* of the law is written in their hearts,[5] and one may certainly not without further examination introduce such a change. When we take the literal text it strikes us that Paul speaks of their *doing* that which the law commands and that they do so *"by nature."*

Especially these words have always drawn the attention of Bible students and many have thought to discover signs of Stoic influence in them. According to Althaus, Paul adopts here "the pivotal word and the basic idea of Stoic ethics," just as when he adopts the word "conscience," which is a linking up with "original Stoic — at that time popular-philosophic — thought of his age."[6] According to this, Paul had adopted the Stoic idea that there is an internal law in every person, a law of nature, corresponding with the rational law which functions in the entire world.[7] All that harmonizes with this law of nature is good, all that does not, is wrong.

Once this dependence is accepted and considered highly important, far-reaching conclusions will be drawn from it. Dodd,

4. *Ibid.*, 21.
5. Cf. Ch. Dodd, *Romans*, p. 35, "a law written on their hearts."
6. Althaus, p. 21; cf. Helge Almquist, *Plutarchus und das Neue Testament*, Uppsala, 1946, p. 85, "Paul adopted the Stoic fundamental rule from the natural moral law."
7. Cf. Dodd, p. 36.

for one, states that to Paul the law of Moses was easily the most complete revelation of the will of God, "but the 'law of nature' is not a different law, but only a less precise and complete revelation of the same eternal law of right or wrong."[8]

And when further it is stated that the Gentiles instinctively obey this law, then it becomes very easy from there on to deny the depravity of human nature.[9]

According to Althaus and Dodd, Paul is simply speaking of the relative "goodness" of the Gentiles. This, then, would supply the crux of Paul's accusation of the Jews who *have* the law. Paul wants to say with regard to this "goodness" of the Gentiles "that the pagan has just as good a chance of being acquitted, on the day when God judges the secret things of men, as any Jew."[10]

He who proceeds from the supposition that Paul's "nature" (*phusis*) is identical with the "nature" of the Stoic natural law and practically identifies this law with the law of Moses, makes a gross mistake because he construes this "by nature" far too much *a priori*. No one will want to maintain that Paul chose all new and original words. But there remains every reason always to consider *how* Paul uses elsewhere existing words and which meaning they take on in his argument. Pohlenz has pointed out that Paul thinks entirely differently from the Stoics because to *them* "nature" was the highest authority in moral questions, whereas the *law* was considered of subjective meaning. To Paul, however, the law, the *torah,* is the highest authority. Now Paul places that which the Gentiles do "by nature" alongside this law. It is therefore absolutely illicit to conclude from the word "nature" which, according to Pohlenz had been used *ad nauseam* [11] in that time, that Paul adopts

---

8. Dodd, *Romans,* p. 36.
9. Dodd, *ibid.,* p. 37. "We note this against the doctrines of 'total depravity' and the complete impotence of the human will, which have been attributed to Paul."
10. *Ibid.,* p. 37.
11. Max Pohlenze, *Paulus und die Stoa,* Zeitschrift, Vol. 1949. 75f.

the Stoic idea of nature and appreciates it like they do; the more so whereas Paul in Romans 2:27 speaks of "uncircumcision which is by nature," by which he means life as it is.[12] When we do not *a priori* overcharge Paul's "by nature" under the influence of the Stoics, then the possibility remains open to ask what Paul has in mind. Therefore, first of all we ask what, according to Paul, is written *in their hearts.* He speaks of "the work of the law." In many translations and commentaries we find that this expression has been made to read "the law" as having been written in their hearts. Especially Schilder has emphatically pointed out that such a shifting of ideas is illicit.[13] If we say that the *law* is written in their hearts we are apt to take it in the sense that Scripture does with regard to the prophecy of the New Covenant. The expression of "the writing of the law in the heart" is very strong and implies that the law is not simply given to man in an outward, general sort of way, but that this writing in the heart results in an inward inclination and readiness of the heart to fulfill the law out of love.[14] However, in Romans 2 we read nothing about that. We only read that the *work* of the law is written in their hearts. According to Schilder this is something entirely different. The *work* of the law implies concrete actions which are in conformity with the demand of the law, it is "acting as dictated by the law."[15] "What is meant here is a concrete acting without questioning or inquiring about the motives, principles, or reasons." They do, according to Paul's word, "the things pertaining to the law."[16] Schilder points to the formal conform-

---

12. Cf. also Rom. 1:26.
13. We already quoted Althaus and Dodd. Schilder also quotes V. Hepp *Testim. Generale,* p. 147, "God writes the law in the hearts of the Gentiles."
14. Cf. G. Ch. Aalders, *Jeremia* II, p. 89, "the writing of the law in the heart results in 'the inward communion with God which is the portion of every subject of the New Covenant.' They all shall know the Lord with a 'spiritual knowledge of the true fear of God.'" p. 90.
15. K. Schilder, *Heidelberg Cat.* I, p. 102.
16. Cf. also Greijdanus. *Comm. ad hoc.*

ity with what the law requires, a certain loyalty as may be found in obeying one's parents, respecting other people's property, etc., but these things alone do not disclose the real intention and motives of human actions.

Thus Schilder has explained Romans 2 in flagrant contrast with those who want to promote it to an ode on *"general revelation and common grace."*[17] The point at issue is 'only' the work of the law which the Gentiles do "by nature," because of their nature, in which they are a law *to themselves.* Because all kinds of things are favorable to their nature, therefore they simply do the work of the law which is written in their hearts, in other words, which becomes part of them.[18]

According to Schilder it is incorrect to deduce from Romans 2 that God "gives his general revelation in the heart of man or that God in his general revelation works from within to the outside." No one may conclude from the mere fact that the Gentiles "by nature" are "law-abiding" in their conduct that this is the result of general revelation.[19] They act simply 'by nature.' That is the cause of their actions and not the general revelation. But then the question arises, according to Schilder, how to explain that heathen conduct themselves in conformity with the law. He gives three reasons why Gentiles, in spite of the fact that they lack the illumination of revelation, do so[20]: *a.* their sinful nature by which they do a certain work of the law out of self-interest; *b.* the remnants of the original gifts; *c.* the preservation of world and mankind as God's providence intends.[21] Especially the last two reasons demand our attention. Schilder points out that our human

---

17. K. Schilder, *Heidelb. Cat. I,* p. 107. In this connection Schilder mentions also Kuyper's opinion that Rom. 2:14 belongs to those passages that shed light on the destiny of the people of this world. (Schilder, *I,* p. 98)
18. K. Schilder, *I,* p. 102f. *Cf.* the difference between *poiein* and *prassein.*
19. K. Schilder, *I,* p. 110
20. *Ibid.,* p. 110.   21. *Ibid.*

nature has not been destroyed by sin but that some light of nature has been left in man, remnants of the original gifts given to man when God created him in his own image.[22]   What Schilder means is that man retains reason and will.[23]   But it is very remarkable that he adds the "sense of responsibility."[24] Next he mentions the preservation of the true human nature, but all this has nothing to do with common grace.   Man remains man but that in itself is not yet grace, but supposition of the covenant of grace *and* judgment.[25]

This continues to prevent man 'from going down in utter bestiality'[26] and so his nature enables him to perform works in conformity with the law.

We are dealing here with an attempt to explain "by nature" purely and solely within man, outside of the general revelation of God and general grace.   But it is important to note that in order to make this solution plausible it is apparently inevitable to make a jump from "reason and will" (as preservation of nature) to the *sense of responsibility!*   The impression is being created that *via this sense* their "law-abiding" conduct is explained.   This, however, is not the case at all.   It is indeed correct that the preservation of human nature enables man to perform acts prompted by will and reason, but man may in this frame of human nature perform acts which are *not* in conformity with the law just as well.   It is absolutely incomprehensible where Schilder all of a sudden gets this *sense of responsibility.*   That fallen man should be responsible is simply evident from his revelation to God but not in the least that he has a *sense* of this responsibility.

It is regrettable that Schilder's valuable expositions on the work of the law and acts in conformity with the law are robbed of their strength by his vehement reaction against common

---

22. *Ibid.*, p. 115.   23. *Ibid.*, p. 116.   24. *Ibid.*   25. *Ibid.*   26. *Ibid.*

grace and his elimination of general revelation.[27]   The basic
weakness of his whole argument becomes apparent just because
of his introducing the sense of responsibility.   Only by insert-
ing this sense in "by nature" can he make his argument hold.
Only then "by nature" can function *without* general revelation
and *without* common grace.   At one point this unsolved problem seems to challenge him when he writes, "Another question
is whether this *nature* itself is not being determined by the
accepted idea of the so-called general revelation."[28]   For an
instant Schilder touches here the central question of the whole
problem, but immediately he continues, "but that is an entirely
different problem all by itself," and he does not allow this
question to have any further influence on his argument.   Yet,
that is exactly the fundamental question of this "by nature" *and*
the revelation! Also the other reason given by Schilder contains important elements of truth: man can only move within
the frame of the law.[29]   But all this is not being made plausible
by *a priori* excluding general revelation and common grace,
because this does not explain the *doing* of works of the law.
Thus the doing of works of the law is not in the least made
clear.   That obedience and disobedience must operate within
the frame of God's law does not explain a thing concerning
*the doing of the works of the law, because also the most radical
disobedience exists and has its place within the scope of God's
providence,* nevertheless it is therefore no less disobedience
and void of all love of God and fellow-man.

Therefore Schilder does not even touch the actual problem
of the doing "by nature" of the things contained in the law.
That problem consists exactly in what Scriptures say about

27. How incorrectly Schilder deals with the problem is evident from what
he writes concerning the illicit conclusion drawn from "by nature," that
they (who perform acts in conformity with the law) do so *by virtue of
general revelation* or . . . by virtue of an innate, an inborn "theory" or morality theory. *I*, p. 110. These two things, connected with "or," imply two
entirely different "forces." Disputing the latter does not automatically involve the former.
28. K. Schilder, *I*, p. 110   29. *Ibid.*, p. 123.

the light of nature as a remnant. They point to the fact that the natural man retains some knowledge of God and shows some practice of virtue and outward discipline. They add that man does not use this light well in natural and civil matters but that he suppresses it in all kinds of ways. The problem mentioned here — slightly and partly practicing virtue and outward discipline — is exactly the problem that has not been solved by Schilder, nor by Hoeksema who also lost the right path on account of his *a priori* opposition to common grace. It is not sufficient to state that man remained man. That is also true of the antichrist and of him who proceeds from sin to sin even without "natural affection" (II Tim. 3:3). It is exactly created man who can commit the vilest sins. Thus neither does it become clear that the totally depraved man still does the things of the law. Of course, one can produce the factor of self-interest and egoism and no one will be able to deny that this egoism can and indeed does again and again play an important part. This, however, is not *the* explanation. Why does not man, who in the corruption of nature follows his own way, allow hatred to dominate his entire existence even though this would ultimately destroy himself? Why should he manifest the slightest interest in acts that somehow are in conformity with the law? There is only one answer to this question possible. But this answer does not leave any possibility for criticizing the praise of general revelation and common grace as Schilder does, because both in general revelation and common grace we exalt God's sovereignty over the created reality, which makes this "by nature" of Romans 2 possible and thus still sustains human life by his longsuffering. Sheer egoism plus the preservation of nature does not explain this "by nature." *If* Schilder wishes to enter the sense of responsibility *here* then he can reasonably do so only in the light of general revelation and of common grace, because the sense of responsibility presupposes the consciousness of having to give an account and the sense of *dependency*. This consciousness, as well as the knowledge of God in the codes, and the knowledge of outward discipline and virtue are conceivable only in connection with natural illumination which still confronts man with the revelation of God and the works of his hands. There is a *realization* of the *excellence* of that which the law requires. The Gentiles do not have the Mosaic law. They do not know nor acknowledge the sovereignty of the Lawgiver. But there are *norms* in their lives which they "acknowledge" without *normgiver* — they are a law unto themselves — and thus they place themselves within the normative framework which *virtually* demonstrates the supremacy of the divine normativity. We notice this supremacy in many ways. The Humanistic League strongly denies that ethics ceases as soon as religion ceases. This humanism maintains that without religion there can be a certain norm-consciousness, norms, ideas, and ideals. These norms — as its followers *see* them — do not transcend man (being a law unto himself) but they are recognized as a reality. *This* extremely important fact cannot be deduced from the fact that God directs history within the boundaries of his orderings but solely from the *excellence* and *majesty* of the revelation of his supremacy over all of human life and from the excellence of his law.

There is objective *evidence* in the reality of life. This is not *another*, a new source of revelation because it is understood by faith only. However, man is everywhere surrounded by it.

Man still *observes* and *discovers* the purity of the law and the limitation of created life. Without this limitation life would break asunder — the unbeliever's just as well. It provides the means to understand the *history* of the moral, the functioning of the conscience and the remarkable role humanism has played in all phases of history.

* * *

"Doing the works of the law" always consists of at least two elements: the evidence of God's orderings and the preservation and government of the world and the capability of yet observing the "blessing" contained therein, even though this blessing may not in the least be recognized as coming from *God*. We see in this the preserving hand of God and his rule over the whole world over which he still stretches out his hand. Not the fact that God still keeps created life within the limits of creation explains the course of human life in its relative stabilization and bearable condition (because the Antichrist, too, is a creature and life without natural love is simply 'natural' life) but that *he* sovereignly directs our natural illumination to the manifestation of *his* power in the maintaining and governing of man and world.

This knowledge will never permit us to declare the human conscience autonomous or to identify it with the revelation or the *voice* of God in the human heart. The idea "conscience" always presupposes reaction to the revelation of God and Scripture itself points out that this "conscience" is not an unchangeable, stable entity which belongs to man as an innate possession. Scripture speaks about those who "have seared their conscience with a hot iron" (I Tim. 4:2), which, among other things, implies that in the continuation of unbelief and apostasy the "fatal moment" may arrive that the conscience deteriorates, resulting in the permanent refusal to allow it to be one's accuser. Thus they may easily become the instruments of the devil having the stigma of servitude in their conscience. It is the same Paul, who in Romans 2 sees the conscience functioning as well as judging others, who is speaking about this. All this does not imply a gradual transition or identification of *law* and conscience so that the conscience even might become the source of knowledge concerning morality, but the functioning conscience does presuppose the relationship to the revelation of God, a relationship in which, however, it may err and deteriorate. Paul never idealizes the conscience but he does call our special attention to it in connection with his argument. God's general revelation in creation, preservation, and govern-

ment,[30] therefore, never leads to automatically exalting the
conscience to God's voice, but it places man by reason of his
indestructible relationship to the Creator, Preserver, and Ruler
of the universe in a condition of responsibility and inexcus-
ability.[31] We are touching here — generally speaking — upon
the profound problem of the *norm-consciousness* which can
never be understood if we proceed from the mere human nature
without revelation.

* * *

In this connection we wish to consider the much-discussed
problem of the so-called *natural law*** which has been quoted in
connection with Romans 2. It is not our intention to go into
the many aspects of this *natural law*. Only a few fundamental
questions which have immediate bearing upon our subject
are of interest to us, especially the one concerning the idea
that a *general*, not specifically Christian, law and law-conscious-
ness must be admitted, a *law of nature*. Despite the confusion
in this matter there has been a continuous search for a common and unchangeable *natural law,* a seeking for a plateau
on which all people and minds could come together in common
conceptions and fundamental ideas without being separated

---

30. Belgic Confession, Art. II., cf. Chapter X.

31. Here lies the solution of the problem W. J. Aalders discussed, namely
towards the transcendence and immanence of the conscience. (*Het Geweten,*
1935, p. 82)   Cf., "Suppose the conscience to be absolutely transcendent,
divine — and it is no conscience any longer. Suppose it to be absolutely
immanent — and it is no conscience any longer either." It would be more
correct to say that the conscience is truly human but then not in the sense
of immanence as in isolated humanity, because this humanity is always "in
relationship" and thus never *isolated.*

** The term translated here is *natuurrecht,* a well-known term in Dutch
and German theological and philosophical discussions, and here literally
translated *natural law,* not in the sense of the laws of nature, or physical
natural law, but embodying the concepts, varied with the particular context, of natural goodness, righteousness, justice, morality, and the consciousness in men's minds of standards expressed in their ideas. In the balance of this chapter this term appears very often, and is roughly the
equivalent of what is covered by *lex naturalis* in discussions of the views
of Thomas Aquinas and others.

by the antithesis between Christians and non-Christians. Also
in our day the battle for *natural law* continues to play an
important role. Pressed by the catastrophic events of our age,
in which mankind is threatened with extirmination, men have
taken up the search for elementary, common conceptions which
should be capable of checking the impending chaos. It should
be possible, it is asserted, on the basis of these concepts to hit
upon sources conducive to the restoration of culture. One
of the striking examples of our day is furnished by the "universal declaration of human rights" drafted by the General
Assembly of the United Nations in Paris in 1948.[32] This
concerned the rights and freedoms of man. Mankind had seen
in National Socialism the violation of human rights, and in
this world-declaration an attempt was made to protect human
dignity in all its aspects. This declaration of 1948 has been
called "the first *international* document describing the rights
of man."[33] It is true we cannot simply speak of it as world
opinion[34] but the object nevertheless was "that all people should
become convinced that it concerns principles which deserve
to be materialized." In his preface (to the U.N. Dutch Info.
Service release) Kranenburg speaks of a "universal consciousness of law which expresses itself, the central idea of which
he calls "the surety of the importance (dignity) of the human
personality, the recognition of the human personality as subject," formulated in "a response of the general human consciousness of right and justice." He even speaks of "a demand
of justice made by the world community." Anyone who goes
deeply into all this is confronted with the basic problem with
which we are dealing in this chapter. It is already important
to at least be aware of the danger of taking the "universal

---

32. *Publication* No. 2 of the Dutch Information Service for the U. N.,
published by J. M. Meulenhoff, Amsterdam. Quotations on the next few
pages are from this U. N. release.
33. *Universal Declaration of Human Rights,* p. 7
34. The document was accepted in Paris with 48 votes in favor. There
were eight abstainers: Ukraine, Poland, Saudi Arabia, Soviet Union,
Czechoslovakia, Union of South Africa, White Russia and South Slavonia.

consciousness of justice" for granted as is done here.   Is there
in such a consciousness, in such a "demand," indeed some
hopeful perspective?   Is it indeed possible thus to make up
"a program of principles" which will show us — and *all* people
— "what *ought* to be"?   Is it really so that these ideals directly
link up with universal opinion, because man is *fundamentally*
an "idealist"?   *Is* there such "proof on the basis of experience
in history," are there such ideals "of which not a single person
has ever in principle denied the importance"; and are these
"formulated ideals of humanity" indeed "the drawing forces
which help mankind proceed on its pilgrimage"?   Considering
that already during the French Revolution a "declaration of
the rights of man and of the citizen" was made, we can
anticipate what a tremendously complicated problem has been
created.[35]   The U.N. release indeed realizes the "influence of
a personal outlook upon life" and so does not want to choose
sides.   This body is after the "general" and it requests examin-
ers to look further into the matter and to "furnish the supplement resulting from their personal outlook upon life."   In
this word "supplement" we face the seriousness of the problem, because it presupposes the principle which all have in
common and which cannot be endangered anymore by this
"supplement."

We cannot now discuss the universal declaration of man's
rights but we do want to point out that these "norms" imply
a very serious problem.   The preamble of the declaration, for
instance, deals with a future world in which mankind will
enjoy freedom of opinion and religion and in which it will be
free from fear and want, a world "announced as the highest
ideal of man."   The human rights will have to be protected
by "the supremacy of justice."   Confidence is expressed in
"the fundamental rights of man, in the importance and value
of man," while in this connection the fundamental freedoms

---

35. Cf. also the "Bill of Rights" of the North American colonies, the
Declaration of Independence, and the U. S. Constitution.

are discussed and also the "conception" which every one *ought* to have of these rights and freedoms. On the basis of these and other considerations the declaration is then proclaimed as "the common ideal for which all peoples and nations must strive" and in which the right to equality and liberty, inviolability and protection are of the first importance.

The real problem lies in the common possession which Kranenburg called "universal consciousness of law," especially with respect to the conception of freedom (for example: of expression) or with regard to the right of *property*.

It is only logical that the question has been raised whether the ideals are really as *transparent* and *general* as they seem at first glance and whether a personal outlook upon life only furnishes a "supplement" to all this. Is the *universal* declaration not too optimistic a product, that, to be true, shows much idealism, but by far not as much *sense of reality?* (A. M. Donner). Is this declaration *more* than just pretense, hiding behind it a reality of great diversity regarding *essential* concepts? The issue at stake is not just a generality but the *foundation* of that which is supposed to belong to the universal conception of right. Donner points to the "Declaration of Independence" which speaks of the *creation* of all men, whereas the declaration of 1948 begins thus: "All men are born free and equal in importance and rights. They are endowed with reason and conscience and it behooves them to conduct themselves toward one another in a spirit of brotherhood." Donner quite correctly comments that "the element which should give depth to the whole thing is missing," and the International Federation of Christian Trade-Unions requested an unequivocal pointing out of the *source* of the rights of freedom.

This whole theory is highly unsatisfactory because of its lack of *depth* and *clear-cut norms*. The more general and the less detailed the statements become, the more vague also becomes their concrete *meaning*. This significantly illustrates the ease with which men so frequently resort to *natural law*.

We do well, therefore, to consider some of the problems connected with this *natural law*.

We may assume that in the doctrine of *natural law* there has always been a certain awareness that there was not simply something like positive law in the world, but that *behind* this positive law another — as its source — must be assumed, which as *natural law* constitutes the *source* of the positive law, or which functions as a *corrective* upon this positive law.

Frequently, through the ages, there has been an intense struggle between the teachers of *natural law* and the so-called *law-positivism*. The doctrine of *natural law* brings color and perspective in the execution of law; law-positivism wishes to consider only the positive, the established law. Many adherents of *natural law* have pointed out that it has always emerged as a form of *original* law in accordance with which the accepted law is *measured*. "Was *natural law* not always the tocsin in the great crises of the nations?" Did it not prove to be "simply ineradicable"? Even opponents of *natural law,* such as Bergbohm, have marveled at the persistency with which it has always restored itself, for it has always had to contend with sharp opposition. Bergbohm, for instance, writes, "This weed, *natural law,* in whatever form or disguise it may appear, must be extirpated root and branch." Instead of *natural law* the *positive* law must be maintained. This is subject to change with respect to times, nationalities, and circumstances. There is only *historical, evolving* law. Attention is called to the differences which are so tremendous that it is impossible to bypass them and return to a normative, generally operative *natural law* which supposedly is the basis of all positive law. Others, however, posited that law is not simply a historic and constantly changing phenomenon but a *normative* law which in its generality gives strength to it. In this relationship to the norm lies the reason why the idea of *natural law* always revives after it was believed to be dead and gone. The most important question, naturally, is, what must be understood by this *natural law* and to what does it owe its origin?

The idea of *natural law* — in this respect there is unanimity — is evident already in Greek antiquity and especially in Aristotle's writings. He differentiates between that which is just on the basis of nature and that which is so according to the law. This virtually indicates a differentiation between *natural law* and *positive law*. Thus *natural law* is the law that by virtue of nature, applies to all people and that is essentially unchangeable. The Stoics accepted this differentiation and finally, in various ways and means, strongly influenced Christian thinking. Frequently *natural law* was connected with the general *logos* which was present and active in the world, and with the "doing *by nature* the things of the law" as mentioned in Romans 2. This was considered the expression of the general application of *natural law*. The Jews had the Mosaic law as the law of God in its particular Israelitish form, but the Gentiles, too, even though they do not have *this* form, have the law of their "nature" according to which they live.

Especially in Roman Catholic thinking this *natural law* received a predominant place, because of the profound influence Aristotle had on Thomas, also in this respect. *Natural law* took on a permanent form with Thomas which it has virtually retained until now in Roman Catholic thinking. To Thomas there was something in *natural law* which was part of "the reasonable nature of man." Man, as a "reasonable soul" simply *must* strive for the good and for salvation. Thomas, and with him the Middle Ages, fancied to be able to explain from *natural* law important things in the realm of nature, which was sharply distinguished from the realm of grace.

Their opposition to extreme supranaturalism was based upon Romans 2. Rommen presents the Scholastic viewpoint thus: "Paul mentions that the Gentiles who do not have the law (from Sinai) nevertheless have it written in their hearts, conveyed by their conscience. Therefore, it applies to Gentiles and Jews, because it is rooted in the nature and being of man."[36]   The lawgiver of this *natural law* is, according to Scholasticism, God, who had put this law in man as *lex* and *jus naturale,* a law which partakes of the "eternal law" in God himself. The *lex naturalis* is a copy of God's *lex aeterna*[37] and that is the reason why, *irrespective* of the Divine Revelation, there are norms and principles in life which concern all,[38] therefore the positive law may never contradict the *natural law,* but the former must be or made to be in agreement with it. This *natural law* is in accordance with the will of God the Creator, founded in the reasonable nature of man, and thus it is indestructible. It is possible to know the *natural law* with one's reason outside of faith. The natural reason knows God to be the source of this law, but does not yet at all imply the *Christian idea of God.*

"When we assume the existence of God then we do so entirely from a purely natural point of view, and absolutely outside of every consideration of faith. We consider God as known only by a natural, sound mind, and as the creator of the natural order."[39]   This known *natural law* in the realm of nature is unchangeable and absolute normative so that it, as the corrective of positive law, exceeds the latter.   Only strict recognition of *natural law* is able to protect justice against arbitrary despotism.[40]   The pivotal problem of *natural law* became the main topic in the controversy between Duynstee and Polak. The latter rejected the idea that *natural law* originated in God as the source of all law.[41]   He does accept "absolute and unchangeable norms of morality," but only "autonomously founded and not heteronomously and theistically."   The elimination of the theistic foundation *does not*

36. Rommen, Die ewige Wiederkehr des Naturrechts, 1936, p. 48.
37. *Ibid.,* p. 57.
38. Ibid., p. 66, 'principia communissima, quae sunt omnibus notae."
39. Duynstee, W. J. A. J., *Natuurrecht,* pp. 9, 10.
40. *Ibid.,* p. 17.
41. *Ibid.,* p. 20 (discussion).

automatically do away with *natural law*. Polak quotes Grotius who stated that *"natural law* is unchangeable to such an extent that even God could not change it, *even* if he so desired."[42] The validity of *natural law* is at stake, "which is absolutely independent[43] of every will, *even* God's will," because even God could not cause two times two not to be four.

The remarkable element in the discussion between Duynstee and Polak is that they do not disagree about the immutability and the absolute validity of *natural law,* but concerning *its foundation in God.* Polak correctly points out that Grotius does not deviate so much from the Thomists and in nearly all principal points adheres to Thomas' teachings.[44] Polak affirms that we derive the knowledge of *natural law* from the law "which is written in the hearts of man," but he interprets this as an "inward spiritual experience" by which we know what is true or not true, good or not good. These ethics are independent of every faith and all metaphysics. We note that Duynstee — as in all Thomism — accepts a theistic foundation, but in such a way that this does not have any further bearing upon the material aspect of *natural law.* The theistic foundation could also be called the roof that arches above *natural law* because it is possible, according to Duynstee as well as Polak, to know it in itself without faith.

When Duynstee commenced to answer Polak's questions he once again made sure that he did not want to proceed from faith or revelation in order to infer *natural law* from this revelation. He says, "we leave faith and revelation entirely alone."[46] His idea of *natural law* does indeed have something to do with "God" but only *in so far as reason is able to prove him* to be the *prima causa!* Duynstee reasons "simply on the basis of a natural knowledge of God." He

---

42. *Ibid.*, p. 21.   43. *Ibid.*   44. *Ibid.*
45. *Ibid.*, p. 31.   46. *Ibid.*

ıurther asserts that it is not necessary "to connect the knowledge of *natural law* with God" and he thinks it quite logical
that Aristotle and Thomas "developed the idea of *natural
law* apart from God,"[47] because when "speaking about *natural
law* there is no need for even once mentioning God."[48] All this
clearly explains the development of the Roman Catholic doctrine of *natural law*. The *natural law* is deduced from *nature
by means of the natural light of reason*. Man *knows* that
the origin of *natural law* lies in God because of his natural
knowledge of God.

This way of thinking is strikingly illustrated by the manner
in which Manser points at voluntarism as being the main
opponent of *natural law*.[49] He refers to the voluntarism of
the Middle Ages and qualifies it by quoting from Abelard
to the effect that good and evil are "only dependent on the
divine will."[50] According to Abelard, says Manser, "there
are no actions which are good in themselves or bad in themselves." He discovers this voluntarism further in Duns Scotus
and Occam, who developed it completely and taught, "everything depends upon the divine will as the ultimate cause."[51]
Just to show how much Manser despises this voluntarism,
we quote his evaluation of d'Ailly: "Most likely there has
never been a voluntarist that equaled the highly esteemed
Cardinal Peter d'Ailly in blunt courage. There is, according
to him, nothing that is good or bad in itself and that God,
accordingly, must love or hate."[52] In this way even righteousness is not "good in itself" but it is good only *out of
divine good pleasure*.

This voluntaristic doctrine was, according to Manser, the
downfall of every unchangeable *natural law* and must inevitably lead to the ruination of "all unchangeable laws and
principles" (p. 45). Thus the *will* instead of the *intellect*

---

47. *Ibid.*, p. 32.   48. *Ibid.*
49. Manser, *Das Natuurrecht in thomistischer Beleuchtung*, p. 41.
50. *Ibid.*, p. 42.   51. *Ibid.*, p. 43.   52. *Ibid.*, p. 44.

obtains priority and this with regard to both God and man. Voluntarism must lead to *nihilism*. It is pernicious because it "denies inward contradiction" (p. 46) and does not acknowledge that God cannot change the essential nature (*Wesenheiten*) of things.

In this bitter conflict between Roman Catholic thinking and voluntarism we certainly may not, because of our opposition to the intellectualism of Rome's conception of *natural law,* choose in favor of voluntarism, which indeed has irrationalistic tendencies, as shown, for instance, in Occam. But the error of this voluntarism is not that it places all law and morality *in the will* of God, but that it interpreted this will as arbitrary, or at least leaves open the possibility for so doing. When Occam claims that something is good because God wills it, then this in itself has nothing to do with voluntarism or irrationalism. Only the *arbitrary* in God changes everything, and the *speculation* which desires to penetrate behind the wisdom of God's will *which became known to us* — this speculation denies the *wisdom* and the *faithfulness* of God and actually left him, as it were, standing every moment at the crossroads. But the Roman Catholic opposition to this voluntarism is certainly not more acceptable because it creates an ontology of "the good" and "the right" which substantiates the good and the right with respect to God and calls the good *good because* it is good *in itself.*

Thus the relationship to God consists solely in the fact that God's essence is considered identical with the *lex aeterna* (p. 91). This *eternal* law consists of two realms: *natural law,* the source of which is *reason,* and *Divine law,* the source of which is *revelation. Natural law partakes* of the eternal law (p. 96). "It is different from the *lex divina* because it has been put into the rational nature of man itself as directive of appropriate conduct."[53] Thus it is made *by reason* "to the highest norm of all purely natural conduct."

---

53. Manser, p. 96: "participatio legis aeternae in rationali creatura."

It is a law for the *being*. It is not placed *above* man but *coincides with him*. In this Aristotelian-Thomistic conception we find the *core* of the Roman Catholic doctrine of *natural law*. It is directed toward a law which ontologically is written in the heart, in the human soul, so that it is knowable to reason.

* * *

Now that we have seen that there is a close connection between the Roman Catholic view of the natural knowledge of God and *natural law,* the question arises whether the Reformation, which abandoned the differentiation between nature and super-nature, did not automatically reject *natural law*. Is it not so that the Roman Catholic doctrine of *natural law* as well as its natural theology was linked up with a conception of human nature which was in flagrant conflict with the Reformed confession of the total depravity of human nature, from which the human reason certainly is not excluded?

It is one of the most remarkable phenomena in the history of Christian thinking that also in the Reformation *natural law* plays an important role, or at least that it has not been set aside radically. Brunner points out "that the Reformers, who, on the basis of a new conception of *God's righteousness,* had just broken with a tradition of a thousand years' standing, unhesitatingly and unanimously applied the idea of *natural law,* as presented by Patristicism and Scholasticism, as an integral element of their social-ethic."[54] The question arises, How could this be possible, and justified? The Roman Catholic camp considers this *natural law* of the Reformation an inconsistency which was not recognized or was over-

---

54. Brunner, E. *Gerechtigkeit,* 1943, p. 104. A. Lang has tried to show that neither Luther nor Calvin were friendly to *natural law,* and he adds, "Calvin's basic idea of the total depravity of human nature was far too strong for that" (*Die Reformation und das Natuurrecht,* 1909, p. 20). The Reformers, said Lang, recognized *natural law* only as "a piece of accepted tradition" (p. 23).

looked at the time. According to Cassian Weier, all objections to *natural law* have their origin *in the doctrine
of the total corruption of human nature,* with which *natural
law* is incompatible. It is an inconsistency on the part of
Luther to maintain *natural law* and the later development of
Lutheran doctrine separates itself from his standpoint towards a more consistent application of Reformed anthropology and hamartiology.[55]

In connection with this consideration the question is of
importance if we are indeed dealing with the probability that
at first the consequences of the Reformation were not fully
fathomed. This question poses another one, namely, what
use is there left for the idea of *natural law* when the conception of reason in Thomistic thinking is confronted with the
sharp criticism of the profession of human depravity. It is
the very question which occupied Bohatec's mind when he
asked himself in how far there exists a tension "between the
pessimism of original sin and the appreciation of *natural
law.*"[56]

We are not concerned with the history of the idea of *natural
law* during the Reformation but with the *problem* which we
formulated above. We let the matter of Luther's idea concerning *natural law* rest, [57] and by way of illustration we only men-

55. Cassian Weier, in *"Die Kirche Christi,"* p. 229.

56. J. Bohatec, *Calvin und das Recht,* p. 229

57. The problem of the natural righteousness became very topical by the
dissertations of Karl Holl, especially in his *"Der Neubau der Sittlichkeit"*
(Luther I, p. 155ff) in which he develops the idea that Luther did not have
much appreciation for the natural morality. "Luther did not refer to any
natural law" (p. 243). He is of the opinion (in contrast with Troeltsch)
that "the entire idea of *lex naturae* as M. Weber and Troeltsch primarily
understand it, is only pre-supposed in Luther," (p. 244) It is now quite
generally accepted that Holl's interpretation of Luther, also in this connection, is very biased. Brunner correctly points out that Holl took *natural law* in a very naturalistic sense and as such did not find it with Luther.
It is true "that the Stoic conception of *natural law* is not to be found with
Luther and Calvin" (Brunner, *Gerechtigkeit,* p. 319), but that does not yet
determine the matter of *natural law* in Luther. F. X. Arnold also mentions

tion Calvin, of whom Bohatec indisputably proved that with him *natural law* played an important role. Bohatec immediately points to the background of *natural law* with Calvin, viz. Holy Scripture, "Like all Reformers and the entire Christian tradition Calvin links up with the well-known Pauline idea of Rom. 2:14."[58]   This is clear proof that Calvin himself least of all considers his conception of *natural law* to contradict the profession of the corruption of human nature. This is one of the main reasons why Calvin always proceeds from the fact that man has not lost all of the gifts which he had received from God. The total corruption of man is, according to Calvin, indeed present, but that does not coincide, according to him, with the *absence* of all of God's gifts to human nature. Calvin is convinced that man *with* his gifts and *in* the *functioning* of these gifts can manifest his total corruption. In the background of Calvin's thinking is a deep sin-conception, we would call it: a total-existential conception, which is *religious* in character and is governed by the question of the attitude of man's heart towards God. The absence of true religious obedience of man to God does not exclude man's functioning with the gifts that are left to him in the world in which he yet receives his place.[59] Man has still retained his faculty of judgment[60] and his natural understanding of some distinction between good and bad. Life

---

Holl's "simplifying of the problem."   Cf. also E. Brunner, *Das Gebot und die Ordnungen*, 1932, p. 609.   When Arnold states that Luther's teaching concerning *natural law* shows a remarkable likeness to the Thomistic position, "except for the absence of the *lex-aeterna*" (quoted work, p. 128) then exactly this shows a decisive difference!

---

58. Bohatec, *ibid.*, p. 5. Melanchthon also referred to Rom. 2. See Ph. Melanchthon, *Grundbegriffe der Glaubenslehre* (loci communes 1521) (F. Schadd, 1931) p. 55. In the 1535 edition all this is of still greater significance to Melanchthon. We read already in 1521 strong expressions, e.g., "The law of nature, therefore, is a generally known voice which all men likewise recognize and that to the same extent as God has imprinted it in every conscience with the purpose of creating (a sense of) morality." (p. 55)
59. Bohatec, *ibid.*, especially note 24.
60. Gloede, *Theologia naturalis bei Calvin*, p. 179

has not yet been imprisoned in the grey and impenetrable fog of utter immorality and anarchy.

Man still has some discernment with respect to that which the believer knows to be the law and the orderings of God for human life. It is along these lines that Calvin arrives at his conception of natural righteousness. It could be said that Calvin's vision regarding natural righteousness is the result of his conception of God's orderings *and* common grace as gifts of God's long-suffering by which man has retained something of the faculty *to notice* something of God's law.[61] The natural mind is a gift of God which has also been granted to unbelievers,[62] and is a general possession. To Calvin this explains the *preservation* of life which in many respects moves within the realm of God's orderings. He is not speaking about the functioning of the heart of man in *religion* and *true obedience* but about his conducting himself within a legal sphere on the basis of his conscience being touched by the objective goodness of God's law, even though man is not at all conscious of this law as being *God's law* and even though he does not recognize him as the *origin* and *Lord* of this law. Thus a certain civil virtue may originate which does not result from a central and religious inclination of the human heart towards God but from seeing and discovering the *goodness and usefulness of God's orderings.* In this way the origin of this marvelous goodness is not known but it is impossible to escape the *superior power* and *obviousness* of this goodness. To Calvin this contains one of the most important points of his conception as is clearly evident from his exegesis of Rom. 2.[63] His starting-point is

61. "Hace documenta apperte testantur universalum rationis et intelligentiae comprehensionem esse hominibus naturaliter inditam" (Bohatec, p. 23).
62. "to unbelievers also" (quoted work, p. 24) "and to those whom God will never regenerate by His Holy Spirit...it is a matter common to both believers and unbelievers to judge (evaluate) things here below," (p. 24).
63. This evidence is undeniable in Calvin's Commentary on Rom. 2:14 (Edit. Tholuck) where he discusses "justitiae ac rectitudinis conceptiones" by which man does not completely turn his back "ab humanitate." This proves superior power, according to Calvin, *"neque enim aliter possent*

not the relativity of corruption but *God's activity in history.*
Exactly this is the reason why Calvin's idea of *natural law*
does not contradict his profession of man's corruption.   We
may say with Bohatec that *natural law* is maintained "in spite
of the burden of original sin, or *perhaps* rather *because of it,* [64]
because *"natural law* is the differentiated faculty of man
which he by common grace retained after the ruin of nature."
With these views in mind we may say that Calvin's approach
is entirely different from that of the *Roman Catholic* doctrine
of *natural law.*   The latter is founded in the reasonable nature
of man, which, according to Rome, *simply cannot but strive
for the good.*   With Calvin we find nothing of the sort.   His
central idea is that out of enmity and disobedience the corruption of human nature is directed *against* the good will of
God.   Rome does not recognize such a total corruption and is
therefore of the opinion that there is room for natural righteousness and natural morality and consequently that it can
point these out.   The reference to Romans 2:14 becomes therefore of an entirely different nature.[65]   According to Calvin
natural man does not live by virtue of a remnant of true, ontological goodness within the ordinances of God, but he moves
within the manifestation and evidence of the divinely ordained
good as the revelation of his holy will.   The predominant as-

---

inter flagitium virtutemque discernere," and what is said in Rom. 2 concerning the law Calvin understands thus, "sic *veritatis potentia* vincuntur, ut
non possint non approbare." Calvin does not make a distinction between
heart and *intellect.* Not true fulfillment of the law is meant, but *notitia,*
a "naturalis quaedam Legis intelligentia."

---

64. Bohatec, *ibid.,* p. 92.
65. Pelagius referred to this "by nature" of Romans 2, for proof for his
dogmatic ideas. This Augustine refuted, because, according to him, the
point at issue was nature under the influence of grace. Lagrange calls this
"a false interpretation" and points to Baius who shared this opinion. See
the denunciation of Baius' thesis (Denz 1022), "Cum Pelagio sentunt, qui
textum Apostoli ad Romanos II:'gentes, quae legem non habent, naturaliter
ea, quae legis sunt, faciunt' (Rom. 2:14) intelligunt de gentibus fidei gratiam
non habentibus."

pect of Calvin's conception is not the goodness of human nature, *but the goodness of God's law and ordinances.* Calvin's doctrine concerning common grace is not the result of his inclination to detract anything from the corruption of human nature but of his certain conviction that this total corruption is being taught by Scripture.[66] We are facing here God's activity with regard to preservation and government. *This* offers the possibility of the connection between the so-called *natural law* and . . . *corruptio naturae.* The *term natural law* will undoubtedly always lead some on the wrong track because it automatically creates the impression that all this evolves out of the nature of man, whom they automatically will want to protect against the profession of total corruption. But the problem itself cannot be avoided without becoming enmeshed in insoluable difficulties.

It is indeed remarkable that human life, in manifesting an innate aversion to God and his holy will and in manifesting that it cannot subject itself to the law of God, (the "natural man" — Rom. 8:7 and I Cor. 2:14) still stands for right and justice, for punishing that which is evil and rewarding that which is good (cf. Rom. 13:3, 4). There is still an appreciation of associating with one another and of the boundaries of the human community. There is still a searching for truth and knowledge. In short, there is still a *working* of the law written in human hearts which neither know God nor serve him. This doing of the work of the law implies that the eye

66. Illustrative of Calvin's conception in this respect is his thesis in his *Institutes* where he proceeds from the assumption that from human nature *nothing* proceeds but that which is damnable. After this description (referring to Romans 1!) he points at those who "with nature as their guide have striven all their lives for virtue." It *seems* that from this may be concluded that human nature is not *totally* sinful. This conclusion, however, is not correct at all, "but we must remember that in the midst of this corruption of nature there is some room for God's grace, not to purge this corruption but to curb it." (*Inst.* II, iii, 3) viz. "so that it does not break loose, as far as he deems it expedient with respect to the preservation of all things." Dr. Kuyper in his *Common Grace* fully subscribed to this viewpoint. (*Gemene Gratie* I, p. 10).

still *observes* as it is being compelled to notice, and that it, in noticing, *cannot* withdraw itself from the goodness of the preserving and ruling activity of God and his holy law. Only in this light can we understand that there is still some contact with civic virtue as the confessions state. Considering the human *heart* of fallen man it would be only consistent *not* to recognize any boundaries which call autonomy and self-glorification or self-deification of the individual man to a halt and consequently life would perish in individualistic self-annihilation as the result of demonizing one's sovereign ego. We still see something different from this descent into hell. We live in a world which knows and recognizes authority, which protests against total anarchy, which recognizes standards of good and evil and judges itself and others accordingly. Every person moves within the superior power of God's doings and of the upholding of his blessed law. In this world there is not only simply a transcendant, eschatologic judgment but also a judgment immanent in sin. The law is holy and good, proceeding from the wise and holy will of God and *in* violating the law not only the heart becomes polluted but also life is desecrated to the ground. Therefore, in human life and history, the superior power of God's law is triumphant, also over man who *cannot* submit himself to the law. He isolates laws and norms from the Lawgiver and in his apostacy uses them as though they were *his* material and property. He does not do so in obedience but still *in* his actions, *in* his conscience, *in* his judging others and *in* his protest against complete anarchy, he manifests the superior power of God's work and law. Only this explains why there always is a reverting to conceptions such as *evidence, intuition, matter of course* and *natural,* when considering *natural law.* Such words, if considered in connection with man's *nature,* and isolated from the permanent presence of God in his revelation, would remain utterly meaningless and incomprehensible. They could be established only as mysterious facts. However, in the light of God's orderings it

is understandable that human life attempts to live autonomously but that it nevertheless goes on by continuously making use of God's ordinances.

To acknowledge this does not result in an optimistic ap-
praisal of man, because the entire life of man clearly evidences
that it has completely turned away from God and moreover
will also in his concrete conduct continue on his way to manifest degeneration. Paul is not speaking of a constant and continuous conduct of heathendom in Romans 2.[67] The process of
sin may ultimately manifest itself also to such an extent that
finally only slight remnants of discernment will remain. Man's
eye can become more and more obscured for the goodness of
God's orderings so that at last he will have an eye only for the
"law" which pleases him and which safeguards his own life.
It is possible for life to develop, as Paul predicts as to what
will happen in the last days, viz., into nearly total and uncompromising opposition against all that which the law of God
makes valuable in life, days in which man will be even without natural love.[68] This may evoke and manifest God's judgment as happened in the "giving up" of which Paul speaks in
Romans 1.[69]

This is clear proof that it is impossible to write a history
of mankind on the basis of human "nature" and its "natural
light." The relationship between the general revelation of
God, the generally restraining grace, and human life is not a

---

67. Cf. "when ... " Lagrange correctly says, "*oran* implies more than a
possibility" (*Comm.* p. 49), but that does not necessarily mean an unchangeable and continuous *doing* of the work of the law by *all*.

68. Cf. II Timothy 3:3, life is uprooted in lawlessness. That holds true
of "the people," people in general (*viz.* C. Bouma, *Commentaar*, p. 312). Love
will be totally unnaturally inclined. Bouma points out that Paul uses five
times a construction with the adjective *philos* (*their own selves, money,* no
love towards the *good,* lovers of pleasure more than lovers of God, II Tim.
3:2-4).

69. Cf. what Paul says concerning practice contrary to nature (Rom. 1:26)
and doing things of which it is a shame even to speak; the unfruitful
works of darkness (Eph. 5:12); worldly-mindedness (Phil. 3:19); shame-
ful practices (II Cor. 4:2); cf. Jude 13, men who are like the raging
waves of the sea, foaming up their own shame.

static but a dynamic relationship which is entirely bound up with the development of history and the process of sin. It will always be impossible to write about general revelation and common grace without also calling attention to God's judgment already in history.

But there is still also the possibility of being touched by what God does in preserving and governing the world, in his limiting orderings, which make life possible. This does not imply a receptivity for the Giver of this law and the Originator of these boundaries, but for the function of the law in the midst of life's corruption. It is in this light that Calvin sees *natural law* and it correctly speaks to him more for the goodness of God and his law than for the goodness of man who is being forced to live in *this* world of God and to open his eyes.

We may argue whether all kinds of expressions which in this connection have been used throughout the ages, fully reflect the light which Scripture sheds on this matter. We are especially referring to the expression "inherent" (*ingeschapen* — "created into") which we find with Calvin and many others.[70] It is evident that here is referred to that which everywhere evolves out of the nature of man and makes us think of "innate or inborn or created ideas" which are unchangeable and *rest* within the inward parts of man. If this is actually meant, then several objections could be raised in the line of those which Bavinck raises against the "doctrine of innate conceptions" as developed especially by *Cartesius* and which Christian theology firmly rejected.[71] But everything shows clearly that such expressions as, among others, Calvin often uses, do not mean what the doctrine of innate conceptions means, *viz.*, the substantiation of the natural light of reason, but that they wish to point out the relationship between the gifts left to man

---

70. Cf. Calvin, *Commentary* on Romans 2:14, "hominum animas esse naturaliter *ingenitas*" and "quaedam justitiae semina esse *indita* ipsorum ingenio."

71. Bavinck, *Gereformeerde Dogmatiek*, II, pp. 30 33.

and God's revelation.[72] This certainly is the case with Calvin as appears from his exegesis of Romans 2, and when Bavinck attacks Cartesius's doctrine of the innate conceptions because it severs the connection between man and God's creation and revelation,[73] then this is certainly wholly in the spirit of Calvin. The subjective correlate in Calvin's conception of *natural law* is not the autonomous, independent, natural man, who of himself creates his ideas concerning God, world, good and evil, just and unjust, but man as he stands there in the world and of whom can be said, in Calvin's words, that God, "not only has put the seed of religion in the heart, as we have said, but also that he has revealed himself in the entire structure of the universe in such a manner and daily presents himself so openly, that man simply must see him every time he opens his eyes."[74]

* * *

The statement has often been made that the idea of *natural law* is already denied by "an almost inexhaustible *variety* of doctrines of *natural law.*" But this argument would hold only if we had to take the so-called *natural law* as a constant unity which would be always and everywhere in all men present. Such a *natural law,* however, does not exist. The attitude towards the divine principles of justice is contained in the dynamics of the reactions of men. Subjectivism may try to get hold of these principles in order to utilize them in its own self-willed interest. The idea of the Enlightenment as to natural goodness may ultimately make man again the standard of all things.

---

72. How difficult it often was to come to a pure formulation is evident from Bavinck's paraphrase of Voetius (Dogm. II, p. 38), "in the same manner as the will by natural inclination strives for the good and the eye of itself observes the light and the visible things." In this parallel between the *will* in its *natural* inclination and the *eye* that *sees* it is very difficult to discriminate between the Roman Catholic and the Reformed anthropology.
73. *Ibid.,* p. 39.   74. Calvin, *Inst. I, V,* 1 & 2

Man's searching and thinking concerned that which could give justice its actual *power*. This search, apart from the Word-revelation, was, naturalistic as well as idealistic, always a groping in the dark. In the realm of the Christian church the idea of *natural law* was finally thought to be part of the reasonable nature of man as the reflection of the immanent *logos*, whereas in modern thinking it was transposed "in a law-idea, which takes its starting-point in the sovereignty of reason."[75] Dooyeweerd points out that the natural reason in the Aristotelian-Thomistic idea of *natural law* at least shows an objective trait as partaking of the cosmic connection and of the eternal law in God, but that the humanistic idea lost this connection and can be qualified only as "reason-righteousness," with timeless validity.[76] This way we can no longer speak of a divine meaning of justice in this world. The remnants of the old idea of *natural law* were retained, but — also through the fault of this old conception[77] — without open windows towards eternity. On account of this the modern conception lost its aspect of depth and could not help but evoke the constant scorn of the positivists.

And yet, the *problem* of *natural law*, even though it lacks the depth and the truly convincing foundation (the rights of men!) points to the divine sovereignty and divine standards against which man may revolt but which he cannot escape. Without divine sovereignty, justice cannot be but a creation of human personality.[78] That the idea of *natural law* remained and again and again drew renewed attention cannot be explained as a

---

75. H. Dooyeweerd, *De structuur der rechtsbeginselen en de methode der rechtswetenschap in het licht der wetsidee.* In: Scientific Contributions, Free University, 1930, p. 237.

76. *Ibid.,* p. 237.

77. This fault lies in identifying the *lex aeterna* with God, from which frequently was inferred that God actually was *subject* to this law. This logically led to a hypostatization of ideas, a *secularization* of Paul's statement, "*He cannot deny himself*" (II Tim. 2:13) and to a caricature of God's *faithfulness*.

78. Cf. H. Dooyeweerd, *Calvinisme en Natuurrecht,* p. 16

longing resulting from the relative goodness and consciousness of justice in the nature of fallen man, but as an evidence of God's dealing which manifests itself everywhere, also in the chaos of lawlessness.

The multiplicity of theories concerning *natural law* warns us earnestly against any optimistic expectation for the future in which all hope is placed in the victory of *natural law* or the universal consciousness of justice. Such an expectation will always inevitably end in disappointment even though it will again and again — especially today — fill many hearts. It is a groping after *natural law,* out of the overwhelming catastrophe and unproportionate tension which seem to threaten to banish all law. Wolf has, in connection with the tension between normativity and positivity of justice, called attention to the relationship between *power* and *justice,* which at present is indeed a very actual problem.

But even he who fully agrees that only in the light of Christian faith can one know the true meaning of power and justice, cannot and may not deny that man's eye is as yet not fully closed for the difference in the varied "exercising of power" in the world. There is still a distinguishing, which is not disconnected from the evidence of divine activity, of the distance between brutal power and the exercising of justice. The revolt against national socialism and its dictatorship united people of great diversity into one illegality. Nobody will want to maintain that they were truly one in their deepest convictions and this became quite evident as soon as the war was over. There were, however, eyes that *saw* and *discovered* something of tyranny in its terrifying nature even though this did not safeguard these people forever against the danger of unchaining some form of tyranny themselves in later years. That is the reason why we may not neglect this "discovery" (the "when" of Romans 2) but we may not build on this "general" consciousness of right, because today it may sound the trumpet for resistance against chaos and tomorrow *natural law* may

be thus interpreted that life once more is being threatened by
(another) chaos. It is also possible — being a law unto one's
self — to construe a "logos" which is nothing but a projection
of the human spirit according to which positive justice will be
measured. And before being conscious of the fact we may end
up with the "myth" of *natural law,* the "myth" of the state,
or of the race, or of the democracy. Then it is again human
reason which, autonomous and sovereign, does not consider
and acknowledge right and justice as being divine, but *produces* and *creates* its own brand. It is also possible to natural-
ize[79] *natural law* and this may take on the form of *humanism.*
Wolf mentions the correspondence between pope Pius XII and
Truman in which Truman also wrote, "I am seeking to renew
the faith in the value and worthiness of man in all countries,
so that the holy rights of the individual which are bound up
with his relationship to God and his fellow-man, will be re-
spected in every country.[80]

Wolf calls this, not incorrectly, a *"natural law* ideology."
More than ever before we may detect the dangers connected
with speaking about *natural law* in this strongly ideologic
phase of history of mankind. But this means that in order to
stem these dangers, we must be on our guard against incorrect
reaction. We see this clearly with Wolf when he makes an
attempt to explain the so-called Christian *natural law* in its
origin. He points out the points of contact with Paul and
other Scripture texts,[81] the use of the decalogue, and the supplementing of the Christian moral which sometimes is con-

---

79. Ernst Wolf, *Naturrecht und Gerechtigkeit. Zum Problem des Naturrechts.* Evang. Theol. 7th Vol., 1947, p. 234. Cf. Joh. Messner, *Das Naturrecht.*
80. Their correspondence of Aug., 1947 (Wolf, *quoted work,* p. 240)
81. Wolf mentions specifically Matt. 7:12 ("Therefore all things whatsoever ye would that men should do to you, do ye even so to them: for
this is the law and the prophets) as the golden rule which as "natural"
rule supposedly corresponds to the law of God. Further is mentioned
Acts 15:20. Codex D, in which is added, "and all things they would not that
men should do unto them, not to do unto others" (Grosheide translation,
Acts, Korte Verklaring, p. 21).

sidered as being "empty." Taking all this in consideration it was asserted "that the originator of the Christian message is a God of order who gives commandments and who causes man to read the laws of his orderings of creation. The Christian doctrine of *natural law* is essentially as much as creation-ordinance-ontology.[82]

This reveals, according to Wolf, clearly "an ideological trademark."[83] Basically Wolf considers the Christian idea of *natural law* as nothing but an *invasion* of theology by *anthropological* motives, even in the line of antique ontology, regardless of whether this is a theology of the orderings of creation or a proclamation of man's rights. Over against all these new or old attempts to construe *natural law* on the basis of the ontologic nature of man, Wolf wants to surmount the dilemma: *natural law or* positivism, and finds important points of contact for that in the studies of Jacques Ellul who wants to give to *law* a Christologic foundation.[84] According to him, human law is founded only *in* Christ. Only God's covenant gives man — every man — in Christ, human rights. This posits a new antithesis over against the "ideology" of *natural law*, an antithesis which runs parallel with the Christologic foundation of the *State* as found with Barth, Cullmann, and others.

The background of this attempt is the fact that outside of Christ absolutely nothing is knowable of the revelation and of the works and the law of God. We may also say, the background lies in the confusion of the *ontic* and *noetic* aspect of the problem of knowledge, or differently still, in the confusion concerning *general revelation* and *common grace*. In Christocentric concentration everything is reduced to the same denominator and . . . "the tyranny is broken down" as if such a *tyranny* were the point of issue in the actual problem of *natural law* and as if Calvin's conception of *natural law* were an ideol-

---

82. Wolf, *Ibid.*, p. 243.　　　83. *Ibid.*, p. 244. Cf. also p. 246.
84. J. Ellul, *Le fondement theologique du droit*, 1946; cf. Wolf, *Ibid.*, p. 249f,

ogy of which the basic idea would be: the glorification of the ontologic "goodness" of human reason. In this Christologic foundation of all justice lies *this* element of truth that, outside of faith in Christ, God's right to and in human life can never be *clearly* and *truly* understood. Outside of Christ we will never get any further than being a law unto *ourselves.* But unsolved in this Christological foundation of law is that which Paul says in Romans 1 and 2 and especially what he says concerning doing "by nature" the things of the law. That is — among other questions — the unsolved problem of all criticism which without further ado treats both the Thomistic and the Reformed idea of *natural law* alike as being manifestations of an essence-ontology of reasonable human nature.

But this does not leave any room to do justice to what Scripture teaches us concerning God's handiwork and it leads, via this "Christocentrism," to a devaluation of God's revelation. One sometimes gets the idea nowadays that the *word* "orderings" alone already evokes resentment and aversion. Such people imagine to detect a creation-ontology in it which has no need of the revelation of Christ because it is self-sufficient. Undoubtedly this aversion is to a great extent caused by the frequent misuse which has been made of the profession of general revelation and of the ordinances of God. Oftentimes an appeal has been made to the orderings of God which evidenced actually nothing but a traditional, conservative desire to protect situations which had historically developed. This appeal was based upon the disparity of races and people but, despite the many quotations of Scripture texts, the penetrating voice of the Gospel was nevertheless silenced.

In violent opposition to such a creation-ideology we now see, despite the total secularization of life, a reaching for the Christologic foundation of *state* and *justice.* This is based upon the assumption that justice in its fullest sense can be known only through belief in Christ, but, it is added, justice can therefore, also ontologically, only be founded in Jesus of Nazareth, *viz.*

in his atonement.[85] On the basis of this it is posited that, regardless of all kinds of ideas concerning *natural law,* Christ again obtained "human rights" since he died for *all* men.[86] Actually, in such a conception, Christ is made to *create* justice in this lawless world by His atonement. The trinitarian aspect of God's revelation is being transposed to the Christocentric aspect and on this basis the attempt is made to creating a new outlook upon the true community. Over against the "antique, cosmic form of the order of nature," which has come down to us via the Roman Empire, a new conception of righteousness is being advocated which does not first of all proceed from one's self-concern but from the *broken* form of human unity which in justice possesses a source of goodness to lead men to true unity.[87] This then becomes the "justification by faith" which in its last presuppositions elucidates man's rights.[88]

Reasoning consistently, this Christological foundation of justice must lead to a complete ignoring of the "consciousness of justice" which also outside of faith is nevertheless still to be found in this world. Is all such discussion of justice indeed not useless if it is to be *ontically* metaphysically founded in Christ? It is a remarkable inconsistency which we find in Barth as well as in Van Oyen that they nevertheless attach some value to this consciousness. Barth says of his "analogies" (in *Evangelium und Christengemeinde*) that they seem to be closely related to what others have founded on the basis of *natural law.* And he adds, "We need not be ashamed of the conformity."[89] He even states, "the divine plan regarding the state makes it quite possible that in its realm there be essentially correct theoretical and practical perceptions and decisions, although we would expect, considering the turbid source from

85. Cf. Karl Barth, "We have not argued on the basis of a conception of 'natural right' but of the Gospel." (*Christengemeinde und Bürgergemeinde,* 1946, p. 35)
86. Cf. Barth concerning "human rights," *ibid.,* p. 28.
87. H. Van Oyen, *Bijbelse gerechtigheid en wereldlijk recht.* In Wending, Nov. 1950, p. 491.   88. *Ibid.,* p. 497.   89. Barth, *op. cit.,* p. 35.

which they originate, nothing but errors and failures."[90] He considers it quite possible that, despite one's blindness, one "may arrive, and again and again has arrived, at objectively correct views."[91] It is very remarkable that the Christologic foundation of justice and state apparently had to result in this. One would not expect this any more than Barth would have expected the truth of the above conclusions. But actually a problem is mentioned here, or rather a fact is stated, which is of fundamental importance exactly in connection with the general revelation of God. That Barth would not even think of mentioning God's general revelation in this connection illustrates the retarding influence of his Christomonistic conception of revelation.

We find something similar in Van Oyen. He discovers another justice, different from the "every one his due" standpoint, viz. that resulting from and in the atonement. And yet he considers — in connection with the general declaration — man's rights of great importance and value.[92] "If the form of life on earth in the mutual relationship of the nations were built up only according to this declaration, what a surprisingly new world we would then be living in!"[93] Van Oyen correctly remarks that the declaration of man's rights does not voice an opinion concerning "these deepest causes of man's misfortune and unhappiness." But that is exactly why the phenomenon of *this* idealism with this *groping* for the normativity remains so remarkable. It was exactly that which Calvin and others tried to express in the doctrine of *natural law* in connection with general revelation. This problem cannot be avoided by the Christologic foundation of state and justice, which, indeed, was not *his* commission, as he brought God's justice into the light again instead of creating it.

Opposition to the doctrine of *natural law* will be necessary and justified if it aims at the apparent attempt to arrive, out-

90. *Ibid.*   91. *Ibid.*   92. Van Oyen, *quoted article*, p. 497
93. *Ibid.*

side of faith, at common convictions as an appeal to a self-consuming world, because then all objections remain, against its superficiality, its idealism, its mythology, and its optimism. But this criticism of *natural law* — rationalistic or irrationalistic — may not become a denial of the unavoidable divine orderings which are truly and correctly known only by faith, but which in their undeniable goodness and wisdom continuously accompany the struggle of mankind in God's doings.

Considered in this light we can only be grateful for that which opposes this chaos. But at the same time we may not build upon this resistance because time marches on in the dynamics of secularization. The alienation of a people or continent from Christ is never a static situation but a fast deterioration and an estrangement also from the general conceptions of justice and righteousness. This is the problematic aspect — also in Western Eroupe — of the "rights of man" and of the appeal to the universal consciousness of righteousness and justice.

* * *

Now that we have discussed *natural law* we finally want to consider in this chapter a remarkable historic phenomenon which today again has become the main topic of discussion, *viz. humanism.* We are not interested in a historical or systematic description of humanism, but in the remarkable problematic aspect of it in so far as it offers a plea for the protection and the powers of humanity. This phenomenon, which in our day took on a new form in the Humanistic League, fascinates us the more so because there are also many pessimistic voices with regard to the possibilities of humanity. The cause of this pessimistic anti-humanism lies undoubtedly in the catastrophic "results" of the humanity which we so recently witnessed. Yet, in spite of many sad experiences, the faith will not die that it will still be able to bring about restoration and revival.[94]

Our interest in humanism concerns the atheistic aspect of it which states that belief in a personal God may not in the least be considered imperative for the foundation of humanity.[95] It strongly denies and rejects the position that without this belief there would be only one way left open, *viz.* the one leading to *nihilism*. It is evident that we are dealing with a situation which runs parallel to the problem of *natural law*. There the foundation of justice in a *source* of justice was at stake, and atheists, too, have advocated a certain *natural law* in order thus to bring perspective into the uncertainty and apparent arbitrariness of the growing idea of positive justice. We have seen that Polak, for example, based his idea concerning *natural law* on the unchangeable structure of the human spirit.

We find a similar line of reasoning in connection with humanity. However, we may not simply proceed from the assumption that all humanism has unlimited confidence in man. We hear often that adherents of this humanity are at least willing to admit that the achievements of "empiric" man in earlier days and in more recent times are not so overwhelming and sometimes we are surprised at the sober judgments concerning this empiric man. It no longer seems to be the proud humanism that almost naively speaks of the innate goodness of man. Hoetink, for one, emphasizes that there is no longer such a thing as optimistic humanism.[96] If there is to be room for humanism then it must at least be "a well-

---

94. Modern humanism exhibits much variation even as much as identification of humanism with communism. "Communism coincides with humanism," quoted by Barth in *Humanismus*, Theol. Studies, Vol. 28; 1950, p. 18; cf. also J. P. Sartre, *"L'existentialisme est un humanisme."*

95. Cf. the book by W. Banning, *Typen van zedeleer*, of which the subtitle is: Episodes from the history of ethics (not founded in religion), 1948.

96. H. R. Hoetink, *Humanisme en Socialisme*, 1946, p. 23

tried and realistic humanism" without optimistic anthro-pology.[97]

This confronts us with a serious problem: is such humanism really possible or is it a contradiction in itself?

Hoetink, when advocating this non-optimistic humanism, points out that if the humanist does not want to acknowledge that there are things which surpass him, he then automatically acknowledges animalism. He who does not transcend the immanent sphere of human existence is imprisoned in his relative humanity. Humanism *must,* somehow, *transcend* man. There *must* be something that transcends man even though the humanist will absolutely refuse every binding force of concrete norms.[98] Not a single *absolute* pretension holds for anyone who is historically and sociologically schooled, but "*in* judging one's own and others' concrete actions this moral judgment[99] is experienced as absolute and thus humanism *transcends* the absolute autonomy of man." It must strike us that this statement shows some formal similarity to what Paul says in Romans 1, concerning the judging conscience. With Hoetink, however, this presents itself in an atheistic frame and therefore this frame is being filled in a strange manner: "the notion that man transcends himself expresses itself under the present circumstances and in the spiritual and social atmosphere in which we live, most convincingly in the conception of human dignity."[100] It is clear that the shifting from that which transcends man to human dignity contains an insoluble contra-diction, which, indeed, does not entirely escape Hoetink him-self.[101]

The more so, whereas the attempt to transcend man ultimate-ly leads to democratic socialism, that ascribes inalienable rights

---

97. *Ibid.,* p. 27. On page 34 Hoetink speaks of humanism's complete ac-knowledgment of human demony.
98. Hoetink, *ibid.,* p. 31.
99. Viz., in the pointing out of the good.
100. Hoetink, *ibid.,* p. 33.
101. He states, "herein undoubtedly lies an *a priori,*" *Ibid.,* p. 32.

to the *human personality* which never may be sacrificed to the collectivity.[102] We are touching here upon a fundamental motive of various forms of humanism, *viz.* the transcendence-motive. Especially Karl Jaspers' philosophy pushed this to the foreground, whose motive differed from Heidegger's who kept man confined within the limits of this world. Jaspers comes to the conclusion that man is a unique being.[103] He cannot be explained out of something else, (*e.g.* the animal).[104] Man becomes conscious of the absolute and of the infinite and ultimately does not unconsciously accept the finitude of his existence. "The illumination of transcendence reaches him and the consciousness of having been created will dawn upon him."[105] When man inwardly stands firm in adversity or looks death courageously in the face, then he cannot do so in his own strength but the assistance which he receives is trancendent help, "an offered hand, which out of the transcendence gets hold of him."[106]

It is clearly evident, however, that Jaspers is not at all referring to the hand of a living, personal God. He most strongly rejects any religious idea of God. The difference between religion and philosophy, and therefore between philosophical faith and religion, is the difference between "Divinity and God, between the transcendence of thought and the living God."[107] Therefore, Jaspers' transcendence-idea has nothing to do with the biblical idea of revelation. He especially rejects the so-called exclusivism in biblical religion,[108] with its claim of absolute truth.[109] On the other hand, he also rejects

---

102. Hoetink, *ibid.,* p. 37.
103. K. Jaspers, *Philosophical Faith,* 1950, p. 53, especially "on account of his corporality" (p. 53) which indicates "incomparable traits of the human being" and sets man "apart from all other living beings."
104. Jaspers, *ibid.,* pp. 53, 64, "the human finitude does not partake of the encirclement which is characteristic of animality." Cf. also for Heidegger, G. Krüger, *Martin Heidegger und der Humanismus,* in: Studia Philosophica, Vol. IX, 1949, p. 105.   105. *Ibid.,* p. 62.   106. *Ibid.,* p. 63.
107. *Ibid.,* p. 78.   108. *Ibid.,* p. 85.
109. *Ibid.,* p. 89; cf. concerning the Christ-religion: p. 100ff.

the deification of man, because man *remains* finite and "incompleteable." We must let man remain man and respect the mystery of his deepest essence.[110] Man is and remains in border-situations in which he becomes conscious of his transcendence and thus is able to thrust through to his actual existence. This transcendence itself can never become object of our thinking into which we by reasoning can penetrate. There are only finite objects which point toward the transcendence like a cipher, a secret writing which has *another* meaning.[111] But although we cannot objectify this transcendence, it does lead us to a self-consciousness of a *finite* existence which is not confined, not closed off.[112]

It is only natural that especially Jaspers drew special attention among the present-day philosophers of existentialism. He was considered a modern philosopher, who, it is true, rejected the Christian religion, but still offered a point of contact for "conversing" with the Christian religion, in contrast to Heidegger and Sartre, who eliminated all transcendence and considered man confined in the cosmos. It has even been believed that Jaspers' writings "analyze man in his awful poverty outside of God and eternal life" by (without Bible and dogmatics) "making man speak out of himself and about himself." He allegedly has showed that "man has been created toward God and in God's image" and thus he might have some influence among the despisers of Christianity.[113] Speaking, thus, sight is lost of the fact that a neutral analysis, which

---

110. *Ibid.*, p. 130.

111. Cf. also concerning Jaspers' transcendence-idea, Hans Redeker, *Existentialisme. Een doortocht door philosophisch frontgebied*, 1949, especially on "the deciphering of transcendence": "what transcendence is, may not be expected to be answered by Jaspers. It is, indeed, not an object for a subject, it cannot be expressed in terms of meaningful and permanent symbols and of the objective reality." p. 177

112. Cf. Jaspers, "But also existence depends upon something else, upon transcendence as this is the only independent origin in the world, because it did not create itself." (*Vernunft und Existenz*, 1935, p. 42)

113. S. H. J. James, *Karl Jaspers en Karl Barth*, New Theol. Studies, Vol. 21, pp. 133, 139

essentially cannot be neutral but is vehemently opposed to the Christian religion, can neither give a "preconception" for Christian faith, nor in the profession of man's creation in the image of God, no more than the cry of the multitudes that the gods were come down to us in the likeness of men prevented Paul's admonishing them to conversion from these *vanities* (Acts 14:11, 15). Noordmans, like Kohlbrugge, did not think adversely of it that the heathen have discovered the knowledge concerning man, as long as the Gospel receives the honor that it has taught us to know God. But that is exactly the question, does not the' Word of God give us the knowledge of man and does not the atheistic anthropology *reach past* (bypass) man? Neither the confined, finite existentialism of Sartre and Heidegger nor the non-confined, open extentialism of Jaspers have anything to do with the *living* God, who reveals himself.[114]   Jaspers does not mention man's creation in the likeness of God because his conception of transcendence is a border-conception and the offered hand not a real hand.[115]   But we may say, however, that this problematic conception, as well as that of others, indirectly reveals the impossibility of avoiding the reality of human life as it came forth out of the Creator's hand. The point at issue in Jaspers' transcendence-motive is certainly not "truth-elements," because to determine what "transcendence" is depends entirely upon *who* the transcending one is. But the problem itself — and that is the curious point in Jaspers' philosophy, more so than in Sartre's and Heidegger's — reveals to us the perversion of the truth, the suppressing of the truth by unrighteousness, also of the truth concerning man, who is created in God's image.

------

114. Cf. among others, J. L. Springer, *Existentie en transcendentie*, and H. Robbers, *De openheid voor het Oneindige*, both in *Hedendaagse visies op de mens*, 1950, p. 129, ff. and p. 147 ff.
115. On page 63 of *Wijsgerig geloof* he speaks about an offered hand, but on page 131 he states, "We cannot directly take hold of God's hand but we can take our fellow-traveler's."

We may not be satisfied by simply determining that *human-ism* here moves in a *vicious circle,* because next we must concern ourselves with the question, what is the origin of this peculiar transcendence problem? More general yet: what is the origin of all kinds of forms of anthropology which engage themselves with "the problem concerning man," and with the peculiar place of man in the cosmos, and with man's innermost "being"? Apparently it is very difficult to ignore man's uniqueness and therefore it seems impossible, even in catastrophic times full of disappointment, to let go of new faith and new expectation, thus giving form to this problem.

It is a striking facet of contemporary philosophic and scientific thinking that, despite all menace from and by man, it nevertheless, more than ever before, shows an interest in "man" and attempts to fathom his innermost depths. This may be done by biologic-evolutionistically or psycho-analytically confining man's actions, or by searching for "man's being," in short, for his transcendence. It must simply be admitted that human thinking bypasses the *reality* of man as he in the light of revelation is explained as being God's image and pictured in both his glorious *and* terrible state resulting from this likeness.[116] *Man,* too, and truly not only an abstract "nature," is part of God's handiwork, in which *he* reveals himself. This reality, the reality of *this creature* confronts man with the insoluble problem. This is evident especially in our day with its almost mysterious interest in man, in his *boundaries* and his *death,* his *fear* and his *liberty,* his *transcendence.* Of course, it is foolish to try to prove the existence of the Creator of human life, as well as man's creation after God's image, from the interest, the tension and impasse of many an anthro-

116. When Jaspers speaks about man's image in its paradoxical contradiction (he is of all beings the most wretched and the most lofty) then this seems to agree somewhat with the biblical teaching concerning God's image and man's fall and with Pascal's teaching concerning the "grandeur and misery of man," but the cause and depth of this two-sidedness is not diagnosed by violating God's truth also with respect to the reality of man. See Jaspers, *Wijsgerig geloof,* p. 65.

pology.   But we may say, in the light of Scripture, that the
reality of God's revelation in man is manifested in the confused transcendence-problem of modern thinking.   But at the
same time we note how God's truth may be crowded out by
a representation of man outside of revelation in which man's
transcendence rivals God's true transcendence or even re-
places it.[117]   This reveals the insoluble problem of atheistic
anthropological thinking which principally *must* find the road
to *true* knowledge of man blocked.

Men may examine and analyze many aspects of human life
but in their synthesis they will not get further than a sum total
of what they discovered in the different realms of human life.[118]
The actual secret of man's existence will still disappear beyond
the horizon of thinking, as this existence can never be fathomed
and understood after first having abstracted and isolated it
from that which is inseparably created into it, *viz.* the un-
removeable relationship to the living God.   This is the drama
of secularization, that from the onset the problem concerning
man is posited wrongly, radically so, on the basis of this
apostate *a priori* and therefore remains insoluble.[119]   There is
no denying, however, that in the analysis of man in his different aspects many valuable elements may be found which are
correct, but the vacuum in the vision regarding the *total* existence of man — which is the object of this search — is still
there and will remain.   And exactly because of its being a
problem and of its vacuum it will continue to fascinate and
confuse man.   The so ardently longed-for synthesis will in-

---

117. Cf. S. U. Zuidema, *De mensch als historie*. 1948, p. 15.
118. Cf. Jaspers' acknowledgment, "Man is object of examination for anat-
omy, physiology, psychology and sociology.   Anthropology with its problems concerning race and inclination studies human corporeality as an entirety.   Very important material has thus been gathered but it remains
partial knowledge, also the totalities remain relative.   What thus has been
found as knowledge cannot be assembled to a completed synthesis." (*Wijs-
geerig geloof*, p. 52)
119. Cf. S. U. Zuidema on Sartre. "'This conception of man is an 'inverse
theology' and as such impregnated with an utter apostate (ir)religiosity."
(*Nacht zonder dageraad*, 1948, p. 8)

evitably take on the form of a question mark.   There is an
uneasiness in anthropologic thinking which, despite many
assertions of confidence and courage, and freedom, is a true
representation of man in his apostasy, who feels himself
hemmed in in his finitude and threatened by death, or, who
knows to be dependent on transcendent help but at the same
time claims that no doctrine may assume a certainty on which
it objectively may rely.[120]

* * *

All this shows clearly that there is indeed much difference of opinion between Jaspers on the one hand and Heidegger and Sartre (each again differing with the other) on the
other hand, but that religiously, with respect to the examination of man's being, there is nevertheless an undeniable harmony.   This agreement consists in the crowding out of the
truth of God, which may take on different forms.   A marked
example of such crowding out of God's truth is to be found
in Sartre's *conception of freedom* which has no resemblance
whatever to the freedom within the reality of creation in the
light of Scripture, because Sartre's conception of freedom
denies norms and transposes God's sovereignty into the sovereign individual.   The influence of Sartre's atheistic existentialism and his conception of liberty must be explained on the
basis of the general structure of human life on account of
his fall, which in rebellion rises up against God and which
creates a "freedom" which leads to utter thralldom (in the
sense of the Gospel).   This must remind us of the threat of
being "given up" in Romans 1 in connection with God's
revelation, which threat applies to concrete life in its entirety.

All this is of great significance, the more so because essentially the point at issue is not simply philosophical abstractions,

---

120. Cf. Jaspers, *ibid., passim.*

but concrete life and the real man.[121]   Modern anthropology concerns itself with man as he is, or, at least, it attempts to. Therefore, all this is directly related to practical life and the work of the law in connection with man.

All concern with man's liberty, his life and death, his limitation and association today is sharply projected against the background of a world in turmoil.   Will a way be found to the concrete need and to the sense of life, or does the vacuum of anthropology also (demonstrate) its results with respect to the concrete life of man in the world?

The remarkable thing is that besides the many who deny the sense of human life there are others who take up the fight against this nihilism. We again note this strongly with Jaspers who rejects nihilism as being "lack of faith and nothing else."[122] because it renders everything relative and nowhere finds a firm foundation, it considers nothing true and real, and everything lawful, and thus allows life to go down in chaotic negations.[123]   It is the inclination and force towards nothingness, towards life without hope.   Jaspers wishes to combat this nihilism.   He indeed acknowledges an element of truth in this nihilism, "When we arrive at the borderline of the reality of the universe, desperation is unescapable."[124] True nihilism is actually irrefutable and "there is something aggravating in the haughty scorn of nihilism." But no matter how true this is, we still should appeal to man's deepest essense. *God* is *the* transcendence.   "However, what God, the tran-

---

121. Cf. R. F. Beerling, *Moderne doodsproblematiek.   Een vergelijkende studie over Simmel, Heidelgger en Jaspers,* 1945, p. 270.
122. Jaspers, *Wijsgerig geloof,* p. 131
123. *Ibid.,* p. 132; cf. S. U. Zuidema, *Karakter van de moderne Existentiephilosophie* (Public. Reun. Org. N.D.D.D.) p. 7, "Jaspers has the evident intention to isolate an undisputed realm in the midst of this 'crisis of man' and 'crisis of uncertainties' and to safeguard it against destruction, viz. the realm of the intimate, personalistic life of the aristocratic humanist — family life, political life, cultural life, mental culture and philosophic friendship and contact.   He attempts to safeguard these by his philosophic conviction." Cf. also p. 8 on Jaspers' crusade against nihilism.
124. Jaspers, *ibid.,* p. 137.

scendence, is, may be endlessly explained and approached witl. negations, it can actually never be comprehended.[125] From this standpoint Jaspers wants to arrive, via nihilism, at a new task. All ruling norms are terminated and nihilism is a self-experienced possibility,[126] but at the same time reflection drives us again to the problem of communication, the association with one another.[127] This communication is so much part of man's being that it must be made possible at all times. In this communication we must materialize being man. The belief in the possibility for man to live is truly at stake. The communication is a fundamental requirement of all of us.

Thus, in the darkness of nihilistic threat, lamps are being lighted which will be lights unto man on his way into the future. Man has come to free himself from reason, to separate himself from the *Logos*,[128] and from the idea of the universal order. This contained at least so much truth that the self-confidence of reason had to be unmasked and also the big, boasting words which camouflaged the mediocrity of life that, in turn, was unmasked by psycho-analysis.[129] But we may not stop with the complete irrationality of life. "Our present task is to establish reason in existence itself."[130] Thus the ideals revive again. In its appearance Being has crumpled down. In the communication we find each other again "in the presence of the Embracing."[131]

Thus the I-you problem comes to the foreground again in opposition to nihilism which is always individualism at the same time. Here anthropologic thinking obtains connection with the work of the law. A fervent opposition to nihilism and absurdism is noticeable. Again the search is on for the meaning of human life in communication, for a task, an ideal. There is — oftentimes out of a profound fear of the demonization of life — a renewed advocating of relationships and ties out of which we cannot and may not withdraw ourselves.

125. *Ibid.*, p. 140. 126. *Ibid.*, p. 165. 127. *Ibid.*, p. 173. 128. *Ibid.*, p. 174. 129. *Ibid.*, p. 160. 130. *Ibid.* 131. *Ibid.*

Words like "fellow-man," "new responsibility" are being re-introduced with an appeal to that which essentially belongs to the essence of man, his responsibility thus to exist in the community.[132]   But it is evident that in doing the works of the law one still is a law unto himself.   The appeal to the deepest humanity is closely related to the fundamental vacuum in modern anthropology, which wickedly crowds out the truth concerning man's creation in God's image.[133]   Therefore this doing of the works of the law is not an unchallenged and con-stant phenomenon in the midst of a threatened world.[134]   There is, it is true, some evidence of the works of the law, but again they are being obscured in a degenerated world by that which estranges man from man and that which causes the crisis to continue and to increase.

Thus the problems of humanism indirectly draw our atten-tion to the light emanating from God's revelation, also in man, in this world.   But on the other hand the humanity of this world is a fearful phenomenon because it does not know the true humanity, nor its *origin* and *meaning* and therefore, despite all humanistic declarations concerning man's being (Jaspers: the communication!) an anti-semitic wave has driven the lives of many to utter desolation and misery.   But again humanism created consternation by pleading once more for humanity and for the rights of man, be it oftentimes only for the individualistic man.   That is the truly mysterious polarity of life, which God in his longsuffering continues to preserve and which is being confronted with the decision

132. *Ibid.*, p. 173.
133. How confusing the dilemma "irrationalism *or* rationalism" is, may be seen with Theodor Schwarz who in his *Irrationalismus und Humanismus* vehemently attacks Klages' and Spengler's irrationalism but next advocates marxistic humanism!
134. Zuidema correctly states that Jaspers' crusade against nihilism "offers little or no resistance against the nihilism of his co-existentialists." It is simply incomprehensible that Kohnstamm considers Jaspers' ideas (viz. his *Wijsgerig geloof*) an important contribution to the realization of common norms by which all of life must be guided. (Ph. Kohnstamm in his *Preface* to Jaspers' *Wijsgerig geloof*, p. 2)

in the preaching of the Gospel, because we may never abstract the history of humanism and nihilism to an abstract relationship between "man" and "general revelation." The Western-European world, for instance, cannot be conceived of apart from the Gospel and it strongly influences anthropologic thought. Zuidema correctly pointed out that Sartre's existentialism has passed *through* Christianity and rejected this faith,[135] and is structurally, therefore, "antithetic-Christian."

The problematic situation of humanism, therefore, is never static, no more than that of *natural law*. Therefore, if we imagine to understand something — in the light of Scripture — of the problems confronting modern anthropology (which claims to be not just subject science of fragments of man but complete philosophical vision) then we shall certainly not draw a straight line from the general revelation to the humanity. Especially the general revelation in God's handiwork is no asylum for confused thinking. But in faith we do understand that God is sovereign and that the preaching of the Gospel, in times when humanism and anti-humanity alternate, brings the message 'across that only Jesus Christ and his redemption and restoration save *humanity*. Without this saving there is no perspective whatsoever,, neither for the future nor for the increasingly threatened works of the law.

In the light of the excellence and wisdom of God's handiwork we can understand the evident power and blessing of *humanity* but outside of revelation this evidence is not in the least transparent to the "natural" man and moreover, actual life is not simply explained on the basis of this transparency. "To the humanist the belief in the creating ability of man is a spontaneous revelation, which, once experienced, possesses such a forceful power and self-sufficient meaning, that every transposition of it into something else appears to him as being meaningless."[136] This statement is indirectly an acknowledge-

---

135. S. U. Zuidema, *Nacht zonder dageraad*, 1948, pp. 16, 17
136. J. P. van Praag (in W. Aalders, *Evangelie en humanisme*, 1946, p. 21)

ment of the *suppressing* of the *truth,* but it thereby demonstrates the helplessness with respect to the dehumanization of life which presents itself in nihilism.

* * *

Karl Barth has emphasized that only a Christologic foundation of *humanity* is possible.

The Christian message is the one "of God's humanism" with which Barth is referring to the incarnation. The Word has become flesh, *that* is the "ontologic and noetic condition" towards Christian knowledge of man. This man is visible only "in the mirror of Jesus Christ" and outside of Christ no real knowledge of man is possible. Man is known only in Christ, who places him under grace, the grace of substitution. To Barth this also means that fallen man actually does not partake any longer of *humanity* and he therefore means something more than that we can learn to know man's being only *in* Christ.

It can indeed be said that outside of Christ there is only a groping and reaching for man's being, but the teaching of the entire Scripture is that fallen man remains man as image of God and that this already implies his permanent responsibility in and before his falling away. The fact that man interprets his own existence outside of his relationship to God does not negate the fact that God's revelation, also in man, comes to us. Within the borders of created reality man is the center of this reality to whom perspectively all things are related and there he becomes the problem par excellence to God-abstractive thinking. Only in the light of revelation is revealed who this man essentially is: this man, the object of Nietzsche's concern until he wearied of it; the subject of Freud's psychoanalytical speculations in order to reveal his obscure backgrounds; man in his "ultimate being" and his "pilgrimage" on which Heidegger focussed his attention, and man in and with his freedom as Sartre saw him. Humanism still puts its confidence in this man by groping for his transcendence, and anti-humanism exhausts itself in a self-condemnation concerning *humanity*. But in all this — whereas man, according to Paul's statement, suppresses the truth by his wickedness, also the truth regarding man — is manifested a struggling with God's revelation, also in human life.

In the struggle concerning man's being and our fellow-man the relationship between human thinking and God's revelation fairly culminates in our day. That this actually involves a struggle is visible and understandable only in the light of the Word of God. Outside of and apart from this Word the modern-anthropologic searching will be considered only a far-advanced stage of science and philosophy. But in the light of Scripture, which shows us the relationship between man and his Creator, we observe the dynamics of this modern struggle. The issue at stake in this struggle is ultimately not the knowledge concerning man as fellow-man but also the knowledge concerning *self*. In the secularization of transcendence we discover the truth of Calvin's statement, "On the other hand it is manifest that man will never obtain a perfect knowledge concerning himself, *unless* he has first beheld God's countenance and then descends from his look to the contemplation of self."[137] If, in connection with self-knowledge, this relationship is not seen, man simply cannot understand himself. He then tries to break out of the nihilistic consequences and still tries to contact the world, his fellow-man, and his real self. He thus finds man's freedom, his "transcendence," and his communication, in strange constructions of his imagination. But the nature of this construction reveals man's problem within the revelation of God. This is the problem of modern-philosophic thinking concerning man. Man's thinking discards the mystery of his origin and preservation and in so doing he

137. Calvin, *Institutes,* I, 1, 2.

avoids the consequences of the problem-less man but creates himself a new problem: a free man or an absurd man. It seems as though man cannot free himself from this longing. Only in the light of God's revelation can this uneasiness, this pondering concerning fear, boredom, loneliness, and especially death, be understood. Outside of Christ there is no way to life out of these depths. The suppressed truth concerning God drags the knowledge concerning our fellow-man and self into an ever increasingly inextricable chaos. Only in Christ the way and the doors open up towards the world, our fellow-man and ourselves. In the light of God's revelation the Greek "know thyself" is being crossed out by the prayer, "Search me and know my heart!" in order to thus establish the knowledge of self in communion and in preservation.

Therefore, speaking about general revelation, we are far from being inclined to advocate a natural theology or a natural anthropology which allegedly would be capable of unveiling the mystery of man's existence. No matter how much in such anthropology is referred to "revelation" [138] and to *being* or to "existence-illumination"[139] it still is nothing short of a caricature of God's revelation. From this revelation, which contains both the meaning and the destiny of human life, there is only one way which can be trod safely, *viz.* the way of conversion, also with respect to thinking. In the self-denial of this conversion, in this dying and being raised again, man will find himself back again, however, not in abstract individuality but in communion with his fellow-man. The depth of the harmony between the first and great commandment regarding love towards God, and the second, *like unto it,* is understood only

138. For instance Jaspers, "history" as "the manifestation of Being" (*Wijsgerig geloof,* p. 150) ; cf. the Embracing, the Being which *manifests itself* (*Ibid.,* p. 29) and especially Heidegger, *Was ist Metaphysik,* 1929, pp. 19, 20.

139. Jaspers, *Vernunft und Existenz,* 1935, p. 46.

333

in the reconciliation. In *this* equality the second commandment becomes not simply an appendix to the first but manifests its full significance. And only this is the fulfillment of the law, "for he that loveth another hath fulfilled the law" (Romans 13:8).

Revelation and Illumination

CHAPTER IX

Revelation and Illumination

A FTER having discussed the relationship between revelation and knowledge and between revelation and the fulfillment of the law, we finally wish to discuss the relationship between revelation and *illumination*. Surely no one will be surprised about this relationship being brought up, since the entire Scripture evidences such a close connection between revelation and *light*.

It even can be said that the idea of revelation itself implies the idea of *light*. When the *"kalumma,"* the covering or veil, is taken from revelation, then the *light* of revelation beams forth everywhere in the *revelation* of the mystery. That is why both the Old and New Testaments refer to God's revelation as *light* and it is therefore imperative that we ask ourselves whether this sheds any "light" upon the problems which present themselves to us in connection with the *general* revelation.

Now it seems that the answer to this question must be negative already for this reason that whenever Scripture mentions the *light* of revelation, it *means* the light of *salvation* which arises in the *special* revelation. Thus already in the Old Testament we hear of the *star* which shall come out of Jacob (Numbers 24:17), of the light which shall arise in the darkness. "Arise, shine; for thy light is come, and the glory of the Lord is risen upon thee."[1] The joy concerning the revelation of salvation resounds in Israel's psalms, "The Lord is my light" (Psalm 27:1, cf. Micah 7:8) and the light of God's

---

1. Isaiah 60:1; cf. Isa. 9:1; in Isa. 60:3, "the Gentiles shall come to thy light, and kings to the brightness of thy rising."

countenance is prayed for, "Lord, lift thou up the light of thy countenance upon us!" (Psalm 4:6; 31:16; 80:7) "In thy light shall we see light" (Ps. 36:9). And God's Word is a lamp unto the feet and a *light* unto the path (Ps. 119:105) while also God's revelation in the law is seen as a light, "For the commandment is a lamp; and the law is light" (Prov. 6:23). Everything Israel saw in the light of God's revelation can be summarized in the priest's blessing. "The Lord make his face shine upon thee, and be gracious unto thee: The Lord lift up his countenance upon thee, and give thee peace!" (Num. 6:25, 26). To Israel all salvation and blessing is contained in this light of his gracious presence and therefore God's people are ever admonished to seek this countenance of God. In his grace God does not hide his countenance (Isa. 50:6) while exactly his hiding his face causes the people to tremble for his terrible anger (Cf. Isa. 21:10; 33:5, etc.). Therefore, the fervent prayer that God not hide his face (Ps. 143:7). In short, innumerable are the passages which speak of this light of God's face, the light of his gracious revelation over Israel. Here is not meant a "general" light which shines everywhere. To the contrary: the light of God's countenance is, we might say, *locally* limited. It is the light of his *grace* upon his people. This is strikingly illustrated in the exodus of the children of Israel and in the battle between God's people and the Egyptians. When the pillar of cloud of God's special protection accompanies the children of Israel it descends between the camp of the Egyptians and Israel's, "and it was at the same time a cloud and darkness to them, but it gave light by night to these."[2] All this shows what we might call the *particularity* of *God's light*. Over against this light of grace is the darkness of His holy judgment: clouds and darkness (Ps. 97:2).

---

2. Exod. 14:20f. Cf. W. H. Gispen, *Korte Verklaring Exodus I,* p. 151, "Darkness and light are two sides of the same pillar."

We note this particularity of God's light also and especially in the New Testament. This is evidenced most clearly in the Light which arises in the Messianic day of salvation. In Zacharias' prophecy there is mention of the Dayspring from on high which has visited us to give light to them that sit in darkness and in the shadow of death (Luke 1:78,79). And although this light is not particularly limited to Israel, but also the heathen who come to Christ shall walk[3] in this light, but exactly *this* illumination proceeds from *Christ*. It is real and full of blessing only in him.

Christ is *the Light of the world* (John 8:12; 9:5; 12:35f). He who follows *him* shall not walk in darkness, but shall have the light of life (John 8:12).

"I am — thus says Christ — come a light into the world" (John 12:46). When Paul meets Christ on the road to Damascus a light above the brightness of the sun shines about him (Acts 26:13). God's revelation as the light includes and comprises the conversion from the darkness to *this* light (Acts 26:18). Paul depicts the glory of God's light in a marvelous way when he compares this illumination with the creative word of God, "Let there be light!" He does so in II Cor. 4:6, "For God, who commanded the light to shine out of darkness, hath shined in our hearts, to give the light of the knowledge of the glory of God in the face of Jesus Christ." What God has done for and unto his people is comparable to the original creation of the light.[4] *This* light leads to *knowledge*. It is the light of *special* revelation which by means of preaching leads to this knowledge.[5] In contrast with the blindness with which the god of this age has struck the imaginations of the unbelievers, here the full light shines forth, the light of the knowledge in *"discerning the shining of the glory of Christ"* (II Cor. 4:4). Because of this revelation of the light of God the believ-

3. Luke 2:32 "a light to lighten the Gentiles." (Song of Simeon).
4. Grosheide, Commentary on II Cor. 4:6.
5. Grosheide, *ibid.*, p. 148.

ers are "no longer in darkness" (I Thess. 5:4) as they have been called out of darkness into God's marvelous light (I Peter 2:9).

Thus — in this light — they themselves are the light of the world,[6] children of the day which is at hand (I Thess. 5:5). Their being light in the midst of the world does not rival Christ's being Light, but is by God's grace the co-expression of the same. All the glory of God's people is included in the light which is Christ. They no longer belong to the night or the darkness and do not sleep as do others (I Thess. 5:5, 6). They are the children of light (I Thess. 5:5), and of the *Father of lights* (James 1:17). "The night is far spent, the day is at hand. Let us therefore cast off the works of darkness, and let us put on the armour of light" (Rom. 13:12).

* * *

It is not without special intention that we dwelled at length upon the message of light of Holy Scripture, because, if we wish to do complete justice to Scripture, we must realize that Scripture speaks of *"the* light" in such a particular manner. Does the message of salvation do *anything* else but call to *this* light? Does the joy of salvation originate anywhere else but in the blessed rays of this light? Does the Sun ever arise anywhere else, the Sun of *righteousness* (Cf. Mal. 4:2)? And is knowledge of God's salvation ever possible without *this* illumination? All of this is so apparent that it is well nigh impossible to question this. It simply seems indisputable that every attempt to "generalize" this light must at the same time obscure it. And therefore it seems to be very dangerous to speak of *general* revelation whereas Scripture thus exclusively speaks about "the light."

However, there is in the quotation of the above light-texts a special selecting noticeable. We did not quote above that

---

6. Matt. 5:14; cf. Matt. 5:16, "Let your light so shine before men."

passage of Scripture which also mentions "the light" and which has often occasioned argument in connection with general revelation. We are referring to *the prologue of the Gospel of John.*

When we include this prologue in the orbit of our attention then we are well aware of the fact that we — especially in connection with our topic — must proceed very cautiously, because it is undeniable that especially in connection with John's prologue all kinds of speculations — light-speculations included — have threatened the church's life and thinking. These perils call for great carefulness in pondering this subject. We are touching upon the many questions which have been brought up in connection with the *Logos* of John 1.

It is obvious, however, that we hardly can evade considering this prologue if we seriously wish to examine general revelation. Grosheide, when considering the meaning of John 1:5 "And the light shineth in darkness; and the darkness comprehended it not," points out that John does *not* discuss the question whether the shining of the light still concerns all men in spite of the resistance by the darkness. And he adds, "The answer may be found in Romans 1:19; cf. 2:14, 15."[7] In this short remark we touch upon a very important problem which, especially today, forms the center of attention and interest. It is factually *this* question: does John's prologue have direct bearing upon the inquiries concerning general revelation? The prologue has been frequently appealed to in connection with general revelation and more particularly to what John says concerning the shining of the light (John 1:5), concerning the life, which was the light of men (John 1:4) and concerning the true Light, which lighteth every man (John 1:9). When Bavinck wrote that God reveals himself in the heart and conscience of every man, he, too, re-

---

7. F. W. Grosheide, *Commentaar op Johannes*, I, p. 75.

ferred also to John 1:3-5, 9 and 10.[8] This connection between general revelation and John's prologue was derived from the fact that John 1 allegedly showed a *general* relationship between the pre-existent Logos and the entire universe, all men included, and only later in the prologue, it was asserted, *Jesus Christ* was mentioned *as the Word made flesh* (John 1:14, 18). It was believed that this showed indications concerning both the general revelation as well as the specific revelation of Christ.

The appeal to John 1 as proof for the profession of general revelation has been attacked sharply, especially recently, since it was believed that this prologue showed far more an affirmation of the conviction that only Jesus Christ revealed God and that it was therefore absolutely unwarranted to assume another, a more general revelation. The basic idea of John's prologue allegedly would point to the *exclusive revelation of Christ* and would rule out any possibility of a *general* revelation.

In order to obtain some insight into the many questions which here arise, we do well to proceed with an illustration from the exegesis of Zahn, especially since it originated before the present-day dogmatic discussion.[9] Zahn was of the opinion that all of John 1:1-18 referred to the *historical* Jesus of Nazareth and *not* to the pre-existent Logos.

This Logos was the historic person of whom John the Baptist must witness. When John speaks of the light, then, says Zahn, "This light is a man" (p. 43), and that this refers to Jesus Christ is supposedly self-evident. According to Zahn it is clear that to John and his first readers the Logos was just another "name of Jesus" (p. 44). This conception in favor of Zahn's exegesis receives great importance especially in verse 4, "in him was life; and the life was the light of men."

---

8. H. Bavinck, *Gereformeerde Dogmatiek I*, p. 282. Cf. also A. D. R. Polman in *Het dogma der kerk*, 1949, pp. 82, 83.
9. Theod. Zahn, *Das Evangelium des Johannes*, 1912.

According to Zahn this does *not* refer to a relationship between the Logos when not yet made flesh and humanity, between the Logos and the created but not yet fallen world (p. 56), because already in verse 5 light and darkness are opposing each other and speaking about light *already presupposes darkness*. Therefore verse 4 must already refer to a period "in which the Logos influences mankind by his light and illumination in a world which, without him, is dark" (p. 58). *Jesus of Nazareth* is the light as he oftentimes referred to himself as such *during his sojourn on earth*. It is not likely that besides Jesus' light there would be a more "general" light shining in the world. He was not just the light of *Israel* but the light of the *world!* (p. 58). Neither is meant a presence of light *before* the fall, because the light *came into the world* and "therefore did not shine before in the world." "Ultimately, the two statements of verse 4 can refer only to the time of Jesus' earthly life" (p. 58). True, Christ leaves this world again, but then "he leaves people behind on earth who . . . . have become children of light" (p. 59). "By them his world-illuminating working continues" (p. 60). Also the statement of verse 9 that the light lighteth every man refers to the time beginning with Christ's first coming and this time continues until his coming again (p. 67). In short, the question whether the point at issue in the prologue is the Logos, not yet made flesh, or the Word become flesh, is answered by Zahn by unequivocally choosing the latter. And it is clearly evident that in Zahn's exegesis John's prologue does not have the least significance as to the questions concerning general revelation. According to him the sole issue is the *historic* and very *special* revelation in Jesus Christ, the Word *become flesh*.

* * *

In our day especially Barth has concerned himself with the prologue of John's gospel in connection with the relationship between *Christ* and the *creation*. This relationship must be strongly emphasized, according to him, because Scripture explicitly mentions that all things have been created *in Christ.*

However, of what *nature* is this relationship?

What does John mean when he says that all things were made *by the Word?* In any event this points to a special "indication and designation of the Person of Jesus Christ."

The prologue does not proceed from the assumption that a "mediator" is needed between God and creature but with "authorizing Christ's Lordship." In order to glorify *him* as the fulfillment of the promises the Bible authors venture to make "the tremendous statement that the world has been created by and in him as by God, in God, in God's eternal will and decree."[10]

John's mind moved from Christ's Lordship to his Lordship "at the beginning of all things." This, however, does not answer the fundamental question regarding the significance of the creation of all things by the Logos. Is the point at issue — Barth questions — in the statements of John 1 the *eternal* Son *as such,* viz. in his pure Divinity, or the Son of God as Son of man, the Word in the *flesh?* If it is exclusively the former, then, according to Barth, it would be difficult to see why Scripture speaks of such a *special* causality of the *Logos* in the creation: *by* him and *in* him, because this implies more than that God's wisdom and power are also the eternal Son's. The point is a *special* relationship. We may not simply think of the Logos when not yet become flesh. That which is said at the beginning of the prologue may not be disconnected from verse 14, "the Word was made flesh." "The Word in the beginning, viz. in God's eternal decree before the universe, was the same as the Word in the flesh when by this event it became historical reality."[11] That Barth is serious when making this statement is evident

---

10. Barth, *K. D. III.* p. 57   11. Barth. *K. D. III*, 1, p. 58.

from the following, "And that it (the Word) was thus with God, thus pre-existed the world; that God from eternity wished to consider, know and love his only begotten Son as the One, as the Mediator, and as his Word in the flesh, was the only true motive for and basis of the creation. This may and must be deduced from the incredible statement in verse 3, 'all things were made by him' " (p. 58). Jesus Christ was "the divine motive of the creation" (p. 59). That is why the prologue speaks of the Word as it does. It does not simply say that the second Person of the Divine Trinity takes part in the creation. The entire conception of the second Person of the Trinity as the Logos not yet become flesh, is, according to Barth, as such, an *abstraction*.[12]

It is actually impossible — in connection with the creation — to speak of the Logos *as such*. Just *because* the Logos became flesh it can be said of the Logos what John 1:1-3 says of him. That is why verse 2 says that the Logos was *with* God from the beginning, viz. the Person of whom verse 14 says that he was made *flesh* (p. 58). To the question, "What or who in this Word, this Logos of John 1:7, Barth answers, this Logos "is unmistakably substituted for: Jesus."[13] "He, Jesus, is in the beginning, is with God, is God himself in essence."[14] He, who has once seen *this* in the Gospel of John discovers also the wide difference between this prologue and all kinds of cosmological logos speculations which present the Logos as a being in between God and the world.[15] The point at issue in John 1 is not the *cosmologic* but the *soteriologic aspect*. It is true, in John 1:3 and 10 "undoubtedly a

---

12. *Ibid.,* p. 58. Barth remarkably adds that this abstraction "it is true, has proven to be necessary for the Christologic and trinitarian thinking of the Church and today is still indispensible for dogmatical searching and definition but in the N. T., although often suggested, it is nowhere directly mentioned." One wonders, however, why Barth then argues on the basis of criticism of this "abstraction."

13. *K. D. II* 2, p. 103.

14. *Ibid.,* p. 103.

15. See what Barth writes concerning Philo in *K. D. II*, 2, p. 204 and III, 1, p. 55.

cosmogenic function is ascribed to the Logos,[16] but . . . "the evangelist has not recorded this idea with this meaning."

It is·obvious that we have arrived at a critical point in the discussion regarding the prologue. This discussion again and again circles around the two ideas: *cosmologic-soteriologic.* It is remarkable that Barth does say that John mentions a cosmological function of the Logos but, nevertheless, neglects this in favor of the soteriologic aspect. And what Barth is doing himself he ascribes to *John,* "he bypasses it without construing anything on the basis of the same" (p. 104). John, therefore, does touch upon "the content substance of the idea" (the cosmogenic function) but then "he hastens toward his own goal" (p. 104), viz. the *soteriologic*: the life was the light of men; the Word is made *flesh.* "That is the Logos of John." John 1 deals already in the first verses with *Jesus.* "He was in the beginning with God; it was *Jesus*" (p. 105). The point is not *eternity. Nothing* is "projected in (to) eternity" (p. 105). Verse 2 "indicates" the name and person of Jesus (p. 105). When it is said that all things are made *by* him and *in* him then this refers to *this* Jesus (p. 106). In the beginning, before creation. God had decreed within himself "that he in his Son wanted to be gracious unto man, that he wanted to bind himself unto him" (p. 109).

Here is expressed "that really the Word — the Word which is God's, which is called Jesus — is in the beginning, by God himself, like unto himself, and with him one in Divinity" (p. 108). This "in the beginning" is the reverse *or* rather the *expression* of God's election *in* Jesus Christ, the expression of God's grace (p. 108). That is the determining — *soteriologic* — aspect of John's prologue.

* * *

After being somewhat orientated as to the — what we might call — soteriologic interpretation of John's prologue,

16. *K. D. II,* 2, p. 104,

it is, in connection with our subject, necessary to go further into the dilemma: cosmologic-soteriologic.[17]   In this connection it is first of all necessary to point out that those who seriously object to this consistent-soteriologic exegesis do not at all wish to present their exegesis as cosmologic and thus being somewhat in *contrast* with the soteriologic. It is remarkable that there is hardly any difference of opinion concerning the fact — which indeed is undeniable — that John's prologue culminates in verse 14 and that already the preceding verses clearly point to Jesus Christ, even though his name is not yet mentioned.[18]   Already the fact that verse 6 mentions *John the Baptist* as witness of the Light points in this direction. History has then already entered our horizon. Bouma comments that verse 6 speaks of the Word with the incarnation of Jesus in mind as the Son of God who entered our history as historic Person.[19]   John's witness is inseparably connected with Jesus, "that all men through him might be-

---

17. It may be said that the question whether this dilemma is legitimate or not creates increased interest. We are thinking of what Stauffer says concerning Paul's students. "The epistle to the Galatians had never been understood by any of them until Luther appeared. The historic-theologic legacy of the Epistle to the Colossians has no one ever executed until the present day" (E. Stauffer, *Die Theol. des N. T.*, 1948, p. 24). The discussion concerns especially Col. 1 and John 1. Cf. also Stauffer, *ibid.*, p. 204f.   For the present situation see M. H. Bolkestein, *Het Woord Gods en de kosmos*, Ned. Theol. *Tijdschrift* 1949, pp. 1-11 with a careful criticism of Barth: "Barth does say that the cosmos is nothing but a prepared table for man; but I am of the opinion, however, that the history which God makes with man does shed some light upon the cosmos as such. We may not anthropologically minimize and humanize the works of a triune God" (p. 4). Elsewhere (in his book) Bolkestein sees a connection with a possible Oriental theology, which would not replace the Reformed theology of justification but would run parallel to it and which could have a "supplementing and correcting" influence upon it. According to him the point at issue is foremost (Colossians) "the cosmos perspectives of salvation." The Orient — as yet not blocked by rationalism and individualism — possesses all the conditions to understand Scripture in this respect anew and better (M. H. Bolkestein, *Theologie in deze tijd en in deze landen.* Lecture for the Higher Theol. School in Batavia. *Vox Theol.* 1948, p. 11).

18. Cf. F. W. Grosheide, *Comm. I*, p. 92 who points to the verses 6, 11, and 12.

19. C. Bouma, *Het Evangelie naar Johannes* I[3] 1950, p. 58.

lieve" (John 1:7). It is, therefore, not true that the soteriologic aspect *does not become apparent until in verse* 14.[20] John
certainly is not a speculative thinker who wishes to lead us
far away from the historic reality in order to let us somehow
entertain ourselves in contemplating the depths of God. No,
the Word is made *flesh* and has declared the Father to us
(John 1:18). If that were meant by the "soteriologic" character of John 1, then no one might argue against it. The
point at issue is certainly not a cosmologic, metaphysical insight which has further nothing to do with the way and knowledge of salvation. The Gospel of John is *Gospel, also* in the
prologue. Neither will anyone be able to object to Vogel's
evaluation of John 1:14 as being "the central and substantial
pivot of the whole."[21]

However, we may not posit that John's prologue *begins*
with John 1:14 and we must do full justice to the copiousness
with which John speaks about the relationship between the
Logos and God. Our objections to many an exegesis of our
day do not consist in the fact that it posits John 1:14 to be the
center, but that it operates with a *dilemma* between *cosmologic*
and *soteriologic*. This dilemma, it is true, is often being
limited as we have noted with Barth, but this betrays, nevertheless, an undeniable tendency *to force* all *pre-temporal* aspects
of John 1 in(to) a peculiarly soteriologic direction. Is it not
possible that John in his wide perspectives transcends this
dilemma and exactly thereby *protects* the soteriologic against
the invasion of the anthropocentric and historic-accidental?

When Grosheide discusses John's prologue in a way which
is quite contrasting with the exclusive-soteriologic conception,
he does not therefore choose in favor of an *exclusive*-cosmologic
view. On the contrary: although he rejects Zahn's exegesis,
he does say that the full purport and solemn tone of verse 14

20. Cf. F. W. Grosheide, *In den beginne was het Woord.* Vox Theologica,
1944, p. 104 ff.
21. H. Vogel, *Christologie, I,* 1949, p.. 112.

creates the impression "that John preaches here what he wished to testify in the first place,"[22] while he at the *close* of the exegesis of verse 14 says, "now we may say, and with more right than before, that John in the prologue, indeed wishes to accentuate this pronouncement" (p. 99). This shows that he, while rejecting the soteriologic, does not accept the cosmologic. But he does attempt to transcend the dilemma and calls John the evangelist *"who does not disconnect the soteriologic from the cosmic"* (p. 76; cf. pp.83, 116). In this striking statement we are touching upon the *core* of the problems surrounding John's prologue. And these questions become of importance to our subject *here* and now, too. If the exegesis of Barth, *et al* were correct, we could simply let the prologue alone, because then it would be speaking about salvation as a strange, *new* salvation which has nothing to do with any general but only with the *special* revelation.

We are of the opinion, however, that for several reasons this viewpoint cannot be maintained. Already the fact that Barth himself must agree that the Logos in John 1 has *also* a "cosmogenic" function points in this direction. For, if this be indeed the case, then we shall have to fully realize this, and moreover, ask ourselves the question, What is the meaning of the fact that John by way of introduction to verse 14 from John 1:1 brings *this* message? When Vogel writes, "The first verses of the prologue are, so to speak, only the quiver for the arrow-point which becomes visible in verse 14,"[23] then this may be with some good will, correctly understood, but we still will have to give an explanation of this copiousness. And anyone doing this is automatically confronted with the relationship between *the Logos* and *the creation*. The point at issue in the exclusive-soteriologic exegesis of the prologue is actually the relationship between *Jesus of Nazareth* and the creation. *Because* God in his eternal decree decided to recon-

---

22. Grosheide, *Comm. I*, p. 91.   23. Vogel, *ibid.*, I, p. 112.

cile the world with him in Jesus Christ, therefore, according
to Barth, the Word (which became flesh) was *in the beginning
with God*. So, according to Barth, the prologue expresses
that Jesus of Nazareth was the "motive" of the creation. Thus
and therefore was it created *in* him. This presents the creation of the world *in* and *by* the Son not *in its beginning* but in
the middle (the incarnation). *In* Christ does not mean, according to Barth, the creation of the world in its original
structure but indicates the creation *on account of, in connection
with*, or, *with a view to* Jesus of Nazareth.[24] It is obvious
that thus this *in* and *by* Christ Jesus is not taken *primary-
ontologic*, but *absolute-soteriologic*.

This exegesis is untenable already for this reason that
John, no matter how much he is concerned with the incarnation of the Word — in connection with the *power* and the
blessing of this blissful event — exactly points out the relationships of this incarnation in the whole of God's works.
It is to him of the greatest importance that this salvation
and *this* glory not for an instant can be disconnected from
the relationship between the *Logos* and *God*. With John
this is not an ontological speculation but it is a reference to
this reality of God by which the blessing of the incarnated
word *fully* and *eternally-powerfully can enter into human
life as God's act of salvation*, God's concern about the world.
We may say that the *issue at stake* in the prologue is Jesus of
Nazareth, but *this* refers to *this Jesus of Nazareth* who is the
incarnated *Word, that* Word and this Logos, which was
eternally with God and which was God himself and in

---

24. The word "with a view to," in my opinion, hits the core of Barth's
idea. He even speaks in this manner in the following statement, "With a
view to this his Son, who would become man and bearer of human sin. God
has loved man and with man the entire world from eternity, even before
he had created it. He loved the world in spite of and in its lowliness, non-
godliness, yea contra-godliness — and he has *created* it because he *loved*
the world in his own Son, who, on account of their sin, stood before his
eternal eyes as the *rejected* and crucified One." (*K. D. III*, 1, p. 53)

whom the life and the light of men was and *by* whom all things are made.

That is the same as what we read elsewhere in Scripture, for instance, when Paul writes of Christ, "For by him were all things created, that are in heaven, and that are in earth; . . . all things were created by him, and for him" (Col. 1:16); for . . . "he is before all things, and by him all things consist" (Col. 1:17; cf. also I Cor. 8:6). No one, reading these words in their context, will be able to get the idea that Paul here suddenly jumps from the soteriologic (verses 13, 14!) to abstract-cosmologic conceptions. On the contrary: everything he states here is *related to* this salvation, but connected as *this* reality which is known to us only by means of revelation: all things are *created by him*. Also in this respect the attempt has been made to substantialize the soteriologic aspect by saying, among other things, that the expression that all things together consist by him *"can be explained only in the contingent of the indwelling as it took place in Christ and in the reality of the congregation as the body of Christ."*[25]

Thus this word of Paul is soteriologically and eschatologically explained in contrast with what we might call the exegesis of all ages that the point at issue here is the relationship between Christ and the creation of which we can speak, not abstract and speculative, but as a reality. The accusation has been made, although entirely without foundation, that this exegesis is possible only against the background of the *"analogia entis"* of Roman Catholic thought.[26] Thus we can only proceed from a narrowing of God's revelation which leads

25. Hermann Diem, *Analogia fidei gegen analogia entis* in, Evang. Theol. 1936, p. 159.

26. Diem, *ibid.*, p. 160.

to a dialectic formulation of the old supralapsarianism[27] by which the power of the expressions of John 1 and of Colossians is weakened *on the basis of the soteriology.*

The result is a stabilization of the relationship between Christ and the creation *in* and *on the basis of* the salvation, while objections are being made (as against an *analogia entis*) against the "stabilization" on the basis of the *beginning* and the Logos *as eternal Son of God.* This view — entirely in line with Barth's thinking — is applied to *all* texts in the New Testament which refer to Christ and the creation. The issue is then always "the Son of God, not *in abstracto,* but *in concreto."*[28]   Barth thus understands Colossians 1 :17 and Hebrews 1 :3 and the expression concerning Christ as being "the firstborn of every creature" (p. 106).   We may summarize this vision in Barth's statement, "If God the Father wished to give this function and form to his eternal Son and if God's Son wished to obey his Father in this form and function, then God as the Creator *must* begin to act, *inasmuch as* — according to what these New Testament texts teach — not only God the Father, but especially also the Son, Jesus Christ, is *propria vi et efficacia et potentia* the Creator of all things."[29]

It is clear that the influence of this — in our opinion — entirely *new* exegesis is connected with its opposition to the *abstractly* speaking of Christ *as* Logos and *as* Son of God.[30]

---

27. I am aiming at the same objective as what Bolkestein says concerning Barth's standpoint "that God created in order to be able to deliver." He considers this opinion "too monistic" (M. H. Bolkestein, *Het Woord Gods en de Kosmos,* in N. Theol. T. 1949, p. 5).

28. *K. D. II,* p. 106.   29. *K. D. III,* 1, p. 59.

30. Cf. also R. Bultmann, *Der Glaube an Gott den Schöpfer,* in: Ev. Theol. I, rp. 174f. Bultmann discusses here I Cor. 8:4-6, also the words, "Jesus Christ, by whom are all things." Bultmann interprets this not ontologically and in connection with Christ's pre-existence, but noëtic: through Christ the world becomes to us a creation of God (186). Christ is man, like us. He died on the cross for us. "And only when we understand this we understand that God is the Creator and thus by him (Christ) the world becomes God's creation — for us." That is, to Bultmann, the meaning of "by whom are all things."

Over against this "abstraction" the *relationship of salvation* is placed in the center. But the basic mistake of this method is that it calls abstract what *may* not be called abstract. We could speak of an abstraction only if this ontologic perspective would be disconnected from the message of salvation and if the world's creation *in* and *by* Christ were to be considered apart from John 1:14 and from the relationships of salvation of Colossians 1. But that is just never and nowhere the case. On the contrary: these relationships become permanently visible. But we may not on the basis of these relationships arrive at a misjudgment of what is said and expressed *in* these relationships, because then we deny the relationships and connections in which the Bible authors have considered *the salvation of God.* When John in his prologue proceeds from the Logos, which was with God and was God, then he does not for one instant abstract from him whom he wished to bring out. He himself points to the witnesses of the light and in *John's* gospel we find Christ's word concerning the way of knowledge, viz. *from* Christ to the Father, "He who has seen me, has seen the Father" and, "No man cometh to the Father but by me." But in full harmony herewith John in his prologue can point out *the perspective of eternity in* the form of the incarnated Word. Here the point is not just simply a relative-historic appearance on which we would have to build in the midst of the relativity of history, but it is Jesus Christ, the *Word* that became flesh, the Logos, *this* Logos who was *with the Father. That* is the perspective of eternity *which exactly reveals the full meaning of John* 1:14.[31] The issue at stake in the prologue is not simply the decree, the plan of God, in connection with which therefore the Logos *was with God, because* the objective of God's plan

---

31. Cf. K. Schilder, *Heidelb. Catech. III,* 1950, p. 139, John "has received a tremendous impression of the Lord's glory, greatness, and majesty; has seen him as God, manifested in the flesh. And now, still under the impression, and still seeing in the spirit, he gives an explanation of this majesty and glory" (from a discussion by Dr. S. Greijdanus on the prologue).

was the reconciliation *in Christ,* but the issue is a *being* with
the Father in the reality of the eternal trinitarian existence
of God, *by which the mystery of the incarnation is eternally
removed from all relativity.* This view of the *real* "in the
beginning" has nothing to do with abstraction or speculation but indicates the reality in God himself.[32]   Therefore
the relationship between John 1:14 and John 1:1ff is not
competitive but we must agree with Grosheide that the dilemma "cosmologic-soteriologic" bypasses the deep coherency of
John's prologue.   Had Barth only fully realized that which
he acknowledges himself (*"also* a cosmologic function") then
he would have had to let go of his soteriologizing of the
prologue, exactly *because of* John 1:14.

* * *

However, he who has once broken with the dilemma mentioned above will be in a position to understand John's
prologue in its depth without having to resort to artificial
exegesis.   And thus the question may be posited whether the
prologue of John has any bearing upon the problems with
which we now are dealing.

Though it is difficult to place sharply-marked *caesuras* in
the course of the prologue and to determine what is the
subject of the acts mentioned in each verse, one thing, however, is clear, viz. that John proceeds from the *being with God*
and *being God* of the Logos to the creation of the world by

---

32. Bultmann considers the Logos of John 1 a figure of gnostic mythology,
a "being-in-between," which at the same time is a cosmologic and soteriologic being" (*Comm. Evang. v. Joh.,* p. 12).   It is of importance that Bultmann acknowledges that the cosmologic and soteriologic are *not* separated.
He recognizes that John's objective is the connection between the pre-
existent Logos and Jesus of Nazareth: "the revelation which the church is
given in the historic Revealer has its origin from before time; the history
of the world and of salvation is based and founded upon the eternity and
unity of the divine will: the Logos is not an act of revelation by God of
that time but the Logos is pre-existent" (*Comm.* p. 181, Cf. F. W. Grosheide, *In den beginne was het Woord,* in: *Vox Theol.,* 1944, p. 105.

the Logos and from there to the relationship between the Logos coming in the world *and* the world.

In the Gospel we find nothing of this tense antithesis against the so-called metaphysical, whereby, as a rule, it is not clear what must be understood by this metaphysical. In order to understand the prologue we must disconnect ourselves from the anti-metaphysical spirit which in the 19th century attacked, among other things, the church's doctrine of the trinity, which was considered as being "metaphysic-ontologic" and it still shows its profound influence upon theology (especially on account of Ritschl and Herrmann).[33]

The Gospel of John speaks with great reverence and liberty about the eternal, pre-existent reality of the Logos, who was with God and who in history became flesh. No matter how many speculations may arise regarding the Logos, this may never cause us to neglect or deny *this* truth.[34] John's mentioning the Logos has nothing to do with speculation. If, however, the prologue is discussed in such a manner that it is hardly comprehensible that John did not *commence* with the incarnation of the Word (John 1:1), then one inevitably must arrive at pushing the so-called cosmic importance of the Logos to the background. But in so doing one resists an "abstraction" which *is* no abstraction but revelation of

33. When Smelik states, "If it be correct to consider him (namely Christ) as the unmentioned subject of verse 1, then there is no such a thing as metaphysical 'being' " (*De weg van het Woord,* 1948, p. 12) then it all depends, also here, what is understood by "metaphysic (al)" which, to our opinion, is in this connection a very confusing expression, especially whereas Smelik later on says that the line of revelation *and* the theological line can be traced in the prologue "which makes mention of a creation by Christ" (ontic). Smelik also speaks of "a cosmic broadness" with respect to John (p. 22).

34. Cf. also I John 1:1ff, especially the expressions: "that which was from the beginning" (I John 1:1) and "the eternal life, which was with the Father" (I John 1:2). See: Kittel, *Th. W. B. IV,* p. 131, who speaks of a new element in the primitive Christian conception of the Logos "whose immediate consent and execution is evident from the prologue of the Gospel." Cf. also p. 132 concerning the main point of the statement on the Logos in the prologue "in the 'Vorzeitlichkeit' (actually "in eternity, in the 'time' before time")."

God. Calvin did not in the least think in abstractions but he did not hesitate to do full justice ontologically to John 1:1 by speaking of the Son's *two* manners of activity, viz. in the creation of the world and his activity whereby he renews and restores.[35]

There is a close and inseparable connection between John 1:1 and John 1:14, but this connection does not in the least compel us to interpret the "in the beginning" on the basis of the incarnation of the Word. John exactly sees the incarnation of the Word against the background of eternity of God's reality in John 1:1. One must resort to speculations only when substantializing John 1 with respect to John 1:14 in the message of the prologue. The activity of the Logos in the world was treated as though this were a truth *all by itself* in Scripture. *This* assertion concerning the Logos was so captivating and *this* light so fascinating that all sight was lost for the reality of the revelation in Jesus Christ that the Word was made *flesh*. On the basis of such a conception of John 1 the Logos thus became an *entrance* to a way of thinking which distantiated itself further and further from the Gospel and ultimately ended up in the realm of Greek thinking. The Logos thus became the mediator, the intermediary between the transcendent-exalted Godhead and *matter*, which without intermediary *could* not have contact with one another. This Logos was considered the "world reason" proceeding from God, an idea which we find already with Philo[36] and which later on also played an important role with the apologetic fathers and especially with Origen. They speak of an immanent Logos which is the source of the natural knowledge of God, since the human reason in all men partakes

---

35. Cf. E. Brunner, *Offenbarung und Vernunft*, p. 63.

36. N. J. Hommes speaks of "the tremendous influence of Philo's ideas upon numerous church fathers" (*Philo en Paulus*, in: Philos. Reformata. 1937. p. 1570; cf. "Philo knew only a logos who avoids all contact with the flesh" (p. 223).

of this Logos.[37]   The striking aspect of all logos-speculation
consists herein that an *unbroken* line is drawn *from* the immanent Logos *to* the *knowledge* of men.   Here the idea of
innate ideas plays an important role.   On account of the
immanent Logos there is a "consciousness" of morality, and
of the difference between good and evil.   The *lex naturalis*
is simply granted *with* the immanent Logos.   By thus reasoning they proceeded from the Logos to natural reason, which
is capable of arriving at all kinds of knowledge and insight.

By the same token the heathen philosophers had known
God by their natural reason and thus originates a relationship between heathen philosophy and Christianity.   "Origen
goes very far in his concessions to philosophy and it is often
very difficult for him, when discussing with Kelsos, to maintain the superiority of Christianity."[38]   Herein lies the core
of any logos-speculation which *must* push the special revelation to the background, at least as far as knowledge is concerned.   It is striking indeed that with Origen the Logos-
idea plays a determining role as *Educator* of mankind,[39] but
that, as a result, it can be said, "that the incarnation itself
as historic event does not play such a marked role in Origen's
spiritualizing conception as it does in other theologic systems."[40]   We could say that Origen is more interested in
the *beginning* of the prologue than in its *continuation!*   The
idea of the Logos *as light* and *life* plays a peculiar, dominant
role with him.[41]   This shows us what dangers are connected
with the logos-speculation.   But it is obvious that this logos-

37. See especially for Origen: Hal Koch, *Pronoic und Paideusis. Studie
über Origenes und sein Verhältnis zum Platonismus.* 1932, p. 49f. Cf. J. H.
Bavinck, *Religieus besef en Christelijk geloof,* p. 135.

38. Hal Koch, *ibid.,* p. 55.   39. *Ibid.,* p. 62.   40. *Ibid.,* p. 63f.

41. Compare, in order to see the dangers, the way in which A. H. de Hartog, in connection with John's prologue, spoke about "the All-organism of
Divine Revelation or Self-information" (*Korte samenvatting van mijn
theologisch onderzoek.* 1926, p. 9).   De Hartog frequently discusses the
prologue. so, for instance. in his *Christendom.* 1922, pp. 57, 63 and in *Zeker-
heid.* 1929, p. 151.

speculation is in flagrant conflict with the prologue of the Gospel of John, which does not create an interest in a Logos "as such" without also calling all our attention to the *incarnated* Word. The speculation isolates the logos-idea "as such" from the whole of the prologue and *on this basis* reasons via the immanence of this Logos to a natural theology as *true* theology which *by nature* allegedly is peculiar to all men.

But John's prologue, which does speak of the Logos as the *light* and *life* of man, does not directly conclude to some form of natural theology or of a natural ethos, but it is going to deal with the *breach* in the world and in the life of man. The world has been made by the Logos but the world has *not* known him.

The light shines in the darkness, but the darkness has not comprehended it. John is not in the least after conclusions from some kind of Logos as "world peace" or the rejoicing of the world about *this* light and *this* Logos, but after the complete breach between *this* light and *this* darkness. After all, it is possible to love the darkness rather than the light. John himself talked about that in connection with Jesus Christ. It is the *condemnation,* that the light has come into the world and that men preferred the darkness, because their deeds were evil (John 3:19).

He that does evil, hates the light, neither comes to the light, lest his deeds should be exposed (John 3:20). That these words refer to Jesus Christ, the Light of the world, is to John in no contrast with the fact that Christ, the Logos, is the *light* of creation. Thus John in his prologue can speak about the Logos without from moment to moment sharply indicating the *caesura* between the Logos who has *not yet* and who *has* become flesh.

The world has *not* known him. "He, the Mediator of Creation, was in the world not as a stranger who stood entirely outside of its life, but he had put his thoughts into it; traces of him had grown into it, apart from sin, and these traces could be found, could be read and recognized. In a creatural sense there was relationship between the world and him. The creature should have recognized and accepted its Creator."[42] *For,* the world has been created by him. "And yet, this is the climax, the dreadful outcome, the world has not known him."[43]

By this John points out the *relationship* between the Logos and "all things." From this he does not conclude that therefore there is knowledge of God by virtue of this life and this light of the Logos. On the contrary, he sees the *ignorance,* the guilt, the darkness.

It is not so that the Logos is the unsearchable, hidden origin of creation, but he was — according to John — the *light* of men. The import of this is underestimated if this "was" is being referred only to the appearance of Jesus Christ upon earth as Light of the world.[44] The creation of the world and of all things simply *stands* in *this* light, in *his* light, no matter how dark and veiled the eyes may be that look around in this world.[45] The light of Christ is not known and recognized. The entire universe and all things are wrongly interpreted, wrongly *seen.* But this want of appreciation and this blindness do not abolish the *nature* of light of all things, created *in* Christ. To the contrary, all that is left here is *guilt.* As far as that is concerned there is a marked harmony between the prologue of John's gospel and Romans 1. It will not do to make a separation in both chapters between the cosmologic and soteriologic. The intention and purpose of John 1 as well as of Romans 1 is to show that man ignores and obscures the glory of God.

It is, of course, possible to arrive at all kinds of speculations from the Logos as the life and the light and in consequence to say that Christ meets us in creation not *personaliter* but

---

42. C. Bouma, *Korte Verklaring op Joh.* 1:3, p. 62.
43. *Ibid.*
44. Cf. Grosheide contra Zahn (*comm.* p. 71)
45. Cf. K. Schilder, *Heidelb. Catechism, III,* 1950, p. 167.

realiter.[46] In this way it is denied that John is speaking of a personal act of the Logos in the creation and preservation of the world. The dilemma *realiter-personaliter* with Dillschneider naturally refers to the incarnation (the *personaliter*) but is absolutely insufficient to shed any light in this respect. There is not simply a strange Christ-like shining in the world, but the Logos *was the light of men.* His transcendence makes it possible that he does not encounter the world, in which he becomes flesh, as a *stranger,* but a world which has been created by him.

Dillschneider further discusses, in connection with the "Christ-cosmos" (p. 288), the question what this revelation of Christ means. Usually, says he, with regard to the revelation in creation we think of the glory and grandeur of the creation (p. 220). But when we recall the book of Job and the catastrophies in the cosmos we observe something else besides the glory and splendor of creation. And *this* world is God's creation (p. 223). Ever since the first days a dimness covers the world (p. 223). God's revelation in the works of creation is at the same time *concealment*. For "this creation is nothing else but the cosmic servant-form of Christ" (p. 224). In this the creation has "its motive and stability." And in this connection Dillschneider speaks of the *silence* of creation (p. 225f). *The* characteristic of the revelation of creation is its speechlessness. "We experience God's revelation as the mute handclasp of a man who is very dear to us" (p. 226). The issue in the encounter with the Christ-cosmos is a *"verbum visibile."*

It needs no proof that *this* conception of Christ's servant-form in creation finds nowhere support in Scripture. The light has not been overpowered and it is *shining*. God's curse on the world and on man may not be made to rival the light of him who created all things.

The problematic aspect of the *fallen world* may not be interpreted as a problematic situation of *revelation*. Such an in-

---

46. Cf. O. Dillschneider, *Gegenwart Christi I*, 1948, pp. 214, 218.

terpretation is basically nothing else but a *flight* from the guilt of blinded eyes and from *responsibility*. And because *this* Logos was the life and, the light of men, and because his light shines in the darkness, therefore John can say in the continuation of the one and only deep argumentation of his prologue, that John came to bear the witness of the Light, of Jesus Christ, the incarnated Word.

On the one hand this finality of the prologue affords the dam against all logos-speculation, but on the other hand the eternal depth of the trinitarian work of salvation is *not* soteriologically narrowed. For it is exactly the salvation which Christ, reconciling and illuminating, brings, that causes man to *live* in the light again. And only on this basis can be explained that the New Testament, which is full of Jesus Christ — the *historic* Jesus — in the middle of the doxology in praise of God's salvation, can speak of the *creation* of all things by him.[47] Unless one wishes here to posit the exegesis "with a view to him," these relationships can be considered only on the basis

47. Colossians 1:16. Especially in Col. 1 we may observe the deep harmony of the soteriologic and cosmologic aspect, because the point is not a dualistic condition of Christ as Creator *and* as Savior, but the absolute fulness of the salvation in Christ, *by* and *in* whom are all things. Colossians mentions this to oppose the heresy which threatens the church from the side of all manner of "powers." See, for a correct description, a.o. "The position of the heretics was that there were powers controlling the natural world, who needed to be reckoned with and that the work of Christ alone was insufficient" (E. F. Scott, *The Epistle of Paul to the Colossians*, etc. 1948, p. 20). Over against this heresy which attacks the universality of salvation, Paul points out "the cosmical significance of Christ" (pp. 20, 22). Scott admits that there has been much speculation in this connection, but also that Paul correctly observed "that a religious issue was involved in the problem which had been raised by the semi-Pagan teachers at Colossae" (*Ibid.*, p. 22). Cf. Kittel, *Th. W. B. IV*, p. 133 about this "background for the clarification of the *soteriologic* statement of Colossians 1:12f. Cf. also the articles by H. N. Ridderbos: "Christ and the Cosmos," 'Christ and Creation," "Christ and the Re-creation," in Gereformeerd Weekblad, Oct. 20, Oct. 27, and Nov. 3, 1950; and K. Schilder, *What is Heaven*, 1935, p. 314, on the inseparable connection between Christ's cosmologic and soteriologic significance, and against the accusation of "cosmic speculations" (p. 315).

of the reality of the trinitarian work of God, and on the basis of Christ's pre-existence of which he himself clearly testified.[48]

Whoever wishes to speak of speculation in this connection, let him beware not to lose sight of the *salvation* of God in Jesus Christ.

It is, therefore, again the same view which arrests us: God's revelation *and* human opposition, human ignorance.[49] Speculation makes a necessary correlation (out) of it and subjectivizes the revelation in its sovereign nature. But God's Word does not speculate. When it speaks of the Logos *with God* from eternity *and* of the Logos who became flesh, then many are inclined to see therein a dualism. *If* one would want to speak of a "duality" in this connection, then it should be understood that this duality in Scripture is exclusively bound up with the guilt of the world. No logos- or light-speculation is presented here, but the message of the incarnated Word which now — historically — takes away the guilt and illuminates the eyes.

But this Jesus is not a *strange* Savior, but he enters *his* world, which, estranged from the Word-revelation, prefers the darkness above the light, which manifests itself again in Israel (his own) when they are offended by Christ's lowly state. It is he, who, as the Logos, has made all things, who was eternally with God and who is God himself, the Revelation of God, *also* in his creation. For he, who is the Revealer of the Father in his historic appearance in the flesh, is the Revelation of God *in* and *from the beginning.* He is the eternal *Word* which God sends forth also in the creation of the world. In *this* Word is the communion with God. He, who is the light of the world in the reconciliation, is the Logos who is the light

48. Cf. E. L. Smelik, "Not everything that has come into being by him does also know him. There are relationships which remain below the consciousness. Not everywhere, where the light illuminates things, is this being perceived." (*Ibid.,* p. 28)
49. Cf. Chapter VII.

of men from the beginning. All communion with God is communion *in* him. He is the Word, God's *speech*.[50]

The prologue of the Gospel, therefore, has significance for the general revelation of God. But that is the reason why it cannot lead us to logos-speculation, because John, like the entire Scripture, thinks in terms of history and does not from revelation come to the calculated conclusion of man's knowledge-by-reason out of creation. But the revelation of the incarnated Word does bring us, it is true, not to a penetrating and fathoming of creation, but to an understanding by faith of the work of creation as it rests in Christ. To us, therefore, the road of knowledge does not run from John 1:1 to John 1:14, as though we could deduce the significance of Jesus Christ as the incarnated Word from the knowledge of the pre-existent Logos. The road runs just the other way, from the incarnated Word to the Father. No gnostic mystery is being revealed,[51] but in the knowledge of Jesus Christ we see the world in *his* light.

What the blinded eye cannot see in this creatural world, the enlightened eye observes in the doxology for him, of whom and through whom are all things (Rom. 11:36). Here psalms of nature become truly possible again and also an understanding of his doing in the history of the world and of the life of man. The issue is not an intuition, which would reveal the keenness of our insight, but the understanding of faith, which is no longer confronted with *abstract* nature and history or abstract human life, but which is facing the creatural reality as God intended it, viz. that we should view it only *in* and *on the basis* of the communion with God. Communion is now possible for us only on the basis of the reconciliation which prevents any autonomous world-conception. There is no need

---

50. Cf. H. N. Ridderbos, *Christ and Creation* (Gereformeerd Weekblad, Oct. 27, 1950) on the creation of the world "by him, who is the Word, the Image of the invisible God, so that in this world there is also the reflection of God's virtues and God has clearly expressed himself also in the world."
51. Kittel, *Th. W. B. IV*, p. 133.

for any interpretation from our side nor do we have *to attach* the seal of revelation to the reality. On the contrary: we can only "perceive" in faith. This faith is not a seeing. Again and again the heart is still obscured by the power of sin and then we do not understand the origin, the stability, and the finality of the entire creatural reality. Our knowing is still in part and we see through a glass, darkly (I Cor. 13:12). God's judgments are still upon the earth and around about his throne are clouds and darkness. We are included in the dynamics of all of life on the way to the revelation of the Kingdom and only *the Lamb* is able to open the book and to loosen the seals (Rev. 5:2) in that Kingdom. But in the way of faith the world is now already stripped of its imagined autarchy and Christ is professed as the *Light* of the world even as he was the light of the world *from* the beginning.

This also explains why, in John's Revelation, in the middle of the doxology on the *salvation* of the Lord, the *Creator* is exalted. "Thou art worthy, O Lord, to receive glory and honor and power: for thou hast created all things, and for thy pleasure they are and were created" (Rev. 4:11).

In the light of this doxology it will be possible with yearning to look forward to the new heaven and the new earth, when all problems and confusion in which the world, on account of sin is chained in servitude, will be taken away.

According to Paul even *creation* itself longs for this day (Rom. 8:22). And this longing will be accompanied by the groaning of the believers and that of the Spirit, until the prophecy will be fulfilled, "He that overcometh shall inherit all things" (Rev. 21:7). All these things will be *new* (Rev. 21:5). Then the light of the entire creation shall eternally illuminate the eyes, and the new Jerusalem, which descends out of heaven, will be full of the glory of God "and her light was like unto a stone most precious, even like a jasper stone, clear as crystal" (Rev. 21:11). Then the *problem of knowledge* will be dissolved into undisturbed stability. Then all problems as to "natural" and "supernatural" revelation will disappear on account of *evidence*. And all "illumination" will find its ultimate fulfillment, "And the city had no need of the sun, neither of the moon, to shine in it: for the glory of God did lighten it, and the Lamb is the light thereof" (Rev. 21:23, cf. 22:5). Then the divine revelation will be general and universal on account of the divine preservation of salvation's bliss in its exclusive particularity, and the particular reconciliation by Jesus Christ, who *dwelled* among us, will find its eschatologic effect in the *dwelling* of God, "Behold, the tabernacle of God is with men and he will dwell with them" (Rev. 21:3 cf. John 1:14 with Rev. 21:3, Greek text). And he who sat upon the throne said, "Behold, I make all things new." All tension between the cosmic and the soteriologic is in the prospect of the Apocalypse vanquished by the absoluteness of the new heaven and the new earth (Rev. 21:1), which is at *the same time* the new *Jerusalem,* into which will enter all those who are written in the Lamb's book of life (Rev. 21:27).

The Controversy Regarding Article II
of the Belgic Confession

CHAPTER X

The Controversy Regarding
Article II of the Belgic
Confession

I N THIS CHAPTER we wish to deal especially with a pronouncement of the Belgic Confession which has played
quite an important role in connection with the controversy
regarding general revelation and natural theology. This particular interest on our part is justified already by the fact that
we are not merely dealing here with a theological opinion, but
with a confessional pronouncement of the Church, which, moreover, is not unique but which is surrounded by other pronouncements of a similar nature.

We are referring to Article II of the *Confessio Belgica,* which
has been thrust into the discussion by an extremely sharp
criticism from Barth. This criticism alone demands that we
answer the question whether it is justified, and whether justice
is done here, to the confessing Church.

The Belgic Confession, after having stated in Article I that
there is one only simple and spiritual Being, which we call God,
and having mentioned many attributes of God, continues to
deal with the manner and the means by which God is made
known to us. We know him — thus we read — by *two*
means. First of all is mentioned that we know God by the
creation, preservation, and government of the universe. This
is before our eyes as a most elegant book, wherein all creatures,
great and small, are as so many characters. To this the confession adds further that, because of the clearness of this rev-

265

elation of God, all excuse is taken away from man, and in this connection Romans 1 :20 is quoted.

Secondly, God reveals himself "more clearly and fully by his holy and divine Word."

For a long period this article was considered a pure reflection of the Scriptural idea concerning God's revelation. But when Barth opened his offensive against natural theology, Article II also became involved in this controversy. Barth had observed that in Germany, besides Holy Scripture, gradually also other sources or means of revelation were accepted, such as nature and history. And in this connection he became opposed with increasing intensity to any so-called *two-sources-theory*, which, according to him, inevitably would become of the same nature as Rome's two-sources-theory: Scripture *and* tradition. In such a theory, according to Barth, it would be inevitable and necessary to accept Scripture as a source also, but the latter would virtually be pushed more and more to the background in favor of the second source.

This same scheme Barth now discovered also in Article II. The fatal aspect of natural theology was, according to Barth, to be found exactly in the fact that it also took roots there, where the exclusive salvation in Christ was explicitly professed. That was the case with Augustine and also in the Reformation. Especially the Reformers proceeded from the "*sola Scriptura*" but they did not, according to Barth, go so far as "to decisively terminate the problem of another revelation and knowledge of God."[1] It was a great achievement of natural theology that it managed to find entrance also into the Reformation, be it unobserved "by the eyes of the Reformers which otherwise saw so sharply."[2] Indeed, "it could again invade a persecuted Church — this time in France — in such a way, that it — contrary to Calvin's example — could become such a misconstruction as can be read in Art. II of the

1. K. Barth, *K. D. II*, 1, p. 140.
2. *Ibid.*, p. 140.

Confessio Gallicana and which from there, immediately was taken up also in the *Confessio Belgica.*"³

It is perfectly clear: Barth discovers in these confessions a dangerous invasion of natural theology, by which the Church is always seduced — sooner or later — not to be fully satisfied with the only revelation in God's Word, with the revelation in Jesus Christ.

* * *

We do well to remember that, before we consider Article II of the *Belgica* more closely, the doctrine of the two means, which is at stake, is not to be found only in the *Confessio Belgica* and the *Confessio Gallicana*. Also in other confessions we find an explicit confessing of the so-called general revelation of God in the works of his hands. Thus we find that the "Hungarian Confession" of 1562 speaks in like manner of the two means, which, moreover, just like Art. II of the Belgic Confession, connect both means comparatively.⁴

In the Larger Westminster Catechism we find the confession that God's works abundantly indicate, reveal,⁵ God's existence, and we read in the Westminster Confession of 1647, that the light of nature and the works of creation manifest the goodness, wisdom and power of God, as to leave men inexcusable,⁶ and several other confessions speak of God's revela-

---

3. *Ibid.,* p. 141. In Art. II of the *Confessio Gallicana* we read, "This God manifests himself thus to men: Firstly by his works, in the creation as well as in the preservation and government of the same. Secondly, and clearly, by His Word, which at first was revealed in oracles and afterwards by His Spirit in books, which we call Holy Scripture." (Müller, *Bekenntn. schr.,* 1903, p. 221f.)

4. "Credimus unam esse divinam Essentiam, quam Deum appellamus. Non ideo tantum, quia rerum naturalium contemplatio et aspectus nos id docet, sed multo magis, quoniam Scriptura Sacra nobis eius rei testis est." (Müller, *Ibid.,* p. 376) .

5. "operaque Dei esse Deum luculenter manifestant" (Müller, p. 612).

6. "Although the Light of Nature and the Works of Creation and Providence do so far manifest the goodness, wisdom, and power of God, as to leave men inexcusable, yet are they not sufficient to give that knowledge of God and of his will, which is necessary unto Salvation" (Westminster Confession, Chapt. I; Müller, *Ibid.,* p. 542).

tion in the works of his hands.[7] It must be admitted, it is true, that none *enlarges* upon this revelation of God on the basis of Holy Scripture. We might say that this confession was commonly accepted by the churches of the Reformation. And also the Belgic Confession speaks out of this common conviction.

* * *

It can hardly be said that Barth's criticism met with general agreement, not even by those who in many respects wholeheartedly accepted his theology.[8] Koopmans, for instance, contradicted Barth when he wrote, "there is no such a thing as 'natural theology' in Article II."[9] He even considers Article II less confusing in this respect than Calvin's *Institutes*. For the issue at stake in Art. II is not abilities in human nature "which are independent organs to know God," as is very clear from the fact that Romans 1:20 is quoted, "so that they are without excuse." Article II places all knowledge exactly in

---

7. Cf. also "Böhmisches Bekenntnis" (1609), Müller, p. 457; "Helvetische Konsensus—Formel XVIII, 1675 (Müller, p. 876) with quotation of Rom. 1:19; cf. also same Confession, formel XX (Müller, p. 867), and finally the revision of the Westminster Confession of 1902: "We believe that God is revealed in nature, in history and in the heart of man; that he has made gracious and clearer revelations of Himself to men of God, who spoke as they were moved by the Holy Word." (Müller, p. 943).

8. We read in *Fundamenten en Perspectieven van Belijden,* in Art. II: "This caused us to fall away from our destiny and we have become totally unable to recognize and follow God's voice." In the explanation (p. 42) is stated: "At the same time the phrase 'We are unable . . .' expresses that there is no natural knowledge of God." Further is added: "The question as to how far and in which respect we may speak of a revelation of God in nature, is left unanswered." Miskotte discusses the difficult problem of *theologia* and (or) *religio naturalis* and considers it correct that *Fundamenten* does not go further into this. He himself states in this connection, "Many are inclined to deny the 'natural knowledge of God.' This does not mean that they deny that God is omnipresent and evident in 'Nature'; but it does mean that the natural man does not discover God, our King, the Father of our Lord Jesus Christ in it, but some other deity. *Objectively* considered, there is no eye and no ear, no heart and no spirit, to meet therein the God whom we confess. The composers of this proof of the confession, however, have *not* drawn this consequence" (K. H. Miskotte, *De Kern van de Zaak,* 1950, p. 36).

9. J. Koopmans, *De Nederlandse Geloofsbelijdenis,* 1939, p. 30.

revelation. "Not only is not the word, but neither the matter
of natural theology mentioned in the confession of faith, nor
in Romans 1." The point at issue is not a general knowledge
of God from nature, but God's *revelation*. However, Koopmans' favorable analysis of Article II does not hold. He considers the opening words of Article II 'unfortunate,' because
"actually, subjectively, we do not know God by two means,
but only by his Word."[10] The fact that another revelation
than the one by the Word is mentioned is only to render all
excuse impossible. In this connection Koopmans objects to the
comparative in this article ('more clearly and fully').

This comparative would make sense if Adam had *not* fallen :
the Lord revealed himself more clearly in his Word than in
'the cool (wind) of the day.' (Gen. 3:8 — A. Kuyper is very
good on this in *To Be Near Unto God*). But "it is, to say the
least, confusing to simply maintain this comparative in the situation we find ourselves in after the fall, since such a relationship between revelation in creation and revelation in Christ,
subjectively and actually, no longer exists."[11] It is evident that
Koopmans does not go along all the way with Barth, but that
he has various objections. At first he speaks of "a less fortunate formulation,"[12] but later the simile changes and he does
discover a real danger, for . . . . if the comparative remains between the "two means," also after the fall, then this always
means that some kind of a pre-form of the Christian faith must
be accepted.[13]

This danger has become more prominent especially on account of the controversy in the German church. Koopmans,
therefore, speaks of "an objection to the confession" which he
finally illustrates with the well-known confession of the *"Be-
kennende Kirche"* against the two-sources-theory. For, in
this supposedly far purer confession the false doctrine is repu-

10. *Ibid.*, p. 32.   11. *Ibid.*, p. 33.   12. *Ibid.*, p. 32.
13. *Ibid.*, p. 34. Cf. also the objections by J. Riemens, *Godsopenbaring en
Aanknopingspunt,* 1946. p. 46f.

diated that the Church, above and besides this one Word of God (Jesus Christ) could and should recognize as God's revelation also other events and powers, figures and truths, as source of her preaching.[14] And his final conclusion is that the relationship between the two means is better expressed by Calvin's well-known simile: "we can read the book of creation *through the* spectacles of Holy Scripture," than by the comparative.[15] So Koopmans does not want to oppose the confession of a revelation in creation, but he wishes to bring out the *aspect of salvation* in the knowledge of God stronger than does Article II. The confession may not have meant this knowledge by "means" of creation as a pre-form of the Christian faith; there is, however, an acute danger that natural theology may penetrate the Reformed heritage,[16] *via this comparative.*

* * *

Haitjema's reaction to Barth's criticism was sharper than Koopmans', since, according to him, this criticism is dominated by a passion which cannot have been evoked by the text of the confession, considering the history of its origin.[17] He does admit that Article II, according to present-day standards, speaks too carelessly about the two means of the knowledge of God and of the elegant book of this universe. But that does not alter the fact that the natural knowledge of God of Article II is *not* such a knowledge of God at all that would result from

14. *Ibid.*, p. 34.

15. *Ibid.*, p. 35. Cf. also A. A. van Ruler, in: *Onder Eigen Vaandel,* 1938 (Nature and Grace) p. 198, who says, that Calvin's simile is "considerably purer" than the formulation of Article II.

16. *Cf.* H. de Vos: "God's love is certainly not known from nature. De Genestet, Woutertje Pieterse, Francesco Campana e. a. bring up a real problem. We shall be less optimistic in this respect than Article II of the Confession of Faith" (*Het Vraagstuk der Natuurlijke Theologie* in N.T.T., 30st Vol., 1941, p. 251). Cf. further H. de Vos on general revelation in *Het Christelijk Geloof,* 1948, p. 21 ff, and his *De Wijsbegeerte van de Godsdienst* (Service Enc., 1950, p. 9).

17. Th. L. Haitjema, *Het "Barthiaanse" Bezwaar Tegen Artikel II der Nederlandse Geloofsbelijdenis,* in O. E. V., 1938, p. 204.

"general revelation," "but very obviously a knowledge of God, by which the triune God of revelation manifests himself to those that are called to the confession, and who can, for the purpose of this self-manifestation, in a sovereign way, make use of the universe, which he created, preserves, and rules."[18] Haitjema attempts to show, on the basis of several proofs, that Article II does not speak at all of the heathen's natural knowledge of God outside of Christ.[19] It is *believers* who are confessing here. This, however, does not solve the problem of the "we" in Article II. It is an unwarranted reducing of the problem concerning the natural knowledge of God, to "limit the scope of the word 'we' to the Western-European cultural world" (p. 208). The confession is confession of *faith* and as such is connected with the preaching. That means it belongs to its nature to let it be heard there, where people are living who never heard about Christ. That is the reason why today the problem of revelation becomes actual again. Haitjema first of all points out the sovereignty of God in choosing his means of revelation. For anyone who, with Reformed Protestantism, professes the sovereignty of the God of grace, remains the possibility of making an extraordinary usage of the first means (p. 214). The church may not go by that, but God can, by exception, make use of it. *When* he does so, no preacher of the church is present as organ, "but man, as by surprise, stands before the open book of the universe" (p. 210).

This attempt at explaining Article II is, in our opinion, absolutely unacceptable, because it is the *church* that speaks in Article II, (be it not in her direct preaching, but in any case in her *confession*), of an actual revelation of God, without showing anything at all of what Haitjema has in view, viz. the *extraordinary* self-revelation of God. To the contrary, it does not speak of an exception but of an actuality of revelation.

In the second place, Haitjema is of the opinion that general revelation is not the point at issue in Article II. We may not

---

18. *Ibid.*, p. 104.   19. *Ibid.*, p. 207.

create a kind of conception of general revelation of which general and special revelation are, as it were, certain "branches" (p. 210). When analyzing Article II the whole idea of "general revelation" must be eliminated. There is only a revelation "in a trinitarian-Christocentric sense" (p. 217). There is a certain similarity between the means of the book of the universe and the means of the Book of Scripture: "I consider them both as witness to Christ, although the first book, the book of the universe, contains only a shadowy witness concerning Christ" (p. 211). They are *both* soteriologic, "even though the voice of the first book is only the dark bass-tone of the angry justice of God" (p. 211). Haitjema himself calls his interpretation of Article II, compared with the traditional interpretation, *uncommon.*[20] But it is not only uncommon, it is totally untenable, because it inserts entirely new elements into this article of faith. Does Haitjema speak of the angry justice of God with regard to the first means, Article II speaks of the *elegant* book in which the creatures are as so many characters. It can, therefore, hardly be understood how Haitjema can speak of a soteriologic revelation and at the same time reject general revelation.

Only then Haitjema's own view becomes somewhat transparent, when he finally moves into the direction of Calvin's simile. For when he, besides dealing with the extraordinary way of God's revelation, also deals with the *ordinary* way, then he includes the *first* means "in Holy Scripture, which is a guiding tunnel," a *pathway in* the tunnel of Scripture. And thus Haitjema considers Article II still a legitimate part of the Reformed confession.

He moreover considers it logical that De Bres expressed it thus and that he apparently subscribed to the Thomistic scheme, because *the* enemies of that day were nominalism and

---

20. *Ibid.,* p. 217; cf. A. D. R. Polman, quoted work 1, p. 173, who correctly states, that Haitjema cannot prove from the sources that this was what De Bres actually meant. Moreover, this attempt is not made either.

socinianism, which sought their strength in the total denial of natural theology. The fathers simply had to defend the natural knowledge of God, "be it then by making use of a theological scheme, which, on account of the Reformed doctrine concerning man and the results of the fall, in principle was already rendered harmless" (p. 218). Also this argumentation in his analysis of Article II must be considered insufficient. For, if Reformed theology deals with God's revelation in the works of his hands, and with creation and providence, then it deliberately does *not* maintain a scheme which the professors of the *corruptio naturae* would have to pierce. It is exactly in *connection* with the corruptness of human nature that they bring up the "insufficiency" of this revelation. ˉThe question may be asked whether this qualification of God's revelation is acceptable. But one thing is certain, that with this "insufficiency" is *not* meant a criticism of God's revelation,[21] but of *man,* who, in his corruptness, was not in a position to know God truly from his works. And the theme of "without excuse" which again and again returns, indicates that their view was connected with the confession of man's *fall.*

Therefore, all we can say concerning Haitjema's defense of Article II against the "Barthian" objection is, that he has rendered this article no service. We can even imagine that this uncommon "soteriologic" interpretation could strengthen the desire of many to stigmatize the reasoning of Article II as "natural theology."

* * *

Before going further into the meaning of Article II we call your attention to Polman's judgment, who, it is true, is of the opinion that there is in Article II not a single incorrect, let alone heretical, idea, but still, when comparing this article to what Calvin says, he cannot admire its wording.[22]

---

21. To this we are referring again in our last chapter.
22. Polman, *ibid.,* I, pp. 158 and 173.

It is true, with this "we" the article places itself from the onset on the standpoint of faith, but the rich ideas developed by Calvin, "although contained in it, do not clearly and purposively come to the foreground." And finally Polman states, "It is not evident that after the fall everyone is in dire need of Scripture as his monitor and mistress in order to come to God the Creator. Only by faith, which finds God correctly and truly described in his Word, and also in the works of creation, preservation and government, the most elegant book of God's beautiful works becomes now legible" (p. 159).

Objectively, however, Polman fully agrees with Article II and he emphatically (and correctly) denies that it would be the intention of Article II to teach a natural theology on the basis of reason and *natural* revelation. We may not read in it that nature and history are clear to us without the spectacles of Scripture (p. 173).

* * *

He who attentively follows the discussion on Article II might come to think that we are dealing here with only a symbolically interesting, but dogmatically unimportant difference of interpretation, because, ultimately, we all can agree with Calvin's simile with respect to the relationship between Holy Scripture and "general revelation." Yet, there are important questions behind all these discussions, as becomes very evident with regard to Karl Barth. The issue at stake in this discussion is not simply the relationship between the two means, but the *reality* of God's revelation. People frequently proceed from the fact that the "natural knowledge" is in a sorry state and then draw conclusions in connection with revelation. And on the basis of these *negative* conclusions Article II is criticized. Therefore it is necessary to ask ourselves the question: What does the confession really intend by these 'two means'?

In the first place, it must be remembered that we are dealing with a *confession of faith,* which is apparent from the "we" with which Article II begins. Haitjema and Polman point out that De Bres' original draft did not read: "we *know* him by two means," but: "we *confess* to know him as such by two means."[23]   This must be fully taken into consideration when interpreting this article, because this determines everything that is said concerning the *means*.   This is especially related to what the confession elsewhere says concerning the authority and the significance of Holy Scripture as norm and source of our faith and life.   This refers not in the least to a natural theology, which is built up upon the light of natural reason, outside of Scripture.   Neither is meant that we can ascend *"via causalitatis"* from the things created to the *"prima Causa."* That is how the Vatican Council reasons, which, like the Confession of Faith, refers to Romans 1:20, but the former points out the relationship between *the natural light of reason* and, *the reality*.   The confession does not mention an independent knowledge by natural reason, but the reality of God's revelation which "we" know.

Yet, exactly this constitutes the problem, that Article II does not just deal with actual revelation, but with the *knowledge* of this revelation.   Many considered it precarious that, in connection with this *knowledge, two* means are mentioned. Out of vehement opposition to the two-sources-theory of a later period, it was believed that Article II breathed the same spirit, and it seemed as though in the relationship: "knowledge -revelation," creation, preservation, and providence formed an independent source from which one could freely draw as much as he wanted, without the light of Scripture.   The fact that many did not agree with this interpretation, proved at least that not all consciousness was lost of the fact that this way an *injustice* was done to the motives of Article II.   For especially in the time of the Reformation serious opposition arose against the Roman Catholic two-sources-theory (Scripture and tradition).   And had the two-sources-theory of the

---

23. "Nous confessons le cognoistre tel par deux moyens" (Bakhuizen van de Brink, *De Nederlandse Belijdenisgeschriften*, 1940, p. 60).

'*Deutsche Christen*' in Calvin's day become dangerous, then
— thus we might say — Calvin's theology and the Reformed
confession contained enough weapons for defense to fight *these*
theories of creation and providence. We are thinking especially
of Calvin's and the Reformed churches' confession that God's
providence can be truly known *only by faith in Jesus Christ*.
For this reason one must be extremely careful, when, in tur-
bulent, troubled times, amid many current problems, one brings
up a confession of the 16th century.[24] We may say, however,
as Polman did, that Calvin's beautiful thoughts with respect to
this point do not fully come to the surface in Article II. But we
must not expect a clear, dogmatic explanation in an article
of this nature. The confession's objective is not to give a dis-
sertation on general and special revelation, neither does it deal
with man's situation before and after the fall, but it does clearly mention the reality of revelation in God's handiwork. And
later on the confession evidences clearly how much it agrees
with Calvin's opinion concerning the corruption of human nature with respect to God's revelation and gifts.[25]

Moreover, we may not underestimate the significance of the
fact that it is exactly in Article II that reference is made to
Romans 1, and more specifically to Paul's statement that, because of God's revelation, man *is without excuse*.

The only question, therefore, we might ask in connection
with Article II is whether in other times — for instance ours
— it would not be possible and desirable to express the truth,
which Article II wishes to confess, in such a way that it
would be simply impossible to use, to *misuse*, this confession
for a two-sources-theory, which obscures the light of Scripture. This question could be answered in the affirmative only
when one would be fully conscious of the fact that such a
formulation may not be the result of a one-sided reaction,

24. *Cf.* also what Barth did, when he approached Groen's phrase: "It is
written; it took place" without further examination on the basis of the
German two-sources-theory. See: K. Barth, *Grundfragen*, 1935, p. 31.
25. Cf. Art. 14 of the Belgic Confession.

and that it certainly may not eliminate the very thing which
Article II, in adherence to Calvin, obviously *meant* to confess.

What, then, is it, that the confession wishes to express at
this point? The answer to this question cannot be difficult.
Article II wishes to express that there are two means by which
God can be known, *viz.* creation, preservation, and government, *and* the Divine *Word*. We could call it *deed* and Word-
revelation. It is true, these two may never be separated, because God's speaking is also his *deed*. No one will be able to
deny this, if he remembers the word of Scripture, "For he
spake, and it was done; he commanded, and it stood fast"
(Psalm 33 :9), and, "By the word of the Lord were the heavens made" (Psalm 33 :6). These relationships between Word
and deed were certainly not overlooked in the time of the Reformation. However, when subjectively they still differentiated
between Word revelation and deed revelation, they meant to
designate by these two words, on the one hand, the works of
God's hands in their creaturely reality, and on the other hand,
the spoken and audible Word of God, by which alone we can
rightly understand God's activity.[26] For this reason Article II
did not speak of an isolated "nature" in order to thus draw
a marked border between "nature" and "history," but of "creation, preservation, and government of the universe." This
designates the creating and continuing activity of God in
all things. And this universe, according to Article II, is before
our eyes as a most elegant book, wherein all creatures, great
and small, are as so many characters. It is very dubious
whether it is correct as Haitjema states, that here, "with respect
to the present epoch, far too carelessly is spoken about the
most elegant book" of the universe. It will be very difficult
to read into Article II belief in a harmonious, undisturbed

---

26. *Cf.* Polman, *Ibid., I*, p. 156, and K. Schilder, *Christus in Zijn Lijden
II* 1930, p. 42ff, on general revelation and common grace in their relationship to special revelation and grace. Also his sermon on "The Wise Men
from the East and the Word of God" (*Om Woord en Kerk* I, 1948, p.
20ff.).

universe, as Leibniz entertained it. Also in the time when
Article II originated, one could be shaken by God's curse upon
the world, and by suffering and death. The "beauty" of
which Article II is speaking must remind us far more of
Psalm 8 than of a "mood" as of the Stoics or . . . Leibniz!
No aesthetic conception of nature or creature is speaking here,
but a confession is made of God's manifest activity in creation,
preservation, and government of the universe.

And if we — under the impression of the danger of two-
sources-theories — should for a moment shrink from *this* positive speaking of God's universal activity, then we shall have
to remember, that in the time of the Reformation there was,
and could be, spoken of this universal activity of God, because
God's *special* Word had been understood and believed. Maybe
the day is not far away anymore, when the meaning and import
of Article II will be appreciated again, and then not as a
falling back into a natural theology but as a confessing of
the majesty and goodness of him who is not the hidden God,
but the God who reveals himself in such an abundance of
evidence, that this glory can be passed by only out of utter
blindness.[27]

Also the comparative in Article II will have to be understood in this light: "more clearly and fully by his holy and
divine Word." Especially this comparative is frequently considered to be the real weak spot in this article. It must be
remembered, however, that the confession deals with God's
revelation on the basis of the "we" and that this revelation of
God is said to come to us more clearly and fully by God's
Word. So, this does not in the least imply that there would
already be a sufficient and true knowledge from the first
means, which would only have to be somewhat *supplemented*
and *completed* by the second means. This has obviously not

27. *Cf.* Dr. A. Kuyper's meditation in *Nabij God te Zijn* (*To Be Near
Unto God*) on Psalm 18:10 and on Matt. 11:27 ("and he to whomsoever
the Son will reveal him").

been the implication of Article II, because the comparative *does not refer to the knowledge itself, but to God's revelation.* This explains how Calvin, whose simile of the spectacles is quoted so often *against* Article II, *also* knows the comparative of Article II.

Calvin first of all places great emphasis on God's revelation by which he has revealed himself "in the entire structure of the universe, in such a way, and daily presents himself so openly therein, that men simply must see him whenever they open their eyes."[28] He has engraved[29] the unmistakable marks of his glory upon each and everyone of his works, so that all pretenses of ignorance are prevented. The Lord clearly manifests both himself and his immortal kingdom in the mirror of his works.[30] But . . . we cannot conclude the presence of real knowledge from this revelation. It is true, God's lamps are lighted in the structure of this universe, but "in vain" they beam forth their light.[31] *Of themselves* they are altogether insufficient to lead us into the right path.[32] Calvin determinedly rejects every possible excuse[33] by reminding us of the effulgence "which is presented to every eye both in the heavens and on the earth."[34] There is only one way by which we can come to the Creator of the universe, namely "because another and better help is added,"[35] viz. the light of his *Word.* Calvin is not yet speaking here of the fall of the world and the corruption of nature. He discusses God's revelation to man in paradise, and points out that God has acted *and* spoken. It is here that the comparative fits into Calvin's thinking. But the remarkable thing is that, in this connection, he urges "in the first place to give ear to the Word."[36]

We must proceed on the basis of the *heavenly* teaching and we must consider it thus, "that no one can obtain even the least taste of the right and sound doctrine but he, who has

28. *Institutes* I, V. 1.   29. *Ibid.*   30. *Ibid.*, I, V, 11.   31. *Ibid.*, 14.
32. *Ibid.*   33. *Ibid.*, 15.   34. *Inst.* I, VI, 1.
35. *Ibid.*, (here Calvin also mentions the glasses).
36. *Ibid.*, 2

been a student of Scripture."[37] God foresaw that his image, imprinted in the most elegant form of the universe, would be insufficient.[38] "We must go, I say, to the Word, wherein the character of God, drawn from his works, is described accurately and to the life, these works being estimated, not by our depraved judgment, but by the standard of eternal truth."[39]

Article II of the *Confessio Belgica* and the *Confessio Gallicana* can be fully understood by following Calvin's line of thought in this matter. The confessor is not speaking here of what he already could achieve and *has* achieved by the natural light of reason, in order to further add to this, as a "complement," the knowledge received from the Word. But he considers the knowledge of God as an indivisible quantity. It is the knowledge of the God, whom article I has already confessed. And on the basis of what has been confessed concerning the two means and their comparative relationship, it tries to give an account of God's manifest activity in the works of his hands, which was truly seen and known only because of the Word-revelation. Therefore, there is actually no essential difference between Article II and Calvin's view. We may, and must, emphatically protest against any two-sources-theory, which places Scripture and tradition, or Scripture and nature, or Scripture and history, on one line, as sources of knowledge *of equal import*. Any such equalization has always resulted in a devaluation of Holy Scripture. But also every attempt to prove, on the basis of fallen mankind's blinded eyes, that God has revealed himself only by his Word, and not already in the works of his hands, must be rejected.

Over against this essentially subjectivistic conclusion, which considers *revelation in the light of knowledge,* it is necessary to see and acknowledge the meaning of Article II. Doing this does not in the least result in a song of praise for natural man and the natural light of his reason. That there is a danger of such praise is not just imaginary, but must be openly recog-

37. *Ibid.*   38. *Inst.* I, VI, 3.   39. *Ibid.*

nized. It cannot be denied that in certain circles there is evidence of a *peculiar enthusiasm* for Article II,[40] which should warn us to be very much on our guard. It simply is a fact that one can read Romans 1:20 in the decrees of the Vatican Council as well as in the confession! And it would be possible to find it quoted also in "modern" confessions, which like to *proceed from* the particular to the general and universal. Therefore, the test of, and motive for, accepting Article II should always be: what is the meaning it wishes to convey? The *nature* of the song of praise on general revelation is all-deciding. And only he who takes heed lest he fall will be able to speak with a deep sense of responsibility of the legitimacy of Article II having its place in the realm of the Reformed heritage.

---

40. We observe that, among others, with A. H. Hartog, who frequently refers to Article II of the Confession. See: *Korte Samenvatting van Mijn Theologisch Onderzoek,* 1926, p. 9, and his Christendom, 1922, pp. 36 and 61. Cf. p. 74 on Romans 1:20. De Hartog shifts the entire picture of general and special revelation, namely as he himself states, that the traditional differentiation, in order to remain tenable, must be *shifted* (*Christendom,* p. 62). *The same* shifting is evident in De Hartog's statement, "The indeterminately promoted doctrine, that 'the human mind is darkened by sin', therefore, calls, at this point, for a necessary revision" (*Christendom,* p. 37).

Universality and Particularity

CHAPTER XI

Universality and Particularity

I N THIS CHAPTER we desire to arrive at summary conclusions on the subjects of our discussion. As has been mentioned earlier, the point of departure must be the fact that all our knowledge concerning general revelation is based upon, indeed, *must* be based upon, the Holy Scriptures. That surely does not mean to say that we arrive at a technical knowledge of nature through the Holy Scriptures or that they are the proper source for our knowledge in the natural sciences.

We have in mind only that, in the most profound sense, no true knowledge of the revelation of God in the works of his hands is obtainable without faith in Christ. Calvin's reference to the glasses (of faith) as the only means whereby we can know God in this book of "nature," is of decisive significance for all reflection on general revelation. This is not a question of our knowledge of nature as such, but rather of our knowledge of God's self-revelation. Stated otherwise, in Dogmatics general revelation is not to be regarded (in isolation) as an independent object of study. Reflection on dogma is in principle different from activity in the natural sciences.

If, however, the revelation of God in the works of his hands can be known only by the illumination of Scripture, then the question arises whether there is any sense to speaking of such a general revelation. It is very significant, in this very connection, that the confessions certainly do not treat general revelation in great detail. Schlink comments, in one place, that the confessional documents are "remarkably uninterested" in the questions concerning a natural knowledge of God and all that pertains thereto. And then he poses the question: Must Dogmatics today break with the reserve (restraint) of the confessions on this point? Is it necessary now to develop a special doctrine of the revelation of God in his works in addition to the doctrine of the revelation of God in Jesus Christ? In reply, Schlink says: "Our answer to this question must be *no*." Indeed, he emphatically rejects a separate doctrine of such a general revelation of God, and he holds that in our dogmatizing it is sufficient to speak of the full riches of the special revelation of God in Jesus Christ who, after all, has revealed the Father unto us.[1] Simple and translucent as this solution may seem to be, it is, however, a one-sided way of thinking on the problem. The issue is not that the revelation of God in Jesus Christ is inadequate and hence we must resort to a more general revelation; rather it is a matter of the light which the revelation of Jesus Christ, and a corresponding knowledge of faith, sheds on the universal actions of God in created reality. The relationship between general and special revelation is not a competitive one; but in special revelation our attention is focused on the universality of God's actions in relation to (the plan of) salvation and the Kingdom of God. It is precisely this salvation of the Lord which calls forth a song of praise about the works of God's hands, indeed, this hymn of praise is a part of that salvation. When we speak of the general revelation of God, then we are concerned with this universality of God's actions in created reality.

* * *

This brings us to a point which has, in our opinion, been neglected too much in thinking on the problem of general

---

1. E. Schlink, "Die Offenbarung Gottes in seinen Werken und die Ablehnung der natürlichen Theologie" in *Theol. Blätter*, Vol. XX, 1941, pp. 1 and 5. *Cf.* also Schlinck, *Theol. der luth. Bekenntnisschriften*, 1948, 3rd ed., pp. 67 ff.

revelation. It is true there is much evidence that general revelation has been viewed in close connection with God's universal activity, of which the Church makes profession in article XIII on the Providence of God; in practice, however, this has frequently been restricted to a discussion of the general revelation of God in nature. This is evident from the fact that in the past "natural" revelation was distinguished from "supernatural" revelation, by which was meant that the *first* revelation came to us through "nature." In consequence, reflection on the doctrine of general revelation was frequently restricted to the so-called nature-psalms. Thus a distinction was made between a revelation of grace and one of nature, and accordingly between natural and supernatural religion.[2] "Nature" was then isolated from the totality of created reality and it was regarded as *the* area of the general revelation of God.[3] This view of general revelation as being "nature revelation" often played an important role in the discussions about the relationship between theology and science. On this view the *Holy Scriptures* were regarded as the book of the *special* revelation of God and *nature* (with or without an appeal to Article II) as the book of general revelation. It was thought that both theology and natural science were concerned with the revelation of God, theology dealing with special revelation and natural science with general revelation. Thus Schouten speaks of general revelation as "God's revelation in the realm

---

2. *Cf.* H. Heppe, *Die Dogmatic der evang. ref. Kirche,* 1861, p. 4 ff. *Cf.* the distinction between "natural revelation and divine revelation in Sergius Bulgakoff" in *Revelation* (G. Aulen, K. Barth, *et al,* 1937, p. 132 and 138). This same confusion becomes evident when Bulgakoff speaks of "natural revelation or paganism" in connection with the reaction of man. (p. 135).

3. *Cf.* A. Schweizer, *Die Glaubenslehre der evang. reform. Kirche* I, 1844, p. 241. "Man is prepared for revealed religion by the pious contemplation of the world of nature in which by reflection the natural attributes of God may be recognized."

of nature,"[4] and he places "nature" and "scripture" side by side.[5] From this it follows that in the main we owe our knowledge of the revelation of God in nature to the natural sciences.[6] And the distinction between general and special revelation is then interpreted as follows: On the one hand, special revelation governs our life and world view (*wereldbeschouwing*), but it does not present us with a complete picture of reality; on the other hand general revelation affords us a cosmic picture (*wereldbeeld*), but leaves us without a life and world view.[7] Our picture of the world is, we are told, our knowledge of general revelation, given by God in *nature*.[8] Thus we have two revelations (existing side by side) and both of these possess absolute authority, since they are two independent sources of God's revelation.[9] This point of view creates the impression that our knowledge of nature is as it were automatically also a knowledge of *God's revelation*. Thus Schouten writes that the study of *God's general revelation in nature* has led to important discoveries concerning the age of the earth[10] and that "in his general revelation" God acquaints us with the form and measurement which he gave to the universe.[11] However, this view ignores the fact that it will not do simply to equate the knowledge of nature with the knowledge of God's general

---

4. W. J. A. Schouten, *De Verhouding van algemene en bijzondere Openbaring.* Chr. Vereeniging voor Natuur-en Geneeskunde 1927, p. 91. Cf. also J. Lever, *Het Soortbegrip en de levende structuren,* 1950: "Besides absolute respect for God's word-revelation, only an absolute respect for God's nature revelation can guard us against such errors," (p. 18), and J. Lever, "Geloof en Wetenschap bij Lijsenko": (*Geloof en Wetenschap,* 1950, p. 182): First of all we shall have to have respect for the facts of nature (God's creation revelation). J. Verseveldt also speaks of "the relationship between the divine revelation in Scripture and nature" (*Geloof en Wetenschap,* 1950, p. 152). (*Bezinning* 1950, p. 142).

5. Schouten, p. 94.   6. *Ibid.,* p. 94.   7. *Ibid.,* p. 96.
8. *Ibid.,* p. 97.
9. *Cf.* the statement of Hooykaas: "Christian faith acknowledges two independent sources of revelation: Scripture and Nature" ("Science, Materialism and Christianity": *Free University Quarterly,* 1950, p. 60).
10. *The Relation between General and Special Revelation,* p. 103.
11. *Ibid.,* p. 97.

revelation, for this revelation deals with the knowledge of God *himself*. In our opinion, therefore, it is wrong to say, as is sometimes done, that the natural sciences "investigate" God's general revelation;[12] and surely it is just as wrong to state that we owe our knowledge of God's revelation in nature primarily to the natural sciences.[13] This, it seems to us, is a toning down of the idea and the reality of revelation, although that certainly is not intended. And we, of course, acknowledge wholeheartedly that it is our calling to investigate respectfully God's handiwork. But the revelation of God in his works is a matter of God's self-revelation, and that is not apprehended first of all by scientific investigation, but through faith, as is evident already in the Psalms of Israel. These psalms of praise are not based on scientific investigation; rather the God of salvation is praised in these hymns in all his greatness and glory. In general revelation we are not dealing with an independent source of knowledge; on the contrary, by faith we understand the act of divine revelation in created reality. The so-called nature psalms are not concerned with the concept "nature" of the natural sciences; but they reveal the insight of faith into the works of God's hands. Consequently, the nature-psalms never deal with abstract aspects of cosmic reality, but rather with naive (in the good sense of the word) reality. That also accounts for the fact that in this outlook nature is never divorced from living history, in dynamic movement, as is especially evident in Psalm 33,[14] but even in Psalm 104, that nature-psalm *par excellence*.[15]

---

12. *Ibid.*, p. 94. *Cf.* (Calvin on history): J. Bohatec. "Gott und die Geschichte nach Calvin," *Philo. Reformata* I, p. 149: "Revelation and history are not of equal value and significance." "History as such is not revelation, it is only the place and means of revelation."

13. *Ibid.*, p. 94.

14. *Cf.* 33:10 (the counsels of the peoples and the thoughts of the nations); verse 13 (all mankind) verse 16 (King and war).

15. *Cf.* Psalm 104:14 about the relationship of cosmic reality to man (herb, bread, wine).

The question is never one of the knowledge of nature *an sich* (itself), but it is a question of the glory of God or of what Paul calls *his* eternal power and divinity. Therefore one must proceed with extreme caution along the path of "nature" and "natural science," lest he arrive at a view of revelation in which the living and personal God is concealed behind the knowledge of nature. Even he who fully acknowledges the revelation of God in "nature," or rather in the total cosmic reality, will not be able to grant that the natural sciences, and they in particular, deal with general revelation.

* * *

A pointer in the right direction is provided by Article II of our confession (previously discussed from another aspect) which does indeed speak of a universal revelation, but then as a means of knowing God, and which the creed further defines as being, *"through the creation, maintenance, and governance of the entire world."* *This* world, as it appears in the acts of God, and as it is an object of the activity of God, is then referred to as a book in which all creatures have a place. It is clear that in *this* description we can hardly recognize nature in the duality of "nature" and "scripture." Neither is "nature" here isolated from "history" and we can hardly over-estimate the significance of the words of Article II (*creation, maintenance and governance*). For we are here confronted with the doings of God, of which we profess — in faith — that *these activities are not hidden or concealed.* This action is not a mysterious happening in the "darkness" of the unapproachable light, but it is an activity within created reality which is directed toward fellowship with, and knowledge of, him who personally acts here in a divinely sovereign manner.[16] The

---

16. In the first edition of the *Belgic Confession* of 1561 we read: "par le monde créé, conduite et gouverné." In 1582: "by the creation, direction and governance of the entire world," (direction) again becomes: preservation. *Cf.* J. J. van Toorenenbergen, *De symb. Geschriften der Ned. Herv. Kerk,* 1869, p. 6 and Bakhuizen v. d. Brink, *De Ned. Belijd. schriften,* 1940, p. 60.

fact that this activity of God in created reality is not *observed* and *acknowledged* is not originally due to the essential incomprehensibility of this activity of God, but to the radical darkening of the human heart which did, and does still, withdraw itself from a full communion with him, who is very close to the world in all his actions.   Opposing the idea of a hidden and distant God, the Holy Scriptures bring the explicit message that God is not very far from each and every one of us (Acts 17:27).   The formulation of Article II is also wholly in accord with the message of Acts 14, namely that "God left not himself without witness in that he did good and gave you from heaven rains and fruitful seasons, filling your hearts with food and gladness" (Acts 14:17).   God witnesses, reveals himself *in* (his) gifts.[17]   Here, too, we are not concerned with a nature-revelation in its own right, but it is a matter of the divine self-revelation in cosmic reality which is directed towards man.

Nor does the *Belgic Confession* deal with an isolated "nature," but its confession is that God reveals himself through *creation, preservation,* and *governance* of the universe.[18]   Thus attention is not focused upon "nature" as a *special* area of general revelation, but upon the universal activity of God. Precisely in this way it is possible to get away from the distinction between natural and supernatural revelation.   By limiting general revelation to "nature," which is, moreover, seldom rigidly defined, the entire history of the world would vanish from our perspective, unless one would be prepared to merge that history entirely with the plan and history of salvation. Accordingly, general revelation is much more extensive in

---

17. *Cf.* Grosheide commentary on Acts 14:17.
18. "Ce Dieu se manifeste tel aux hommes: premièrement par ses oeuvres tant par la création que par la conservation et conduite d' icelles." Muller, *Bekenntnisschriften,* 1903, p. 221.   *Cf.* in this connection Calvin in his exegesis of Psalm 19:1, where the poet mentions the heavens, which Calvin regards as a *selection:* "non tamen dubium est quin sub nobilissima parte et cuius excellentia magis conspicua est, totum mundi opificium per synecdochen designet." (*Comm. in Psalmos,* Ed. Tholuck, p. 134).

scope than "nature" revelation, although quite obviously "nature," in the non-scientific sense of the term, also belongs to the reality in which God reveals himself.[19] Indeed, it is utterly impossible to isolate and abstract this "nature" from the totality of cosmic reality as if it were a part of cosmic reality which could be studied apart from *history* and from *man*. The nature aspect of reality is inseparably linked up with history and human existence. To appeal to the so-called nature psalms in support of general revelation is undoubtedly justified, but this nature is not an abstract nature, detached from the totality of relationships within cosmic reality. And the (bold) stroke of the Reformed Confessions in not relinquishing, but rather in retaining this outlook on the universal actions of God, we may regard as extremely fortunate and theologically sound.[20]

* * *

Only from a scriptural point of view can the relationship between general and special revelation be rightly understood; only then is it possible to oppose all sorts of dangers which have continually threatened the church and theology. For in this manner general and special revelation do not stand beside or opposite each other as a duality in a relationship of rivalry and competition (the natural and the supernatural), but they find their unity in the sovereign activity of God. Nor

19. *Cf.* Sunday X, which includes under preservation and governance: herb and grass, rain and drought, fruitful and unfruitful years, etc.

20. Bavinck breaks very clearly with the limitation of general revelation to "nature": "All that is and takes place is the work of God in the real sense of the word, and to the believer it is a revelation of his virtues and perfections. Thus the Scriptures view nature and history. Creation, preservation and governance are one mighty continuing revelation of God" (*Geref. Dogmatiek* I, p. 278). *Cf.* also pp. 281-2: "Nature and history are the book of God's power and wisdom, of His goodness and righteousness." General revelation is frequently spoken of as "the book of nature" (W. H. Gispen, *De Geloofsbelijdenis der Ned. Gel. Bel.*, 1932, p. 16), but this does not signify a limitation to abstract "nature." Gispen speaks of 1. nature; 2. history; 3. conscience.

is it possible to do justice to this distinction by abstract reasoning from a concept of revelation in general and then proceeding to special revelation as the logical individuation of this general revelation.   Such logical deduction certainly never was the intent of Reformed theology.   The distinction between "general" and "special" revelation is related to the fact that the universal activity of God is seen to manifest a revelatory activity of God which extends to the entire world and to all men. Whether or not the designation "general revelation" is the clearest and best is certainly open to dispute.   Korff says that "it is not very fortunate" and he adds: "Revelation *qua talis* (as such) will no doubt always be "special.""[21]   General revelation, according to Korff, "unconsciously suggests something at rest, something static."

As a matter of fact, this danger is not at all imaginary, and in discussions on general revelation in "nature" men sometimes lose sight of the living and personal God who reveals himself sovereignly and mightily; and thus they make the indentification: nature = revelation; and thus the natural sciences which investigate nature are regarded as investigating *God's revelation* and in this way arriving at the knowledge of God.   Nevertheless Korff admits that it is not easy to arrive at another, altogether satisfactory designation.[22]   He has objections to the term *"grond-openbaring"* (basic revelation) or creation-revelation, and he concludes: "We retain the name while emphasizing the right interpretation."[23]   According to this interpretation "general" signifies "that this speaking of God is always and everywhere present";[24] and this dogma of general revelation he regards as being "without doubt a sound biblical idea."[25] In our opinion it is possible to eliminate all misunderstanding by speaking of general revelation which is inseparably tied

21. F. W. A. Korff, *Het Christelijk geloof en de niet-Christelijke godsdiensten,* 1946, p. 71. *Cf.* also F. W. A. Korff, "Openbaring" (*Vox. Theol.* 1940, p. 73: "The expression 'general' revelation is most unfortunate: revelation is never general, but always it is personal."
22. Korff, 71.   23. *Ibid.,* 72.   24. *Ibid.,* 71.   25. *Ibid.,* 72

in with the preserving and providentially governing activity of God, and the universal character of this activity is such that no one is left without witness. Therein lies the "general" character of this revelation of God.

Accordingly, we are confronted with the important question of the relationship between the universality and the particularity of the actions of God. To all intents and purposes the Christo-monistic view of revelation focuses its attention exclusively on the particular, concrete and historically limited activity of God in his election of Israel, in the forming of the people of God, on prophecy as *Hinweis* (a pointer) and *Erwartung* (expectation) and above all else on the activity of God in the incarnation. This particularity alone, most profoundly the appearance of "God himself" in the flesh, was related to the revelation of God. Only there did God *actually* become manifest. The basis for determining the modality of revelation was in the flesh of Jesus Christ. This modality was the modality of the cross, i.e., of the *mystery* in revelation and of the *revelation* in mystery.

It seemed as if this manner of speaking and thinking was in line with the Holy Scriptures, which, after all, also speak of the "revelation of mystery" (Romans 16:25). But essentially something different was meant. For they began to speak about the hidden God, who hid himself in the (act of) revelation, for the express purpose of placing men before the decision of faith. This dialectic between mystery and revelation has continually governed all discussion, also that on general revelation. The modality of revelation was determined by *that* revelation which had become necessary through the fall and perdition of the human race; moreover man's knowledge and acceptance of his situation sometimes became the basis for construing revelation.

Therein lies the basic reason for the opposition of many to so-called direct revelation and general revelation, which are then posited over against the indirect revelation in mystery, which was regarded as the *only* possibility of a God-revelation. As we have previously observed, revelation and the atonement were identified by some, and in this way they arrived at a "theology of the cross" which gave expression to a concept of revelation having its center in the humiliation and in the cross. The "theology of the cross" was posited over against the "theology of glory," supported in particular by an appeal to Paul and, in the history of dogma, to Luther.   Whoever objects to such a view of revelation, is certainly not left in the position of having to minimize the absolute significance of the cross.   For this "indirect" view of revelation was not concerned with honoring only the cross of Christ, but rather a particular theological methodology which was intimately related to a special fixed concept of revelation, the proponents of which appealed especially to the contrast between foolishness and wisdom as made by Paul in I Corinthians 1.   God revealed his inscrutable wisdom exclusively in the foolishness of the cross: "The foolishness of God is wiser than men and the weakness of God is stronger than men" (I Cor. 1:25).   God, they said, *never* reveals himself directly, visibly, as wisdom and power, but *always* indirectly, in the weakness and darkness of flesh (the Word has become flesh), and in the mystery of the cross.   In this world his revelation is never a visible given, immediately cognizable and recognizable, but it is always simultaneously the veiling, the concealing of God (Golgotha).   Hence it is not as though God first remained hidden, thereafter to remove the shroud of mystery, substituting for it his becoming manifest, his self-revelation.   No, the cross reveals and conceals at the same time and therein lies the tension which must be overcome each time again in faith, and that in contrast with the Jews who are offended by the cross, and with the Greeks, for whom the cross is foolishness. Thus it is not simply a matter of the message of the cross as the *content* of the Gospel, but the cross as an *epistemological principle,* a guideline for the methodology of dogmatics, and a

pointer to the indirectness and (the incomprehensibility) of
revelation. The "theology of the cross" is not merely dogmatizing upon the cross as the atoning act of God,[26] but it is a way
of thinking which proceeds from the cross as *the* form of revelation, and in consequence of which all the relations between
man and the divine revelation receive their stamp. Barth,
especially, has developed this "theology of the cross."[27]

This theology is closely bound up with the fact that God
reveals himself in created reality. The creature then becomes
"the representative of the objective existence (*Gegenständlich-
keit*) of God," but by virtue of this the creature also hides or
veils God. "While God makes himself visible to us through
them, he tolerates the fact that he remains invisible as the one
he really is, and as he is known to himself. And he becomes
known to us, he becomes alienated from and untrue to his real
self in the very means and symbols which he employs."[28] Therefore all revelation is at the same time *humiliation,* as is evident
in the cross of the *man* Jesus Christ: "It is precisely the humanity of Jesus Christ which signifies in the highest degree
the humiliation and the self-effacement of God whereby that
which distinguishes him from all creatures remains invisible,

26. This line of thinking one finds in Bernhard Steffen, who developed a
program of stauro-centric theology (*stauros,* cross), which is concerned
with the cross as a historical fact. (B. Steffen, *Kreuz und Gewissheit,* 1929).
27. There is a great deal of literature on the theology of the cross, notably
in connection with the *deus absconditus* in Luther. We mention only W. v.
Loewenich, *Luthers theologica crucis,* 1929; H. A. v. Bakel, "Theologie des
kruises," (in *Circa Sacra,* 1935, pp. 330 ff.); F. Kattenbusch, *Der ver-
borgene Gott bei Luther (Festschrift für Kaftan)*; Theod. Harnack,
Luthers Theologie, 1927, I, 84 v; general works: G. Stählin, *Skandalon,*
1930; K. Schilder, "Skandalon," *G. Th. T.* 1931; G. C. Berkouwer,
"Theologie des Kruises," *Calvin, Weekblad* Vol. I, October 4, 11, 18. Van
Bakel writes: "The profession of the mystery of God is the heart of the
theologia crucis (p. 343). Schilder correctly points out, that the *skandalon*
may not be restricted to the coming into the flesh of Christ, but that everything which comes from God, and makes that its pretension, encounters
the resistance of the natural man and can thus become *skandolon. Op.
cit.,* p. 124); cf. also K. Schilder, *Heid. Catech.* III, pp. 317 ff.
28. K. Barth, *K. D.* II, I, 1940, p. 59. Cf. *K. D.* I, I, 175 and I, I, 338
concerning *deus absconditus* and *deus revelatus.*

and his self-existence becomes veiled in that of the creature which is wholly other from him." To be sure, God manifests his glory in this way, but "one must not overlook the fact, that as he reveals it, he also *conceals* it." Faith only can behold this mystery of revelation, but that means: "Revelation takes place for the believer, not for the unbeliever."[29] In this way the revelation of God consistently has reference to his humiliation and "self-alienation" and it is clear that Barth's thinking here is governed by his view of the foolishness and weakness of the cross. For Barth the foolishness and weakness of I Corinthians 1 does not refer to what *men* regard as weakness and foolishness,[30] (viewed from the wisdom of the world!) but it refers to the modality of revelation, so that God reveals himself in a "form which he himself is not." Consequently, "he remains hidden from us precisely in his divine existence and essence" (*gerade im Sein und Wesen seiner Gottheit verborgen*).[31] The instrumentality or agency whereby God reveals himself is simultaneously the instrument which conceals him, and which creates the possibility of offense in this "sacramental reality."[32]

Clearly, on this basis of this view of revelation in which revelation and "self-alienation" are linked inseparably together, Barth cannot have an eye for "general revelation" as it is represented in the Scriptures.[33] For this *Welthaftigkeit* (revela-

---

29. *Ibid.*, p. 60.
30. K. Barth, *K. D.* II, I, p. 56. Schilder rightly criticizes Stählin for saying in his *Skandalon* that the *skandalon*-idea is blurred even in those scripture passages which speak of the *sound* doctrine, and likewise in Hebrews 2:10, "it *behooved* him," etc. (K. Schilder, *op. cit.*, p. 111).
31. K. Barth, *K. D.* II, I, p. 63; *cf.* p. 64: "that as ego (*ich*) he at the same time remains unknown to us.
32. *K. D.* II, 1, p. 60.
33. Barth's view on the instruments of revelation may be designated as his doctrine of the *Welthaftigkeit* of revelation (*K. D.* I, 1, pp. 171 ff.). According to Barth this *Welthaftigkeit* means that the occurrence of God's revelation is *nowhere* and *never* distinguished (set apart) from all other (natural) events in such a way, that it might not instantly be interpreted as being a part of those other events. (church and sociological unit; preaching and declamation; sacrament and symbol; Bible and other docu-

tion is indistinguishable from natural events, it is "earth-bound" or "earthly") is consistently Barth's point of departure in his approach to God's revelation, the nature of which is accordingly paradoxical and contradictory (insofar as it related to created reality).[34]

However, it cannot be denied, that the Holy Scriptures speak much more plainly; they tell us of the majesty and eternal power of God which comes to man so undeniably (in created reality), that man is left without excuse. The problem of revelation and concealment, as it is posed by Barth, does not appear *thus* in either the Scriptures or in the revelation of Christ, because what the Scriptures state about the offense of the cross is inseparably connected with the antithesis toward the wisdom of the world.[35]

---

ments; Christ and other religious teachers; "The veil is closed. We do not possess the Word except it be in the mystery of its *Welthaftigkeit*." *K. D.* I, 1, p. 171. It is, therefore, *always* a question of the modality of revelation in connection with the *instrumentality* of revelation. "We always possess it in a form, which is *not* per sé (*als solche*) the Word of God, and it does not per sé disclose the fact that it is indeed the form (Gestalt) of the Word of God." Subsequently, Barth expresses himself even more poignantly: This form is "not a suitable, but rather it is an unsuitable agency for the manifestation of God. It does not corroborate, but it rather contradicts that manifestation; it does not reveal, but it conceals (*K. D.* I, p. 172). Barth does indeed relate this to the *fallen cosmos,* but this adds nothing new to his argument, and Barth goes on to say concerning the *Welthaftigkeit* of revelation: "It (the cosmos) is no more capable of revealing God to us, than we for our part are capable of recognizing God in it. Whenever God's word becomes manifest in it, then that certainly takes place "through it," but in such a way, that "through it" also means "in spite of it." (*K. D.* I, 1, pp. 172-3). The main objection to this argumentation can be summarized in an objection to the recurrence of this *"an sich,"* which is nothing more than an abstraction, an abstracting from the actions of the living, majestic God.

---

34. Barth's view on revelation and concealment also affects Christology as is evident, among other things, in his *K. D.* I, 2. pp. 161 ff. in connection with the assumption of human nature by Christ.

35. Without desiring to go into detail at this point, we call attention to the significance of the miracles of Jesus in connection with the Christological incognito, *cf.* Jerôme Hamer, *Karl Barth, L'occasionalisme théologique de Karl Barth,* 1949, pp. 35 ff. The simplicity of the Holy Scriptures comes

The possibility of the cross being an offense to some by no means implies that — due to the instrumentality of its communication — God's revelation is in essence hidden or concealed. That mystery is related to the fact that now — in the present lost state of the world — *God pursues this pathway of atonement*.[36] In this way God has made the wisdom of the world to be foolishness (I Corinthians 1:20). *This* foolishness of God is wiser than men, and *this* weakness of God is stronger than men. It is altogether unjustifiable to determine the nature of all of God's revelation on the basis of *this* propitiative act of God in Jesus Christ. For *this* act, this *modality* of revelation, *this humiliation* is aimed at guilt and alienation. This propitiation presumes alienation from the glory of God, that glory in which he revealed himself in communion with man. And in this communion he did not hide himself, nor was hidden by the creatureliness of the instruments of revelation, but he revealed himself in inseparable fidelity to his words and deeds. Those who do not bear this in mind make the cross the normal modality of revelation and they no longer realize that the particularity of this revelation in Christ does not imply that (before sin) the world was without revelation and lay inaccessibly hidden in the mystery of darkness. They do not understand that in the particularity of his gracious revelation God comes to destroy the illusion of sin, which denied the

---

into sharp focus when they point out the hardening of the heart which is confronted with the miracles of Christ. The marveling of the disciples at Jesus' walking on the sea is explained as follows: "For they had not given heed to the miracle of the loaves for their hearts were hardened" (Mark 6:52). One must have this utterance clearly in mind in order to see how different it is from the theology of the cross in reference to the instruments of revelation. Nothing less than this delineation of a personal hardening precludes both a subjective view of revelation and the "unsuitability" of its instruments for the *power* of the revelation of God.

36. In Luther this element plays an important role. His opposition to the *theologia gloriae* is opposition to those who ignore the cross and seek by speculation to arrive at a true knowledge of God. *Cf.* v. Bakel, *op. cit.*, p. 341 and 344; Th. Harnack, *op. cit.*, I, p. 87.

revelation of God in communion with man, and continues to oppose that fellowship in perpetual enmity.

In treating the subject of the providence of God one needs to be very much on his guard. Even as we write this, we are aware of the danger of human arrogance which desires to fathom the will of God and which does not want to acknowledge the total dependence of man on God's revelation. But this danger may not prevent us from bringing into sharp focus the fact that one can also treat the mystery of God while fleeing from his mighty revelation; the revelation in which he governs and manipulates the instruments of his revelation so majestically and sovereignly that they do *not conceal* him as he reveals himself in them. The proponents of the "mystery of revelation" are on dangerous ground when they *appeal* to the *Scriptures, viz.,* to Romans 16:25. That verse is not in the least concerned with a dialectical tension between revelation and mystery, but it deals with an aspect of *history,* to wit, that the mystery which has been kept in silence through times eternal, but *now* is manifested.[37] This is not a matter of revelation and mystery in a state of great tension, but it is a question of the historically redemptive deeds of God continuing in the fullness of time.

We certainly do not mean to suggest that every reference to the mystery of God stems from this view of the creatureliness of the instruments of revelation. For the *Scriptures* do speak of God who *conceals* himself. But this concealment is never one which can be construed *on the basis of a particular construction or modality of revelation.* For in the Scriptures God hides (conceals) himself in his wrathful judgment against *sin.* Of this we read in Psalm 51 where the psalmist prays: "Hide thy face from my sins" (Psalm 51:9) and this agrees in substance with that other prayer: "Hide not thy face from

---

37. Cf. also Col. 1:26 and Eph. 3:9. Barth in his *Römerbrief* comes to the conclusion that Romans 16:25-27 "is not of Pauline origin" (pp. 506-508). In his *Kirchl. Dogmatik* I, I, 1932, p. 122, however, this passage is quoted in a discussion on revelation. In other writers the appeal to Romans 16:25 plays an important role in reflection on revelation and mystery.

me" (Psalm 27:9; cf. 69:17; 102:2; 143:7). These and many similar expressions most certainly do not express an idea of concealment or mystery which must be inseparably related to the overall concept of revelation (*met de structuur der Openbaring*). They are concerned with a very concrete, dynamically active and holy attitude of God; it is not the essential modality of revelation to which they refer, but to the revelation of God's *wrath*. Thus God himself speaks: "In overflowing wrath I hid my face from thee for a moment." (Isaiah 54:8). We even read that "your iniquities have separated between you and your God, and your sins have hid his face from you, so that he will not hear" (Isaiah 59:2).[38] It is exactly for this reason that one cannot — from the aspect of the instrumentality of revelation — speak of revelation and mystery in an intrinsic dialecticism as if it were possible to draw conclusions from revelation as such concerning the modality of revelation. However, this certainly should not be taken to imply that revelation enables us to know God as he is. The Scriptures plainly indicate that revelation is adapted to human comprehension. The content of revelation is determined by the sovereign will of God,[39] so that John, without doing injustice to the reality of revelation, can write: "It is not yet made manifest what we shall be" (I John 3:2). We also think of other passages, such as Deuteronomy 29:29: "The secret things belong unto Jehovah our God; but the revealed things belong unto us and our children forever." However, *this* mystery does not nullify fellowship; nor are the instruments of revelation the *necessary* cause of this "concealing." Nothing less than the insufficiency of revelation arouses the awareness of God as the exalted and merciful one, the unapproachable and incomprehensible one, who gives himself in profound and perspicuous fellowship. This communion is possible only because he is the reliable one

38. *Cf.* Isaiah 64:7 for the tremendous tension in this concealment.
39. *Cf.* Calvin *Institutes* I, 13, 21, who quotes Hilarius at this point: "He alone is a fit witness to himself who is known only to himself."

in his revelation. Accordingly, it is certainly open to question whether the problem of the mystery of God has always been treated rightly in the history of church and theology. In itself, it is very well possible that by *deus absconditus* it was intended to refer to the exaltedness and the incomprehensibility of God. That would be in full accord with the Scriptures which say, that "there is no searching of his understanding" (Isaiah 40:28), and likewise: "how unsearchable are his judgments, and his ways past tracing out! For who hath known the mind of the Lord? Or who hath been his counsellor?" (Romans 11:33, 34).

However, all of this is within a framework which differs from that of the dialecticism of revelation and mystery. In support of the latter, appeal has been made to the words of Isaiah: "Verily thou art a God that hidest thyself, O God of Israel, the Saviour" (Isaiah 45:15). But it is clear that the conclusions which are drawn from this text frequently are quite unwarranted. The text does confess that the ways of God are incomprehensible, this his work "is shrouded in a veil of mystery"[40] which cannot be penetrated by the human mind. *In* this mystery, however, *revelation* is shed forth which is indubitable in its trustworthiness, for *this* God has saved Israel (Isaiah 45:17). And in *this same* chapter we behold the creator of the heavens, who laid the foundations of the earth, which he created not as a chaos, but as a place of habitation. This creator, who *is* the Lord, is not an arbitrary God, for he expressly says: "I have *not* spoken in secret, in a place of the land of darkness; I said *not* unto the seed of Jacob, Seek ye me in vain! I, Jehovah, speak righteousness, I declare things that are right" (Isaiah 45:19). God who is the incomprehensible and *simultaneously* the God who reveals himself *reliably* is combined in a most remarkable manner in Isaiah 45.

---

40. J. Ridderbos, *Korte Verklaring op Jesaja.* In Kittel, *Th. W. B.* IV, p. 970, the text is interpreted differently: "From the enemies of the people of God, however, the divine governing finally presses the admission, that for them the God of Israel was a God who concealed himself."

This is not the place to enquire in detail how the Scriptures speak of the mystery of God, but it certainly is in order here to warn against all *casual* use of the idea of the *deus absconditus,* as if that concept *of itself* were clear and manipulatable in dogmatic reflection. For frequently it may be observed that discussion on the mystery of God, takes place where according to the Scriptures it should be possible only to speak of human *blindness* and *insusceptibility* to revelation.

Of this we read in the gospel when Christ prophesies his suffering and the evangelist adds: "And they understood none of these things; and this saying was hid from them, and they perceived not the things that were said" (Luke 18:34). This "being hidden" is shown in its *subjective* origin. The relation of concealment to revelation is not one of dialectical tension as is plain from the words of Jesus: "Let these words sink into your ears: for the son of man shall be delivered up into the hand of men" and . . . *this saying was hid from them* (Luke 9:44-45). That "being hidden" is brought out even stronger, not only in its subjective aspect, but also as the act of God, in that other statement: "I thank thee, O Father, Lord of Heaven and earth, that thou didst hide these things from the wise and understanding."[41] Concealment is here the divine reply to the pride of the wise. The true wisdom of the wise passes away in this mystery; their eyes are not opened to discern the revelation in Christ. Of this Paul speaks in another connection: "at the reading of the old covenant the same veil remaineth, without being taken away" (II Corinthians 3:14). This is true of Israel — says Paul — "in the hardening of their minds." Thus God's judgment can be executed in and through this hardening of the heart, and likewise, concealment can be an act of God which manifests itself in them who are blind towards the revelation of God. It is only when the revelation of God comes to hearts which are not receptive, that this conceal-

41. Matthew 11:25; *cf.* the question: "Where is thy father?" and the answer of Jesus in John 8:19.

ment is an act of judgment. Therefore one should always be very cautious even in the use of the concept *deus absconditus*. For it is so easy *seemingly* to honor God's exaltedness and unapproachability, whereas *in reality* one fails to do justice to the sovereignty of God in revelation.

All of this has great significance for our confession of general revelation. For although it is true that the Scriptures state that the natural man suppresses the truth of God's revelation (in his works), yet it will never be possible to say, that God does *not* reveal himself in nature and history. "Concealment" in both history and nature is always the "concealment" of the Scriptures: "And they perceived it not." That is, it is "being concealed or hidden" in and through non-receptivity and spiritual blindness. Therefore the particular revelation in Christ is never the revelation of God, who, as it were, now for the first time is concerned with the world. That was the basic heresy of Marcion, who wanted to separate God, the Creator, from God, the Redeemer, and accordingly taught that the true God first became manifest in *Jesus* as the God who previously had been hidden. The particularity of God's redemptive deeds are in this way severed from the universal actions of God in the creation, maintenance and governance of all things. Anyone who begins to think along these lines today will not very likely take over Marcion's separation between God, the Creator, and God, the Redeemer; but he will not be able to break radically with Marcion's gospel of the hidden God who really had nothing to do with the created world which he was to redeem in Jesus Christ.

Only by making this radical break can we speak of the universality of God's revelatory acts and still avoid those modern generalizations about general revelation, which one encounters everywhere in the offense which men take at the particularity of the way of salvation in Christ, the only way to the Father. Because of this offense, men flee from particularism to universalism, thus relativizing and doing violence to the revelation in Christ. And the necessary inference drawn from these universal actions of God in created reality was, that for every man true knowledge was naturally attainable as the human response to the general revelation of God. In this way *the drastic gulf* between the activity of God and the knowledge of man was not acknowledged and thus in theological thought general and revelation began to stand opposite each other *as competitors.* Having failed to recognize this gulf, men, in and through the darkness of their hearts, could now arbitrarily conceive of all kinds of forces, manifestations and created magnitudes as *direct* "revelation of God." And in this way the universal actions of God were reduced to an arbitrarily *particularistic* form of revelation. The mystery of the universalistic concept of revelation is *this fact*: although beginning as a universalism, it always ends as a *new* particularism, *subjectively determined!* The fault of German Christians was not that they once again began speaking of "general revelation," but that they *misused* this concept and in consequence they gave their blessing to some very "particular" events, such as the seizure of power by Hitler in the year 1933. And it is most regrettable that the legitimate and necessary opposition to *this* particular "revelation" stimulated Barth even more in his offensive against the confession of a general revelation, which — when rightly understood — most emphatically had nothing to do with the "particularism" of German Christians.

This was true especially for history as an area of God's activity. When particular events were designated as real and distinct revelation on the basis of some probable evidence, this was not wrong because the people wanted to find the hand of God in history. The Tenth Sunday of the Catechism does this too. But their error lay in thinking that one could rashly infer from given facts what the mind and intent of God was.[42] They forgot that although God does reveal himself in the works of his hands, the ability *to see him* in them is dependent

---

42. *Cf.* G. C. Berkouwer, *The Providence of God*, 1950.

on the illumination of our knowledge by Jesus Christ in the
true knowledge of faith.　There was a failure to acknowledge
the incomprehensibility of the ways of God in his acts of judgment and mercy.　That is the sin of an *over-simplification* in
speaking of the general revelation of God.　The antinomy of
such speaking lies is the inevitable transfer from universalism
to particularism.　And what a particularism!

*　*　*

Serious though the dangers may be which attend all thinking on general revelation, yet we may never be tempted not to
do justice to the significance (revelational significance) of the
universal acts of God.　For *in* the particular revelation in Jesus
Christ the way is again opened to us whereby we know God,
the Father of Jesus Christ, in his universal doings.　This knowledge which confesses the living God in his almighty working
in all things, is not a knowledge which gives a subjective *interpretation* to the deeds of God.　For that very reason we must
always assert the priority of revelation over knowledge.　As the
wisdom of God is seen — by faith — in the particular revelation of God in Jesus Christ, that wisdom also being present in
reality, so faith also *sees* that the universal doings of God teach
us to confess the *reality* of those doings.[43]

*　*　*

It goes without saying, that attempts have repeatedly been
made to establish a unity and harmony between general and
special revelation.　Such attempts were always beset with various dangers.　Thus it was possible to reduce the area of God's
universal activity and to permit it to become obscured behind
the particular acts of God.　Then, too, the particular doings of

---

43. Compare also John 1:14: "And the Word became flesh, and dwelt
among us (*and we beheld his glory*, glory as of the only begotten of the
Father), full of grace and truth." *Cf.* II Peter 1:16: "We were eyewitnesses
of his majesty."

God could become so obscured that they were no more than a transparent aspect of God's universal activity. Or again, it was possible by means of an exaggerated supralapsarianism to conceive of the unity of God's doings in a Christological, Christocentric synthesis. The striking thing about all such views is the fact that they always terminate in speculation. Accordingly, one can arrive at a speculative view of the general revelation of God, or it is possible to conclude, from the viewpoint of eternity, that the *Logos* would have assumed human nature even without the fall. In contrast with all such views, however, the Scriptures teach us to be modest in our thinking, also in seeking a synthesis. They limit us to the utterances of God to prevent us from going astray in our thinking. Within these limitations we know by faith the *unity* of all God's doings. The confession intuitively and respectfully made profession of this when it treated the revelation of God in the creation, maintenance, and governance of the world, and these same words it also employed for the act of God's providence, for the activity of the Father in Jesus Christ. In *him* the sovereign unity of God's universal and particular activity is contained. But confessing this unity by faith is quite different from perceiving and comprehending it. If the human mind insists on comprehending the dual character of God's actions, then it always ends in one of two ways: either it proceeds from the universal acts of God and declares the particular actions to be superfluous, or at best grants them illustrative value; or it proceeds from the particular deeds of God and represents the *majesty* of God as being exclusively present in the sign of the cross, and the power of God in cross and resurrection. In their urge to arrive at a synthesis, men again and again have found themselves groping in the dark about this or that mystery. This must be attributed to the fact that it is never possible to deduce the universality and particularity of God's dealings from the *nature* of God's revelation. For in the light of the Scriptures we learn only (and that is sufficient for us) that betwixt them is our *guilt,* corruption and basic blindness. In the Scriptures, which speak to us of the doings of God, we are always confronted with and bound by this historical guilt. He who attempts to go beyond faith in making a comprehensible rational synthesis, fuses two matters which historically are not discrete in the dealings of God, and which can be differentiated by us only in the light of the Scriptures. And the remarkable thing is that true faith does not experience this as a duality in the doings of God; but in the pathway of particularism it hears the answer of God to that dualism which sin provoked between God and man in all its terrifying reality. In this way we shall avoid generalizing about the history of salvation out of offense at the exclusive character of *"hic et nun."* And at the same time we shall be able to guard against that other danger of *secularizing* world-history. And *in* the sanctuary of reconciliation, the *particular* sanctuary, the windows are open for the unity of the dealings of God, as a result of which the desire to speculate is once and again taken from us.

* * *

This historical aspect in our discussion of God's revelation (the fall) also helps to explain why theologians have repeatedly discussed special revelation in relation to the fall and to the period after the fall. To be sure, they also spoke of God's revelation in connection with the pre-fall world, namely of his revelation in word and deed; but this revelation was then regarded as being God's revelation in creation and the communion of man with his creator.

In this communion the works of God's hands were a testimony to him; and in this communion man received the *word* of fellowship, of favor, and of *commandment.*[44] The first chapters of Genesis show us man living in the midst of created reality. It testifies of a reality in which there could not yet be a

---

44. *Cf.* H. Bavinck, *Gereformeerde Dogmatiek* I[4], p. 281

question of "nature in its own right," or of man attaining to the creator via "nature." The *absence of that which is problematical* in this created life, and which is due to its being founded in communion with God, is certainly not the least aspect of its profundity and glory. Not until after the fall[45] can there arise in human thinking the problems of natural and supernatural theology, of "proofs" for the existence of God, and the like. In the paradise narrative we read of the deeds and words of God (Genesis 1:28-29). Word and deed were inseparably united in the abundant riches of this fellowship (Genesis 1:16-18). According to the Genesis account all of this has changed radically. All that had been one, in indivisible harmony, now falls apart. We do still hear the voice of God after the fall: "they heard the voice of Jehovah God walking in the garden in the cool of the day." (Genesis 3:8).[46] It continues to be *his* voice, *his* sound, and one can also say: these are *his* footsteps in reality, which come to man in his concealment.[47] It remains a remarkable fact that the Scriptures first speak of concealment in connection with *human* concealment or hiding. This is an indication that harmony has been interrupted. The presence of God, his being not *far*, but *near*, becomes a *problem* for the first time in the trouble conscience. *Man* seeks concealment after he has heard the word of

---

45. *Cf.* "Between the original and the actual is the Fall, which decisively alters the whole problem of knowledge and revelation" T. H. L. Parker, "Calvin's Concept of Revelation," *Scottish Journal of Theology*, 1949, p. 36.

46. *Cf.* G. Ch. Aalders: "The meaning is, that they observed the presence of God in a definite activity in nature."

47. Therefore J. Severijn's criticism of Dr. A. Kuyper's view of the *accidental* character of special revelation is incorrect (J. Severijn, *Encyclopaedie der theologische wetenschap*, 1948. p. 17). Kuyper does not deny that man has never been without the Word of God (p. 18) and that is not an argument against Kuyper's view. Kuyper speaks of "supporting-revelation," of "central revelation" (315 and 317) and of the "abnormal" (323), expressions which can be understood rightly only against the background of guilt and estrangement. *Cf.* Kuyper on the "mirror" of *revelatio specialis* which one day will belong to the past (325). Kuyper's intention becomes clear when he denies *in this same connection,* that the Reformed Confessions intended to express "juxtaposition or coordination" (II, 328). *Cf.* also on Romans 1: *Enc.* II, 332.

revelation: "and the man and his wife hid themselves from the presence of Jehovah," that is, after hearing the voice of the Lord (Genesis 3:8 and 10). In this distress of concealment, God reveals himself *anew* in a historical act of mercy, in the revelation of the enmity which he posits, and which is consequently an act of reconciliation. In this revelation lies the beginning of the particular dealings of God, which, in the midst of the universal doings of God among all peoples, paves the way for the particularism of salvation in Israel and the proclamation of his salvation *exclusively* to Israel. This does not merely concern an announcement which remained concealed from other nations; but it concerns first of all the very particular dealings of God with Israel, and this history of special revelation leads to, and ends in, the fullness of times: God revealed in the flesh (I Timothy 3:16). Along this pathway of revelation, the revelation of salvation to a fallen world, God reconciles the world to himself (II Corinthians 5:19). This way is particular in character and it is tied to concrete, historical data and events. This activity is in fulfillment (of promise), it is saving, but *its taking place is historically limited*. This revelation cannot, and may not, be *generalized*. No man comes to the Father, except it be through Jesus Christ.

It need not surprise us that the entire Scriptures are filled with *this* revelation of God. *These* deeds and words of God receive fullest attention in the Scriptures. In so doing, they emphatically do not deny the universal doings of God, and on numerous occasions the relations between the universality and particularity of the divine activity is illuminated *within* the particular line of revelation. But this occurs especially as *judgment* of this particularity, even as the relation between Israel and the heathen nations is regarded by the prophets as *serving* the preservation of God's people. If, in this connection, we speak of *the* divine revelation, then we do this from the viewpoint of the blinding of the world and its falling away from God. In view of this guilt and "lostness," the church speaks of the new, special revelation of God. Most profoundly, the distinction between general and special revelation does not concern subtle speculation, but a confession of *separation* and *guilt*. We confess *God,* who graciously comes to the world in Christ, the world which does not know him, nor find him in the works of his hands. Therefore the confession of a general revelation, when it is sound, can *never* constitute a threat to the exclusive earnestness of special revelation. For this confession does not signify an escape from the decisive Christ-revelation, but it arises from the knowledge of guilt and darkness, knowledge of what remained "hidden," although God's revelation came to the world. And therefore God does not correct general revelation in special revelation, nor must special revelation be regarded as "supplementing" general revelation. But special revelation is God's coming to a world which has fallen from a non-problematic communion with God, and accordingly has lost the pure and immediate attitude of faith toward God, and hence also toward created reality.[48]

*   *   *

This view also sheds light on the question of the sufficiency or insufficiency of general revelation. Frequently general rev-

---

48. On this view it will be necessary to raise objections to various typifications of general revelation which are sometimes in vogue, e. g., in G. Aulen: "this revelation in itself appears as imperfect and fragmentary: it does not reveal the heart of God" in *Revelation* (Aulen, Barth, and others 1937) p. 287. The hymn which Aulen quotes by way of illustration, does *not* prove what he posits. It reads as follows:

> *True, nature glorious and rich*
> *With thousands voices' sound*
> *Has said to my fainthearted thought*
> *That Thou are great, my God.*

> *But yet Thy meaning was concealed*
> *Thy heart I did not find.*
> *And in a dark and endless space*
> *I vanished like the dust.*

elation has been designated as being insufficient.[49] However, it
is necessary to examine what this means. The term was used
to indicate that general revelation was not sufficient to lead us
to true and pure knowledge of God. Article II states that it is
sufficient to convince men and to leave them without excuse.
Accordingly, when we speak of insufficiency, we certainly do
not intend to cast any reflection on the divine act of revelation
in this general revelation. On the contrary, it only points to
human guilt and blindness. This insufficiency is not a deficiency of revelation, but it is a deficiency which is historically
determined, *i.e.* in connection with the *fall of man*. Hence C.
Van Til surely was not wrong in emphatically asserting the
sufficiency of general revelation.[50] By this he does not mean
that we do not need special revelation, because general revelation is enough for *us*. But he points out that just because
we cannot arrive at true knowledge of God through general
revelation, that does not mean that this revelation as such is
insufficient. For it all depends *how* and *with what purpose* this
revelation of God comes to man. Van Til is right when he
says "revelation in nature was never meant to function by itself." He then relates the sufficiency of general revelation to
"being left without excuse." In any event, when we speak of
the insufficiency of general revelation, we may never diminish
and relativize the greatness and majesty of this revelation.
The fact that man does not behold and recognize the superior
power of the working of God in the creation, maintenance and
governance of the world, can be explained only in terms of
his guilt. God's works are always great, profound, and won-
derful, and they shed forth the light of his eternal power and

---

49. H. Bavinck, *Geref. Dogm.* I, p. 284: "There can hardly be any doubt
concerning the insufficiency of general revelation." Gispen, *op. cit.*, p. 17,
speaks of it as "'insufficient" for salvation and sufficient to remove all
innocence.

50. C. Van Til, "Nature and Scripture," in *The Infallible Word*, 1946, p.
267. Van Til speaks of the "sufficiency of natural revelation," but he is
thinking of general revelation.

divinity.[51] Man who is out of communion with God faces this revelation blindly.

Contact with God in the community of life is broken and man, though continuing to take his place in created reality, accordingly no longer understands its purpose, the language or song of creation. God's greatness and glory are no longer observed by a lost humanity. Word and deed revelation are sundered in the historical course of history. The natural theology of Rome creates the impression that nature (created reality) *was intended* to function independently as a reality, from which man could conclude to its first cause, if need be without Word-revelation. However, that is not at all the case. Whatever is severed in the course of history (because of the fall of man) belongs together according to God's original purpose and revelation. And for this reason we speak of special revelation as a *new* revelation. That which is "new" concurs with the *changed* situation, which has come about due to the fall of mankind. It does not arise out of human life as such, nor is it an extension of general revelation.

Special revelation confronts us with a new, historical working of God in Word and deed revelation, the revelation of God's mercy, which did not arise in the human heart, but in the Father-heart of God. So clearly does this revelation stand before us in the entire Scriptures, that it alone explains why men could think of special revelation as the only true revelation. In this way men seek to express the unexpected and startling character of the act of God's gracious self-revelation to lost humanity. In it men see the free and historical working of God, to which he is neither obligated nor bound, and which opens to lost mankind the only way to the knowledge of God and salvation.

---

51. Consider various facets of the book of Job, particularly in Job 40-41 and and also in Job 42, where Job knows his eyes to be opened after God speaks in a storm (40:1): "I had heard of thee by the hearing of the ear: But now mine eye seeth thee" (42:5). In the light of the divine Word-revelation (*cf.* Job 38), Job learns to lay his hand on his mouth (40:4).

Anyone who fails to do justice to this exclusive way radically misjudges the earnestness and profundity of special revelation. For there we behold — in Christ — the good pleasure of God (Luke 3:22). Here man must listen and obey, kneel and believe. "This is my beloved Son, in whom I am well pleased; hear ye him" (Matthew 17:5; Mark 9:7; Luke 9:35). Whoever desires to point out and follow another way than *this* revelation, fails to hear *this* revelation and gropes in the dark. However, this may never lead us to denying the revelational character of God's universal working in created reality. Knowledge and revelation are *not* identical. And from the fact of human blindness we may not conclude the absence of God's revelation. It is our conviction that this point is decisive for all discussion on the general revelation of God.

In this situation, which is historical, we understand something of the disturbed history of theology in the church insofar as it pertains to general revelation and natural theology. For one thing, there was the assumption of general revelation as an independent source of knowledge, equal in value with special revelation. The result was always — there are no exceptions! — a levelling and supplanting of special revelation. The process here was the same as that in the juxtaposition of revelation and tradition, or of revelation and reason. By way of reaction, the existential and actual character of God's revelation was stressed, and general revelation, which was looked upon as an "extension" of special revelation, was ruled out. Many individuals have been caught in this dilemma and its influence is still being felt. Therefore, it is necessary to see clearly the unsoundness of this dilemma and the misconceptions which are constantly multiplying around it. For the question: either natural theology or Christo-monism — does not pose the problem soundly, but is rather a product of abstract and speculative thinking. This abstraction is evident in both natural theology and Christo-monism. In natural theology, because it abstracts, *at least temporarily,* from the existential earnestness of special revelation, thus making room for a true knowledge of God through the natural light of reason. And in the Christo-monistic view of revelation they abstract from the fact that the revelation in Jesus Christ does not come into an unqualified vacuum of "fallenness," but comes in the guilt and lost estate of man, who walked and still does walk in the light of God's great works, but who suppresses and darkens that light in unrighteousness.

One who avoids and overcomes these abstractions will be guarded against the danger of failing to acknowledge the true sufficiency of the revelation of salvation in Christ. This danger is by no means imaginary, as the Scriptures plainly teach and history confirms from century to century. The cross is both offense and foolishness, and this reaction repeatedly seems to arouse nostalgia for another revelation, or for the *universality* of revelation. Only true faith in Jesus Christ will be able to overcome *this* nostalgia in all its particularity, even as we find this faith in Christ's disciples, when Andrew exclaims joyfully: "We have found the Messiah" (John 1:41), or when Peter confesses: "Lord, to whom shall we go? Thou hast the words of eternal life. And we have believed and know that thou art the Holy One of God" (John 6:68-69).

In this faith alone do we know and confess Christ as the door (John 10:7, 9), the way, the truth, the life, (John 14:6), the vine (John 15:1). This is the *heart* of all preaching.[52] Thus Paul knows *nothing*, save Jesus Christ and him crucified (I Corinthians 2:2). *Every* competing force (in) nature or history is excluded *here*. Psalm 73 takes on its most profound meaning: "Whom have I in heaven (but thee)? And there

---

52. Therefore Calvin, without doing any injustice to the confession of the general revelation of God, can write: "God would remain far off, concealed from us, were we not irradiated by the brightness of Christ" (*Inst.* III, 2, 1). In this same connection note Calvin's protest against the manner in which faith is treated in the schools: "by simply representing God as its object, they by empty speculation, hurry wretched souls away from the right mark instead of directing them to it. For seeing that God dwells in light that is inaccessible, Christ must intervene" (*Ibid.*).

is none upon earth that I desire besides thee" (Psalm 73 :25). Only those who have learned to understand God's salvation in the particularity of his revelation, can speak of God's gen-- eral revelation without falling into that confusing dubiosity of rivalry and levelling, which was manifested on numerous occasions in history. In our reflection on these problems, we can only warn ourselves and others that faith alone overcomes the offense. The riches of the revelation in Christ is not menaced by general revelation in this faith. On the contrary: the utterances of the Scriptures on general revelation will never let us fall into the dilemma of rival revelations. They confront us with the message of our lost estate and of our spiritual blindness which, moreover, are not presented to us in the light of God's concealment, but rather of his *revelation*. The harmony of the scriptural witness to general and special revelation lies in the fact that in the history of man and world it impresses us with the depth and breadth of guilt, and of the miracle of redemption.

* * *

In this connection still another question remains to be answered. If, in the light of the particularity of the revelation of salvation, our eyes are opened to behold the universal working of God in creation, maintenance, and governance, then what is the significance of this working? Or stated differently: *how* does God reveal himself *in* this general revelation?

First of all, we must reply that in this confession there is a° radical rejection of the pantheistic doctrine of revelation, according to which God, by virtue of his identification with nature, *necessarily* becomes manifest in nature. There can be no question of an *act* of revelation here, and still less the revelation of a living, personal God. When we profess that God reveals himself in the works of his hands, then this in no respect implies a deification of nature or of anything in created reality. Pantheism in all its forms identifies nature with divine revelation and thus it does violence to the Christian profession of the personal sovereignty and freedom of God.[53] Consequently, the knowledge of God's revelation cannot be said to deal with the knowledge of nature as such. Our faith (and obviously that of the believing scientist likewise) apprehends God, also in the works of his hands. By no means is it true, that a deeper understanding of the secrets of nature, of the course of history, and of human life, also implies a richer knowledge of the living, self-revealing God. In our earlier discussion we have observed how men sometimes thought that in general revelation (frequently identified with "nature") God revealed all kinds of things about the form and properties of nature. This must be qualified as a toning down of revelation. For it is God who reveals and makes *himself* known.[54] Our thinking on general revelation follows the lines laid down by Calvin who constantly speaks of reality as a *mirror* in which God's glory is reflected, a glory which is no longer beheld by eyes which are blinded.[55] Calvin speaks of the "indubitable signs of his glory," which are engraved in *all* the works of his hands, [56] and whereby he visibly displays himself in the midst of the "palace"

---

53. One may observe this very clearly in Schleiermacher: *Ueber die Religion. Reden an die Gebildeten unter ihren Verächtern* (Deutsche Bibl. M. Rade) in which he described religion as "beholding the universe" ("that on which my whole speech hinges") (p. 40) and in this connection he says of the idea of God: "In religion, therefore, the idea of God is not as lofty as you think" (94), *cf.* "God is not everything in religion, but he is one thing, and the universe is more" (96). The process of obscuration is complete in the utterance: "But the universe speaks to you, as it is written: 'Whosoever would save his life shall lose it: and whosoever shall lose his life for my sake shall find it'" (96). *Cf.* Schleiermacher on miracle and revelation: *Reden*, p. 86. Behind this "natural theology" looms the figure of Spinoza, to whom Schleiermacher in 1799 pays tribute: "Join me in worshipfully offering a lock of hair to the spirit of the saintly, rejected Spinoza" (*Reden*, p. 40)

54. This activity of God is pointed out especially in Job 38:1-39:33, where the uninterrupted relationship of all things to the living, active God is expressed.

55. Cf. Calvin in the Geneva Catechism (previously quoted on p. 26); also Inst. I, 5, 1 and Calvin's *Commentary* on Psalm 104.

56. *Inst.* I,V,1.

of his glory.[57] According to Calvin, this is true in nature, in history,[58] and in every human life in which the signs of divinity may be observed. Thus man has in his own person, "a magazine stored with treasures of inestimable value."[59] One can certainly question whether the three-fold division, "nature, history, and man," constitutes a completely adequate portrayal of reality. But there can be no doubt that the *intent* of this popular portrayal was to indicate the totality of created reality as it was, and is included, in the sovereign working of God. For those who by faith have learned to know the Father in Jesus Christ, this reality is the mirror of his virtues. They again understand this reality in its very creatureliness. Those things which outside of faith can become abstract nature, history and human life, the secret of which must be unravelled, are in faith restored to their relationship with the Creator. His name is glorious in all the earth. We have learned to know this name in a very particular way in the setting-aside of guilt and alienation, but there is then no longer a dualism between the first and second article of the confession, between the God of creation and of redemption.

This knowledge which we have of him, who is the one and true God, is not free from the danger of unbelief. It is still possible to begin thinking, seeing and analyzing outside of faith, to be captivated again by the idea of an abstract and self-contained nature, of a meaningless history in which man attempts to discover some purpose. The possibility still exists of viewing man in the threat to his existence, in his ennui and absurdity, and in his self-satisfied humanity. Our feet can again begin to slip on the pathway outside the sanctuary of God (Psalm 73:2 and 17). In these perils we can only cry out: I believe, help thou my unbelief! With this *help*, however, it will also be possible to resist the temptation of secularization, and in faith again to confess the glory of God. It is not as though we are in the least able to fathom the works of God, for his

57. *Inst.* I,V,1.   58. *Inst.* I,V,7.   59. *Inst.* I, V, 4

thoughts are not our thoughts and his ways are higher than our ways (Isaiah 55:8-9),[60] but the Word went forth, and it did *not* return void (Isaiah 55:11). It illumines the eyes and restores our vista of reality in the light of God. Nowhere in the Scriptures do we find a dualism between salvation and the revelation of God's power and glory in the works of his hands. Theological problems have frequently been insolvable, simply because the problems were not posed correctly. The Scriptures refer quite unproblematically to God's mighty deeds in the works of his hands within the context of his special Word. Thus the Lord says to Abraham: "Look now toward heaven, and number the stars, if thou be able to number them: and he said unto him, So shall thy seed be" (Genesis 15:5). In this passage the numerous stars become an analogy of the numerous seed of Abraham. The message is even more pronounced in Isaiah 40: "Lift up your eyes on high, and see who hath created these, that bringeth out their host by numbers; he calleth them all by name; by the greatness of his might, and for that he is strong in power, not one is lacking" (Isaiah 40:26). This greatness of God in the starry heavens is employed as a *motive* in connection with the greatness and power of God's promise of salvation, and which they may not *doubt*, even in times of trouble. "Why sayest thou, O Jacob, and speakest, O Israel, My way is hid from Jehovah and the justice due to me is passed away from my God?" (Isaiah 40:27).

In this passage we are struck by the fact that the Word points to the greatness of God's works as a consolation and as a motivation for assurance and trust.[61] The true creatureliness

---

60. *Cf.* especially Job 40:10-25.

61. Neither is Isaiah 40 merely concerned with "nature." *Cf.* Isaiah 40:23: "that bringeth princes to nothing; that maketh the judges of the earth as vanity." Isaiah's book of comfort also deals with the foundations of the earth, but there is no suspense or tension. (40:21). *Cf.* likewise the psalm about the city of God (Psalm 46) which treats of the works of the Lord in the midst of destruction and war (verse 9). "Be still and know that I am God: I will be exalted among the nations, I will be exalted in the earth" (verse 10).

of these created things is not denied hereby, but it is emphatically asserted.[62] In faith the power of God over and in all things is perceived and confessed. However, it is not a formal "concept of power" which directs and terrifies our thoughts by the immense proportions of this divine activity; rather it is a matter of knowing the power of *this God*, who is known in his immensity and inscrutability (Isaiah 40:28). In this way life in and among created reality receives its mark once and for all. For this human existence does not find itself in a daemonic world without salvation or expectation. Bavinck seems to be positing a dangerous thesis when he states that the believer finds his place in the world, is *no stranger* in it, and *feels at home* in the world.[63] Is this not in conflict with the idea of scripture, that the believers are *strangers* (sojourners) in the earth (Psalm 119:19), that they have no abiding city here, but seek after the city which is to come? (Hebrews 13:14; cf. Hebrews 11:10). And do not the believers themselves confess that they are strangers and pilgrims on the earth? (Hebrews 11:13) One cannot presume that Bavinck wishes to contradict these explicit statements of the Scriptures. This is evident, moreover, from the fact that elsewhere he refers to this same passage in Hebrews 11 to show that the believers have their citizenship in *heaven* and are still *strangers* here on earth.[64] Accordingly, when he speaks of believers as being "no strangers," then he most obviously has something quite different in mind. When the Scriptures speak of "being strangers," then they direct our attention to the eschatological fulfillment of God's salvation. There is then no contrast between a spiritual heaven and an earthly earth, for the new

62. Isaiah 40:18 ff.

63. ڲ quote the entire passage from Bavinck: "The believer who professes Christianity also finds his place in the world; he is no stranger in it and he beholds no other God ruling the world, than the one he calls his Father in Christ. Because of this general revelation he feels at home in the wo.ld; it is the Fatherly hand of God from which also all things in nature come to him (*Geref. Dogm.* I⁴, p. 293).

64. H. Bavinck, *Geref. Dogm.* IV⁴, p. 701.

heaven and the new earth are both included in the scriptural eschatological perspective. But there is indeed an alienship in the prospect of fulfillment, and in the anticipation of the city which has foundations and whose builder and maker is God. Those who have their citizenship in heaven long and wait for their heavenly home (Philippians 3:20). But this longing is different from that of the soul which despises the body and the earth. It is not dualistic, but it is eschatological and is filled with longing for the coming of Christ, who by his power will make this body of humiliation to conform to his glorified body (Philippians 3:21). Consequently, there is a two-fold view of alienship,[65] that is, of being "strangers or sojourners." There is an alienship which is not in conflict with that other statement of Scripture: "So then are ye no more strangers and sojourners, but ye are fellow-citizens with the saints, and of the household of God" (Ephesians 2:19). "Being a stranger" is here viewed in the light of "being of the household of God," of "not being a stranger." This alienship stands in relationship to the promise of fulfillment in the heavenly mansion of the Father. As such it is totally different from the alienism which arises from that dualistic alienation from the world which disqualifies and despises what God has restored.[66] For this reason Bavinck can speak of "being at home" and "not being a stranger" in the context of his discussion of the works of God. This has no reference at all to making the Christian faith a "world-citizenship" (*verburgerlijking van het Christelijk geloof*) or of putting the damper on the ardor of eschatological expectation; but it points to an initial restoration of uninterrupted fellowship with God, in which the problem of "nature" and "super-nature," and of *independent* nature (de

---

65. *Cf.* Stählin in Kittel's *Th.W.B.* V. p. 32, *xenos*: "The N. T. representation of the alienship of the Christian as demanded by Christ, and the Greek belief in the essential alienship of the human soul, are rooted in basically different views of God and man."
66. *Cf.* Stählin, *op. cit.* p. 35: "The point of departure of the Gnostics is the soul's experience of alienship." *Cf.* also: The N.T. versus Marcion, p. 35.

natuur *op zichzelf*) is removed. It is the pathway back to a reality in which God works, and in which he is known and glorified in faith. In this knowledge of the Almighty all fear is banished, according to the Word of Scripture, because all things fall within the broad scope of *his* Divine working.[67]

There is a remarkable commentary on all of this in the numerous controversies about astrology, which exercised a fairly considerable influence on Western European thought. In this connection we are struck by the fact that though men did not intend to look upon the stars as a source of informa- tion rivaling the providence of God, nevertheless in practice the course of the stars became an independent *source of knowl- edge* of the workings of God. *Here* they found a kind of "general" revelation, irrespective of how "particular" its ap- plication usually was. It intensely engaged the attention of many as real "nature revelation." Calvin, in particular, op- posed such astrology most emphatically. He was firmly con- vinced that God was active in all things, in the maintenance and governance of all of reality. The fact that Calvin's sense of calling toward the church of Christ demanded his concern with this problem is understandable, when one considers its great influence.[68] Bohatec points out that natural astrology, the knowledge of the destiny of man, was regarded as a gift of God, being as it were a revelation of God through nature.[69] Calvin combatted the astrology of his day as superstition, as

-- ---

67. *Cf.* Romans 8:31 ff. and the spectacular postulate of Psalm 46: "There- fore we will not fear, though the earth do change, and though the mountains be shaken in the heart of the seas" (verse 2).

68. *Cf.* J. Bohatec, *Budé und Calvin.* Studien zur Gedankenwelt des franzöz. Humanismus, 1950, p. 271: "Despite the violent attacks on it by several scholars, Astrology was highly esteemed. Also in France." The Sorbonne alone closed its doors to astrology. Bohatec adds: Even Queen Renata de Ferrara, who was well disposed to Calvin, desired to be initiated into the mysteries of this science" and "even the papal chair hearkened to the sign language of the stars." *Cf.* also Bohatec, *Calvins Vorsehungslehr,* in Calvinstudien, 1909, p. 345 ff. and 356 ff.

69. Bohatec, *op. cit.,* 272

belief in the old fatalism, in which piety and the belief in God's righteous rule over the world were not acknowledged.[70]

Calvin is concerned with giving due honor to the sublimity of God's sovereign acts, and towards it he directs the trust of believers. At the bottom of Calvin's polemic against astrology is the desire to maintain a pure concept of revelation. Therefore he distinguishes sharply between astronomy and astrology, and he sees in the astrology of his day a kind of mythical given, which fatalistically charms man and estranges him from the true God, not to mention other secondary arguments, which Calvin, like Augustine before him, raises against astrology.[71] This struggle of Calvin is so important for our subject, because it admits us into the secret of the true view of God's revelation in his works.[72] In our knowledge of this revelation we are not dealing with an independent source of revelation *in addition to* special revelation, but we are concerned with seeing, recognizing and confessing God in the works of his hands. Aided by the knowledge of God, given to us in the way of salvation, we no longer see in those works the irrational, unintelligible power of the distant, unapproachable creator, but we behold in them the hand, the working of God. That is seen by faith, and as Calvin states, in beholding those works we may be led to an increasing amazement at his greatness and majesty. And even as the greatness of God's majesty over the stars brings about courage and confidence in the people of God (but the analogy is contained *in* the Word-revelation), so the believer in the knowledge of his salvation praises *this* God, who

---

70. Ibid., 274. *Cf.* on Melanchthon, *op. cit.*, 276.

71. *Cf.* Detailed exposition of the view of Augustine: L. De Vreese, *Augustinus en de astrologie*, 1933.

72. *Cf.* Calvin *Inst.* I, 16, 3, where Calvin refers to Jeremiah 10:2 in connection with the heathen's fear of the stars instead of fear of him, whom they should fear. Re: astrology and the wise men from the east, *cf.* J. Blauw, *Goden en mensen*, 1950, p. 123 ff.

has made and governs all things, and from whom, through whom, and unto whom are all things.[73]

* * *

This knowledge of God, which is obtained along the pathway of salvation, guards us against unsound views of the work of God's hands. For it is aware of the relatedness of all things to God's purposeful working. This once and for all removes all possibility of a dualistic view of the cosmos, which assumes — within the cosmos — a radical division between a higher and a lower world.[74] This separation has played a very incisive role in the thinking of mankind. Thus separation was made between that which was higher and more useful and that which was lower and less useful or even useless. On the basis of this division it was thought that the relationship of the transcendent God to the cosmos was exclusively, or at least primarily, with the higher rather than with the lower world. Out of this view there frequently arose the thought of the mediating function of the *Logos*: God could not come into actual contact, or at least not in direct contact with the lower world, and hence he required the *Logos* as mediator. There is a chasm running through the cosmos, which is often indicated as a gulf between form and matter. This dualism recurs in many forms.[75] Faith in the working of God in all of created reality excludes all possibility of such a gulf. And hence Article

---

73. *Cf.* also chapter in L. Vreese (*op. cit.* 75 ff.) on Augustine's view of the value of observing the stars, which "witness to the beauty and power of the creator" (79). It is not a coincidence that Vreese finds these expressions of Augustine most frequently in the latter's sermons (80).

74. Compare what Bohatec writes about Calvin and aristotelian-scholastic nature-philosophy: "Therefore Calvin combatted the aristotelian-scholastic nature-philosophy, which divided the cosmos into a hierarchy of heavenly and earthly parts, and which judged the isolated entities of the world by the proximity of their elements to God, the unmoved mover" (*Budé und Calvin*, 1950, p. 264).

75. *Cf.* H. Dooyeweerd, *Reformatie en Scholastie in de wijsbegeerte*. Vol. I Het Grieksche voorspel, 1949, p. 28 ff. en passim. *Cf.* on nature-grace and nature-freedom, p. 35 ff. and 38 ff.

II of the Belgic Confession is able to speak of the world which is before our eyes "as an elegant book.".

This phrase has frequently become the basis for an optimistic, but unwarranted, view of the cosmos. The elegance of this book and the letters written in it, are understood as a purely formal concept of beauty, which does not take into account the darkness and corruption which have entered the cosmos.

But such an interpretation does great violence to the doctrine of general revelation. It is altogether out of the question to say that we here encounter beauty which, *without qualification,* as unobscured beauty, is attributed to the totality of created reality. We are, after all, dealing with the work of God's creation, maintenance and governance of all things; the beauty of the world *in his working.*[76] Because there is this working of God in the world, the world also witnesses to that working, viz. his eternal power and beauty.

The view of the confession is quite different from that of the Greeks who extolled the beauty of the world. Sasse points out that the Greek cosmos-concept includes, among others, the following elements: the *unity* and the *beauty* of the cosmos.[77] The Greeks "sing a mighty hymn of praise to the beauty of the world." In its *essence* the cosmos is beautiful. This is a purely esthetic view of the cosmos. "To behold this beauty is blessedness." The Scriptures do not present such an unshaken and undisturbed hymn of praise to the cosmos. They speak of the fall, of a fallen condition, and thus speak differently than does Greek thought about the cosmos. The Scriptures also view the world in its relationship to man as the crown of creation, and in this connection they state, that the *entire* "cosmos" is under the judgment of God (Romans 3:19), and *lieth in the evil one* (I John 5:19), while Satan is called

76. Kittel, *Th. W. B.* cf. *kosmos,* p. 873.
77. *Cf.* Calvin contra the Epicureans, *Inst.* I, 16, 4 and the *otiosus inersque Deus* (Bohatec, *Calvinstudien,* 355. In this connection Calvin makes appeal to John 5:19 and Acts 17:28 (*Inst.* I, 16, 4).

the prince of this world (John 12:31),[78] although the passage
depicts his judgment: his being cast out in connection with
the death of Christ.[79] The Scriptures never refer with *unqualified* optimism to the beauty of the world. They never
present an *abstract* concept of beauty in which the cosmos in
all its beauty is viewed by itself, because such a view of the
world "in itself" is strange to the Scriptures. We can speak
of such beauty only in the light of faith in God, who creates,
maintains and governs. This is bound up with the fact, that
the world which has fallen from God — in man — is not left
to its fate by God.

In the Scriptures we learn that God has loved the world
(John 3:16) and that God has reconciled the world unto
himself (II Corinthians 5:19). Therefore the entire world is
involved in the kingdom of God and is an object of God's
working. When Greek thought, however, discovers unity,
beauty and harmony in the world, it does not understand reality correctly. For it does not take into consideration either
the shadow which is cast over reality, or the *Light* which enables us to understand the meaning of reality. Hence it is of
critical significance *how* one speaks of the world as "an elegant
book." It is possible to take an abstract, optimistic view of
the cosmos in which one abstracts from the living God, but
this view is not tenable. Such a view of the cosmos will always disappoint us by its esthetic abstraction. For it cannot
do justice to the reality which Paul describes as the groaning
and travailing of the whole creation (Romans 8:22) and as
the bondage of corruption (Romans 8:21).[80] An esthetic view
of the cosmos glosses over this reality or else permits the dis-
sonance to disappear in the harmonious beauty of the whole.
An analysis of the essence of the cosmos without the benefit of

78. *Cf.* J. Bohatec on Calvin's view of demonology in history: "Gott und
die Geschichte nach Calvin," *Philos. Reform.* I, 140.
79. *Cf.* Grosheide, commentary on John II, 1950, p. 225.
80. *Cf.* Luther on loveliness and terror in nature. (H. A. v. Bakel, *Circa
Sacra,* p. 343.

the illumination of faith may indeed discover something of its *unity* and *beauty,* its *organization* and *orderliness* (het bestand en het wetmatige), but these are *not* understood *in their most profound significance* (essential meaning: *in hun diepste zin*). For they become self-evident "properties" of the world, whereas they can be understood only in the light of revelation. On such a view men also may have some impression of the intimate relationship between the reality of the cosmos and the place which man occupies in the cosmos.[81] But because man is not known as he exists before God, their understanding of this relationship is also warped. Faith alone is truly aware of these relationships and beholds the whole world in the light of him, who may truly be called the *Light* of the world.

* * *

At this point the question may be raised whether on the basis of the relation between general and special revelation, we should not conclude that really there is no *actual* revelation of God, and no "beauty" in the cosmos; but that we can speak only of a *conception* or view, an *as if,* an *interpretation* of the cosmos which, however, is not an *essential* part of reality. To employ the terminology of Barth, is it not rather a matter of a *"hineinlesen"* or *"hineininterpretieren,"* to which no creaturely reality corresponds? Is this not really a subjective insight, be it the insight of faith?

This question must be answered negatively, because the function of faith is never creative, but only receptive; related to this there is a perceptive, discerning function which sees reality, subjectively it is true, but always as the work of God. A sound view will be possible only if we resolutely reject this creative function of faith. In speaking of the works of God, the Scriptures always refer to seeing, discerning, and observing, but it should be noted, always as a seeing of *reality*. It

---

81. Kittel, *Th.W.B.* under *kosmos* (III, 873).

is not a matter of subjective projection, but one of a real hymn of praise. Thou hast set thy glory upon the heavens! (Psalm 8:1).

This rejection of the creative function of faith and the acceptance of the *reality* of general revelation is so important, because the issue at stake is a correct view of created reality. The ever present threat of a subjective view of creation (*de beschouwing van een subjectieve creatie*) is most evident in the cosmos-view of Renaissance man, as described by Cassirer.[82] The characteristic feature of this view is that there is present in the human spirit, as it were, a *creative* moment which constructs the beauty and harmony of the world.[83] To be sure, the beauty of the universe is traced back to God, but against this background the creative function of man becomes apparent. It is the thought of the *microcosmos* in which man's function is such that "the religious destiny of the universe is determined in him, as it were" (*in ihm gewissermaszen das religiöse Schicksal des Kosmos entscheidet*).[84] The thought of man as crown of creation then loses that essential element of creatureliness, and hence man is viewed as a creator. This explains why the Renaissance man seemingly delighted in the works of God's hands, but actually took delight in his *own creativity* and in consequence the insight into the real revelation of God's works was lost. It is — as Cassirer says — "the self-affirmation of man, which at the same time becomes the affirmation of the world."[85] Basically, it is the creativity of the *human* spirit which impresses form and objectivity on things. Man becomes the *lawgiver* of the cosmos, a thought which is to play a decisive role in philosophy centuries later. Beauty is now no longer the beauty of the working of God, nor the revelation of

---

82. E. Cassirer, Individuum und Kosmos in der Philosophie der Renaissance, 1927.
83. *Ibid.*, 67.
84. Cassirer, *op. cit.*, p. 68. cf. also W. Dilthey, *Weltanschauung und Analyse des Menschen seit Renaissance und Reformation* (Ges. Schr. II). 1923, p. 7.
85. *Ibid.*, 71.

his eternal power and divinity, but it is an *act* of man. "Ultimately, all beauty of the material world does not originate in itself, but it owes its origin to the fact that it becomes, as it were, the medium with which man's free creative activity is occupied, and in which it recognizes itself."[86] Thus there emerges what Cassirer designates as the Prometheus motif: "man is a creature, but he is separated from other creatures in that his originator has given him the gift of creativity."[87] God's revelation is made into a subjective correlation between creator and creature, in which the divine revelation in the works of his hands becomes a self-revelation of man. The view of nature becomes the view of the creative power of man. God's revelation is obscured behind that of humanity.

* * *

It is evident, therefore, that the doctrine of general revelation is closely related to numerous other weighty problems. Many dangers beset it on every side, as we have seen. In summing up these dangers, we find that they are really two-fold in character. In the first place then, we everywhere encounter offense at the particularity of special revelation, and the tendency to generalize about God's revelation in order to avoid the *hic et nun* of divine revelation to mankind. All liberal and modernistic theology falls into this danger. It suppresses the earnestness and responsibility of revelation and permits it to become obscured in generalizations. We cannot warn too earnestly against this danger, because it is symptomatic of the offense of the cross. Neither can we disassociate this threatening danger from natural theology, although orientation and application are different here. For it points out a way to God via the *undisturbed natural reason* and it assigns to special revelation an *augmenting* function. On the basis of such a relationship between natural and supernatural theology it is

86. *Ibid.*, 71. cf. also p. 89 Pico's microcosmos-motif.
87. *Cf.* on Prometheus motif, *op. cit.* p. 100, 128.

understandable that gradually a rivalry developed between these two forms of revelation.[88] History proves that in most instances "natural" knowledge becomes the *criterion* of "supernatural" knowledge, and the secularization of the nature-grace theme leads in later times directly to rationalistic theology and its criticism of special revelation.

A second danger, frequently intensified out of reaction to the former danger, consists of letting general revelation share in the darkness of this human reaction (to the particularity of the Gospel); in failing to separate the problem of sin from God's sovereign revelation, and even finally denying that (general) revelation. As we have seen, the root of this reaction is a subjectivizing of God's revelation, which culminates in being able only to speak of "*hineinlesen*," thus distorting the clear witness of the Scriptures.[89]

If we remain alert to these dangers, we shall be capable of offering resistance to all attempts "to generalize" God's particular revelation. In times such as ours, when life is shrouded in darkness, men are in danger of seeking new "revelations"; particularly in our time it is necessary both to understand and

88. *Cf.* Cassirer, *Individuum und Kosmos, etc.* p. 59: "And the process of secularizing finally culminates in the contrasting hereafter of the revelation of "the book of nature" with the biblical revelation. There can be no opposition between these two as a matter of principle since both present the same spiritual meaning (Sinn) in varying form, and since the unity of the divine originator is manifested in them. If, nevertheess, we are confronted with such an apparent conflict, then it can be resolved only by giving preference to the revelation in *work* over that in *word*." Cf. Gustav Aulen in "Revelation". (Aulen, et. al., 1937, p. 286) on the "risks connected with the idea of a 'general' revelation," among others, the idea of supplementing.

89. A typical example of this we find in H. P. Wolmarans, "Die betekenis van die openbaringsbegrip vir onse tijd," Pretoria 1938; From the fact that the Reformers place all emphasis on the darkening of human reason, he concludes that "in the final analysis they reject both the natural knowledge of God and natural revelation" (p. 8). cf. p. 9, "reduced it to a minimum" and "the worthlessness of natural revelation and of the natural knowledge of God." The entire speech of Wolmarans is based on the simplistic combination of *knowledge* and *revelation*. *Cf.* what he says about the "typically heathen" character of the doctrine of general revelation.

to affirm that the doctrine of general revelation neither has, nor may have such origins.

General revelation truly has a different origin. That became clear to us from the *historical* character of God's working in the midst of the guilt and lost estate of the world. This enables us to see those two facts which in history are distinct, but which God's revelation relates, namely: the *Work* of God and *Word* of God. When God's Word is not heard, his working is no longer understood. In this state of blindness, God in a new, gracious working pursues his course with the world. He is close to the world in Jesus Christ, and his *working* is explained by his *Word*. It is the way of suffering and death, a historical way, concretely demonstrable in time and place. The way leads from Sinai and Mount Zion to Jerusalem, Bethlehem and Golgotha. The (outstretched) finger of John the Baptist points to *him*: "Behold the Lamb of God, that taketh away the sin of the world" (John 1:29, 36). This way ends in death, yea, in the death of the cross (Philippians 2:8). The Scriptures speak of "necessity" according to God's good pleasure: "Was is not necessary that the Christ should suffer these things and enter into his glory?" (Luke 24:26).[90] There is no arbitrariness in the particularity and absoluteness of this way of salvation. For this necessity is the expression of the will of God and "finally it unveils to man his lost condition and demands of him faith in God's work of salvation."[91] In this faith communion with the Father is restored, *"for whom are all things, and from whom are all things"* (Hebrews 2:10). This faith is rooted in the midst of *his* works, because it is directed toward *him*. When the guilt of alienation has been reconciled and human autonomy broken down, then man can again find his way into the world. He remains faithful to the world, which *God* has loved. And he also finds himself again,

90. Luke 24:26 (RSV); *cf.* Hebrews 2:10.
91. Grundmann in Kittel, *Th.W.B.* I (p.23); *cf.* Acts 4:12: "neither is there any other name under heaven, that is given among men, wherein we *must* be saved."

not in egocentric obstinacy and blindness, but in the joy of a hymn of praise. And in the *proclamation*, which fills his life in the world, the proclamation of the excellencies of him, who called us out of darkness into his marvellous light (1 Peter 2:9).[92]

92. *Cf.* Isaiah 43:21: "That they might set forth *my* praise"; LXX: my excellencies (cf. Kittel, *Th.W.B.* I, 461)

General Index

Adam — 80 ff
Althaus — 16, 37, 47ff, 177f

Baal worship — 124f
Barth — 15f, 21ff, 37ff, 70, 73f, 102, 106, 112, 118, 132, 154, 158ff, 162ff, 177, 210, 212, 215, 227, 239ff, 265ff, 296ff, 327
Bavinck — 205f, 292, 308, 320f
Belgic Confession — 33, 54, 83, 153, 187, 265ff, 290, 312, 325
Brunner — 13, 15f, 37ff, 102f, 112, 197, 199
Bultmann — 90ff, 100, 248, 250

Calvin — 30f, 39f, 42, 46f, 152f, 197ff, 205, 210, 213, 266, 268, 270, 272, 276, 279f, 285, 301, 315, 317f, 322ff
Christomonism — 25, 48, 51, 54ff, 92ff, 99, 101f, 108ff, 117, 133, 213, 294, 314f
comparative religion — 12, 155f, 161ff

Dillschneider — 16, 53f, 256
Dodd — 178f
Dooyeweerd — 168ff, 207, 324

grace — 26, 32, 37f, 41, 44, 46, 119, 182, 202, 234

Haitjema — 270ff
Heidelberg Catechism — 93, 105, 305
humanism — 214ff

Jaspers — 217ff, 229

Kant — 48, 68, 76
knowability of God — 28f, 40ff, 184ff, 266ff, 285ff
Koopmans — 269f
Kuyper — 165ff, 269, 278, 309

Lütgert — 55ff
Luther — 42, 197f, 295f, 299, 326

natural law — 187ff
"Nature Psalms" — 119, 127ff, 137, 287, 289ff
natural theology — 14f, 21f, 26ff, 39ff, 61ff, 153, 168
noetic — 31f, 44, 52, 55, 132, 210, 227, 248
ontic — 31f, 44, 52, 72, 132, 210, 227, 248, 251

pantheism — 119ff, 316
phenomenology — 16f, 82, 151, 160
Polman — 272ff

revelation in the O. T. — 24, 38, 102ff, 110ff, 118
Roman Catholic — 15, 27f, 39, 43, 46, 49, 62ff, 146, 148f, 192ff, 201, 206

Scheler — 75ff
Schilder — 180ff, 255, 257, 277, 296f
Schleiermacher — 49, 317
Söderblom — 155, 161
Söhngen — 65f

Troeltsch — 12, 25, 156f, 160f, 163, 165, 198

words for "revelation" — 94ff

Index of Scripture References

335